Prolegomenon to a Theory
of Argument Structure

Linguistic Inquiry Monographs
Samuel Jay Keyser, general editor

Prolegomenon to a Theory of Argument Structure

Ken Hale and Samuel Jay Keyser

The MIT Press
Cambridge, Massachusetts
London, England

This book was set in Times New Roman on 3B2 by Asco Typesetters, Hong Kong, and was printed and bound in the United States of America.

Library of Congress Cataloging-in-Publication Data

Hale, Kenneth L. (Kenneth Locke), 1934–2001
  Prolegomenon to a theory of argument structure / Ken Hale and Samuel Jay Keyser.
    p.   cm. — (Linguistic inquiry monographs ; 39)
  ISBN 0-262-08308-6 (hc. : alk. paper) — ISBN 0-262-58214-7 (pbk. : alk. paper)
  1. Grammar, Comparative and general—Verb phrase. 2. Grammar, Comparative and general—Syntax. I. Keyser, Samuel Jay, 1935– II. Title. III. Series.
P281 .H35 2002
415—dc21   2002024420

Contents

Series Foreword

We are pleased to present the thirty-ninth in the series *Linguistic Inquiry Monographs*. These monographs present new and original research beyond the scope of the article. We hope they will benefit our field by bringing to it perspectives that will stimulate further research and insight.

Originally published in limited edition, the *Linguistic Inquiry Monographs* are now more widely available. This change is due to the great interest engendered by the series and by the needs of a growing readership. The editors thank the readers for their support and welcome suggestions about future directions for the series.

Samuel Jay Keyser
for the Editorial Board

Preface

The work represented in this volume began almost a quarter of a century ago with the Warlpiri Dictionary Project in Building 20 at MIT. The year was 1979 and the participants included at the outset Ken Hale and Mary Laughren, who were joined shortly by David Nash and Jane Simpson. In subsequent years, under the aegis of the now defunct MIT Center for Cognitive Science, numerous students and visiting faculty contributed to the project. In the fall of 1983, when Ken Hale was on sabbatical in Tilburg, Jay Keyser, then director of the Center for Cognitive Science, set up the Lexicon Project with the understanding that, on Hale's return, he would assume leadership of the project. Unfortunately, the best laid schemes o' mice an' men gang aft a-gley. On his return, Hale formed a collaboration with Keyser that has endured for the past eighteen years, outliving even the Center for Cognitive Science itself.

Over that period of time, Hale and Keyser produced a number of papers, mostly, though not exclusively, on English. These included

- "The Basic Elements of Argument Structure" (Hale and Keyser 1998),
- "Bound Features, Merge, and Transitivity Alternations" (Hale and Keyser 1999),
- "Conflation" (Hale and Keyser 2000),
- "A Uto-Aztecan (O'odham) Reflection of a General Limit on Predicate Argument Structure" (Hale 2000b),
- "Hopi -na" (Hale and Jeanne 1999),
- "Navajo Reflections of a General Theory of Lexical Argument Structure" (Hale and Platero 1996), and
- "Theoretical and Universal Implications of Certain Verbal Entries in Dictionaries of the Misumalpan Languages" (Hale and Salamanca 2001).

These papers comprise the major body of work from which the present volume has been assembled. In every case, however, we have modified the published work in some instances significantly. What we say here supersedes the research acknowledged above.

Having said that, we wish to thank the editors of the volumes where those papers appeared for providing us a public platform from which to air our work. The comments and criticisms engendered by this airing have been of great benefit to us. We thank them and all those who have commented on earlier versions of our work.

In addition, we would like to thank the following people for their help, either directly or through their work: Joan Bresnan, Noam Chomsky, Marcel den Dikken, Anne-Marie Di Sciullo, Nomi Erteschik Shir, Tom Givón, Jane Grimshaw, Morris Halle, Teun Hoekstra, Paul Kiparsky, Beth Levin, Alec Marantz, Shigeru Miyagawa, Tova Rapoport, Malka Rappaport Hovav, Tom Roeper, Juan Romero, Peter Svenonius, and Leonard Talmy. (Thanks, finally, to Sara Hale for her invaluable help in proofreading the manuscript and to Anne Mark, whose skills as a copy editor are second to none./SJK)

As we look back over the work presented here, we are struck by an important limitation. We have imposed on ourselves a very restricted notion of argument structure, and we have limited the range of empirical data to argument structures. Consequently, we do not deal with the wide range of constructions one normally finds in discussions of this kind. In particular, we do not deal with verbs that take clausal complements of the type found with *promise* and *believe*. We assume, however, that the properties of these verbs will prove to be a natural extension of the lexical properties we examine in detail in this book. We plead guilty to this lack of coverage. However, now seemed like a good time to stop, catch our breath, and gather what we have done in one place.

We trust it will be of use.

Ken Hale and Samuel Jay Keyser

Ken Hale died on October 8, 2001, just two months after completing this text. There would have been so much more to add but his illness was unrelenting. Having collaborated with Ken for eighteen years, I realize as well as many and perhaps more than some how much has been lost to the field and to the world of humane men and women.

All good things must end, ¿pero por qué tan pronto, amigo?

Samuel Jay Keyser

Chapter 1

The Basic Elements of
Argument Structure

1.1 Introduction

We use the term *argument structure* to refer to the syntactic configuration projected by a lexical item. It is the system of structural relations holding between heads (nuclei) and their arguments within the syntactic structures projected by nuclear items. While a lexical entry is more than this, of course, argument structure in the sense intended here is nothing other than this.

Argument structure is determined by properties of lexical items, in particular, by the syntactic configurations in which they must appear. There are just two syntactic relations, complement and specifier, defined so as to preclude iteration and to permit only binary branching.

These assumptions delimit a certain project: that of ascertaining the extent to which the observed behavior of lexical items is due to structural relations, rather than to the interaction of structure and some other component, that is to say, to matters we will refer to as "questions of interface."

We take (1) and (2) to be structurally distinct.

(1) The pot broke.

(2) The engine coughed.

This structural difference in turn accounts for their behavior in relation to the standard causative-inchoative transitivity alternation.

(3) I broke the pot.

(4) *I coughed the engine.

The properties that distinguish these two verbs are the following. The verb *break*, as illustrated in (1) and (3), consists of two structural elements: a root (R) and a verbal host (V).

(5) R, V

The verbal component takes a complement, realized here as the root. The latter contains the semantic and phonological features associated with the dictionary entry *break*. The root component requires a specifier, as shown in (6).

(6)

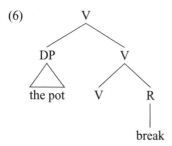

This is an essential feature of the root (R = break), accounting for the central syntactic feature of the verb, namely, the transitivity alternation observed in (1) and (3).

The verb *cough*, illustrated in the grammatical sentence (2) and the ungrammatical sentence (4), likewise consists of two elements: a root and a verbal nucleus. Unlike the root component of *break*, however, the root component of *cough* does not require a specifier; thus, the verb does not, and cannot, project a specifier.

(7)

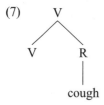

A verb, in and of itself, does not project a specifier, and the verb's complement in this case (i.e., root element) does not motivate the projection of a specifier. These properties account for the ill-formedness of (4).

Transitivization of the type represented by (3) is in principle automatic, by virtue of the complement relation. The structure of (3) results from the combination, via Merge, of (6) and a verbal nucleus V, as in (8).

(8)   V₁

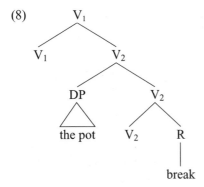

Comparable insertion of (7) into the complement position of a matrix verb is impossible—(9) cannot converge as a transitive, there being no internal argument (specifier) to be licensed (e.g., Case-marked) by V_1, assuming that to be a requirement for convergence.

(9)   * V₁

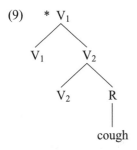

This follows from the fundamental nature of the root ($R = $ cough), which does not force the verb to project a specifier. In general, but with some exceptions, this property is shared by R elements that exist independently as the lexical heads of nominal projections, that is, as nouns. This is in contrast to adjectives, for example, which generally do force the projection of a specifier.

While we attribute these effects to structural factors, a full understanding of these verbs requires addressing other matters as well—there is more to the grammar of verbs than structure, to be sure. We take some such nonstructural factors to be matters that can be understood only in terms of one or the other interface.

Sentences (1) and (2) are identical in "profile," representing the canonical intransitive frame DP V. But they are not structurally isomorphic, we maintain, since their behavior in relation to transitivization distinguishes them in a manner that implicates structure, not some other factor.

The following sentences also share the same profile superficially.

(10) a. He saddled a quarter horse.
     b. He made a fuss.

However, they behave differently in relation to the middle construction.

(11) a. A quarter horse saddles easily.
     b. *A fuss makes easily.

This asymmetry is due to a structural factor, we believe. A verb can participate in middle formation if and only if its complement is a dyadic projection and therefore contains a specifier, as exemplified in (12), the structure associated with (10a).

(12)

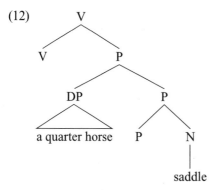

The middle construction involves a number of issues and problems, amply discussed in the literature (see, e.g., Ackema and Schoorlemmer 1995; Condoravdi 1989; Fagan 1988, 1992; Kemmer 1993; Keyser and Roeper 1984; Levin 1993; Rapoport 1997). However, from the point of view of its grammatical essence, we claim that the middle simply cancels the Case-binding ability of the governing V, forcing the specifier to raise into the position associated with the sentential syntactic subject. This prevents the appearance there of the external subject that would otherwise combine with VP to give the transitive structure of (10a).

By contrast, the verb *make* in (10b), although it is transitive and might be expected to undergo middle formation, evidently cannot do so, at least not in our speech, as indicated by the judgment we have indicated for (11b). The reason, we believe, is that the structure assigned to *make* in this use fails the basic requirement: its complement, a DP, projects no specifier (in the required sense).

(13)
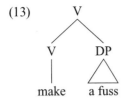

As mentioned above, a complete understanding of the middle construction will involve other linguistic components. The middle is another construction in which purely structural considerations interact with other linguistic objects and principles.

Among other things, the purpose of the following sections is to examine certain cases in which argument structure, as defined above, interacts with other linguistic systems, including the following:

(14) a. conflation and selection,
     b. merge and obviation,
     c. active and stative.

The first problem relates to the fact that the phonological matrix associated with the nominal root *cough* is realized in the verb of (2), and not in its complement. The second problem is semantic in nature. It has to do, among other things, with the fact that the semantic features of the root component of a verb are sometimes linked with an internal argument (object or specifier) and sometimes with the external argument (the sentential syntactic subject). The consequences are straightforward in the syntactic behavior of the relevant verbs. The third problem involves an issue we have not previously dealt with in published work, although we have alluded several times to an opposition (i.e., central and terminal coincidence) that may be relevant. The problem will be to determine the role of structure in this domain.

1.2 Argument Structure Types

Projections of verbs like *make* in (10b) represent a good place to start the study of argument structures. The verbs that head these projections share a certain property, characteristic of the argument structure type they represent: namely, they take a complement (the object DP in (15)) and the structure they project does not include a specifier. We will refer to argument structures having this characteristic as *lp-monadic*. That is to say, the lexical projection ("lp")—the argument structure configuration projected by the head—contains just one argument, the complement. The complement is defined as the unique sister to the head, as exemplified by the DP *a fuss* in the configuration repeated in (15) (where head, projection, domination, and sisterhood, not linear order, are the relevant structural features).

(15)

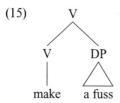

In sentential syntax, of course, these verbs are ordinarily thought of as dyadic, since they have both a subject and an object.[1] We use the terms *monadic*, *dyadic*, and so on, not in relation to sentential syntactic adicity but strictly in relation to the arguments (complements or specifiers, irrespective of morphosyntactic category) that must appear internal to the lexical configuration associated with a lexical item. For lexical items of the type represented in (10b), the sentential syntactic subject (e.g., *he* in *He made a fuss*)—and the subject in countless other like cases, such as *The cowboys made trouble, They had/took a fit*, and so on—is an external argument, we claim, and therefore not an argument (specifier or complement) internal to the lexically projected configuration.[2]

In the latter respect, the situation represented by the argument structure type attributed to the verb just considered can be contrasted with the configurations projected by the prepositions in (16).

(16) a. (put) the books on the shelf
     b. (get) the cows into the corral
     c. (pound) nails into the wall
     d. (drip) paint on the floor

We are concerned here just with the structure following the parenthetic verb (itself irrelevant to the immediate issue). In each case, the relevant structure is headed by a preposition (e.g., *on*, *into*), and the structure illustrates fully the essential lexical character of heads of the type normally realized by prepositions in English. These elements take both a complement (a DP in the present examples: *the shelf*, *the corral*, etc.) and a specifier (also a DP in these examples: *the books*, *the cows*, etc.). The complement is the unique sister of the head, and the specifier is the unique sister of the initial projection of the head (i.e., the substructure formed by the head and its complement). This arrangement is dyadic—that is to say, it is the structural configuration defined by a head that projects two internal argument positions, in accordance with its elemental lexical properties. The dyadic structure projected by the preposition in (16a) is presented diagrammatically in (17).

(17)

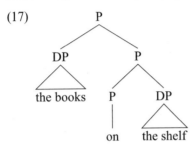

Of course, the presence of a specifier argument is the essential structural difference between the dyadic lexical configuration of (17) and the monadic configuration of (15). While the verb of (10b), projecting the structure of (15), has a subject and is in that sense also dyadic, the subject is an external argument, not a specifier in the lexical configuration. The evidence for this lexical difference is straightforward. The structure depicted in (17) can—in its entirety, specifier and all—appear as the complement of a verbal head within a lexical projection, as in (18). This is the enabling condition for an indefinite number of transitive verbs of "placement" or "location," like *put (the books on the shelf)* and others (see (16)).

(18)

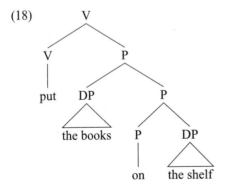

The argument structure of the lexical item *put* is a complex configuration consisting of a P-projection (dyadic), embedded as the complement within a V-projection (itself monadic). The specifier within the embedded P-projection will, in the normal course of events, appear as the grammatical object of the verb in sentential syntax (i.e., it will be assigned structural Case (accusative) in the active voice and, in the passive, it will be forced to raise into the specifier position of an appropriate functional category).

Crucially, the specifier of the embedded P in (18), and the corresponding position in all such cases, is within the structural configuration associated with the lexical entry of the verb. It is properly an internal argument, lexically. This is not true of the subject argument of verbs like *make* in (10b). There are no lexical structures comparable to (6) or (17) in which the subject of *make* (and other verbs of its type) occupies a lexically internal position comparable to that occupied by the specifier *the books* in (17).[3] This follows from the fact that the subject of the verb in (10b) is an external argument. The same is true of the subject of (2).

We take it to be an inherent and fundamental property of canonical prepositions that they project a structure containing both a complement and a specifier. Prepositions are prototypically "birelational"; they specify a relation (spatial, temporal, or other) between two entities (or two events, circumstances, etc.). And the syntax of argument structure— permitting both complements and specifiers—defines an entirely local structure corresponding to the birelational character of prepositions. It is at least intuitively appealing to think of the structure of a prepositional projection as involving a kind of predication. According to this conception of the structure, the head (P) and its complement (a DP in the examples considered so far) combine to form a predicate. By definition, a predicate requires a "subject," which is supplied by the specifier. Thus, the appearance of a specifier, as well as the appearance of a complement, is an inescapable consequence of the nature of the head. Since it is the head that fully determines the dyadic structure in these cases, we will refer to them as *basic dyadic*.

There is another argument structure type whose character compels us to attribute to it an internal specifier argument. It differs from the type represented by (17) in certain respects, however. Consider the following sentence pairs:

(19) a. i. The leaves turned red.
        ii. The cold turned the leaves red.
     b. i. The coconut split open.
        ii. The blow split the coconut open.
     c. i. The liquid froze solid.
        ii. We froze the liquid solid.

    d. i. The safe blew open.
      ii. The charge blew the safe open.

Like the prepositions exemplified in (16), the verbal heads in the sentences of (19) take both a complement (an adjective in these cases: *red, open, solid*) and a specifier (a DP: *the leaves, the coconut*, etc.). It is apparent that the specifier is, in our sense, internal to the lexical projection, because it appears as the sentential syntactic object in the transitive alternant (the (ii)-sentences). The transitive, we claim, is formed by embedding the intransitive lexical structure (dyadic) in the complement position of the monadic structure.

The intransitive verbal projections of (19) have the form shown in (20).

(20)

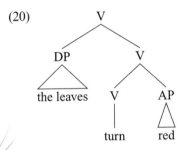

As in the prepositional constructions, the head (V) forms with its complement (AP) a substructure that demands a specifier (in the manner of a predicate requiring a subject). Here, however, it is the complement, not the verbal head itself, that has the fundamental property of requiring the projection of a specifier. It is an essential characteristic of adjectives (in languages that have them as a distinguished category) that they must be attributed of something, regardless of the structure in which they appear. In verbal constructions like (20), this property is satisfied by the specifier (i.e., a "subject" of sorts): the verbal head supplies a structure in which an appropriately positioned specifier can appear, as required by its complement.

It is fitting to view argument structures of the type represented by (20) as "composite." They are, in fact, made up of two monadic structures, one being the type already discussed (a head that takes a complement) and the other being the structural configuration inherent to the category to which English adjectives belong (heads that do not take a complement but must appear in construction with a specifier). The combined structure satisfies the requirements of the two lexical nuclei: the adjective satisfies the complement requirement of the verb, and the verb supplies a place for the specifier required by the adjective. The adjectival phrase is, so to speak, parasitic on the verbal projection. But the reverse is true as well, for the verbal head projects a specifier position solely by virtue of appearing in composition with a complement that *itself* requires an argument in a local specifier position.[4]

For obvious reasons, we will refer to dyadic structures of the type represented by (20) as *composite dyadic* whenever it is necessary to distinguish the two dyadic types.

The intransitive members of the pairs in (19) are lexically based on composite dyadic configurations depicted in (20). As actual sentences, of course, they appear in construction with specific functional projections required in sentential syntax (e.g., Tense, Complementizer). The same holds, of course, for phrasal arguments in syntax. The DP occupying specifier position in (20) is a nominal construction licensed in part by the determiner (D) projection that dominates it. But this is not enough to license a "fully projected argument phrase" in sentential syntax. The DP must at least satisfy the further requirement of Case. Accordingly, in English at least, it must raise out of the specifier position and into a position where nominative Case can be assigned (e.g., the specifier position of an inflectional category, such as Tense). Our concern here is lexical, however, and we therefore focus primarily on what we take to be the *basic* position of an argument, in this case the specifier of (20). While the DP occupying that position comes ultimately to function as subject in the sentential syntax of the intransitive sentences of (19), it functions as sentential syntactic object in the transitive ones. This is fully consistent with the claim that the argument shared by both transitive and intransitive alternants is a specifier internal to the lexical argument structure. We take the transitive alternant to have the form in (21).

(21)

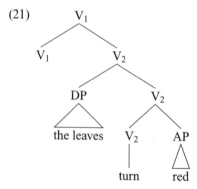

Here V_1 is a monadic nucleus taking V_2 as its complement. The latter is the dyadic structure just discussed. There is, of course, just one overt verb in the actual sentences of (19). This is also true in (21). However, in (21) we are imputing to the transitive *turn*, and to other transitives of its type, an argument structure configuration essentially isomorphic to that of the location verb *put*, as in (18), the difference being that the upper head, V_1, is an empty head in (21), unlike the overt *put* of (18). The parallel is important, however, since the transitive verb *turn* and the transitive location verb *put* come to share a fundamental structural property in sentential syntax. Specifically, the internal specifier DP is in a position in which it can, and must, receive Case; it is governed and locally c-commanded by a verbal head.

In order to fully realize the parallel between *put the books on the shelf* and *turn the leaves red*, we must contrive to get the verb *turn* into the syntactic position it actually occupies in the transitive predicate. This brings us, in fact, to a topic that will henceforth figure prominently in our discussions: namely, "conflation" or "incorporation."[5]

We have adopted the hypothesis that the upper verbal head in (21) is empty. In fact, given our general proposal, this must be the case, since the configuration involved here is built upon the intransitive substructure headed by *turn*, the sole overt verbal head. The upper head, a member of the monadic class of heads, is not separately realized phonologically. Let us say—perhaps only informally, but nonetheless conveniently for our expository purposes—that the upper head, V_1, has an empty phonological matrix. And let us assume further, as a general principle, that an empty phonological matrix must be eliminated from the morphosyntactic representation of sentences. This is accomplished, we assume, through conflation. Conflation may be a specific kind of incorporation, conforming to an especially strict version of the Head Movement Constraint (Travis 1984; Baker 1988; but see chapter 3), according to which the phonological matrix of a complement replaces the empty matrix of the governing head. Of course, by *"phonological matrix of a complement,"* we mean the "phonological matrix of the *head* of a complement." Thus, the observed structure of (21)—that is, the "surface form of the verb," the form presented to sentential syntax, so to speak—is as depicted in (22).

(22)

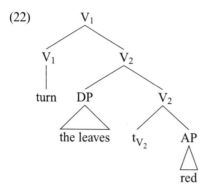

In general, we will use the term *conflation* rather than *incorporation* in reference to the process involved here, in order to distinguish it from incorporation in the sense used by Baker (1988), noting, of course, that the two notions are closely related and may ultimately prove to be the same thing. For present purposes, however, *conflation* is restricted to the process according to which the phonological matrix of the head of a complement *C* is introduced into the empty phonological matrix of the head that selects (and is accordingly sister to) *C*. This is the circumstance represented in (22), where the matrix *turn* is transferred from the lower head to the upper head—leaving, we suppose, a trace of as yet unknown character, perhaps simply a copy of V_2.[6]

Conflation, in the sense just defined, is a major process in English morphology, accounting for an impressive range of forms available through so-called zero derivation, including denominal verbs (e.g., *dance, laugh, box, saddle*) and deadjectival verbs (e.g., *clear, narrow, thin*). Conflation also accounts for certain derived words in which overt morphology appears (e.g., *redden, widen, enliven*). Zero derivation and conflation will occupy much of our discussion (see chapter 3), but before embarking on that topic, we would like to review the elementary structural types that are defined by the fundamental relations in argument structure—namely, head-complement and specifier-head. We take these to be maximally restrictive, in accordance with the informal definitions set out in (23).

(23) *The fundamental relations of argument structure*
  a. Head-complement: If *X* is the *complement* of a head *H*, then *X* is the unique sister of *H* (*X* and *H* c-command one another).
  b. Specifier-head: If *X* is the *specifier* of a head *H*, and if P_1 is the first projection of *H* (i.e., *H'*, necessarily nonvacuous), then *X* is the unique sister of P_1.

The relations defined in (23) straightforwardly permit certain lexical structures. First, a head that takes a complement but no specifier projects the structure we have termed "monadic," corresponding to (24a), in which *Head* represents the head and its categorial projections, and *Comp* represents the complement (cf. (15)). Second, the definitions permit a structural type consisting of the head alone, that is, a head whose essential property is that it takes no complement and projects no specifier, corresponding to (24d)—the "atomic" and simplest type. Third, the definitions permit a basic dyadic type in which the head projects a structure embodying both the head-complement relation and the specifier-head relation, as in (24b), in which *Spec* represents the specifier. Fourth, the logic of the definitions permits a type of head that requires a specifier but excludes a complement. This type can be generated only by composition. The head that has this property must itself appear as the complement of another head, *Head**, as in (24c), in which Head can be seen as endowing Head* with the ability to project a specifier.[7] (Throughout the book, these structural types will be known as the "(a)-type," the "(b)-type," and so on.)

(24) *The structural types of lexical argument structure*

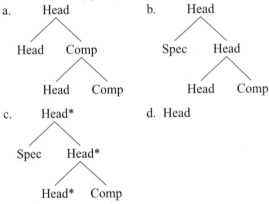

The structural configurations set out in (24) are neutral with respect to the morphosyntactic category (V, N, etc.) of the head. We think it is right to keep these things separate. While there is, in English, a favored categorial realization of these heads, it does not hold crosslinguistically, and it does not hold universally in any one language, including English. In English, the predominant realizations are as follows: (a) V, (b) P, (c) A, (d) N. However, while (a) and (d) are relatively stable in category, (b) and (c) are less so, being realized often as V. In some languages, of course, the category A is not distinguished: in Navajo, for example, the (c)-type configuration is headed by V universally; and in Warlpiri, of Central Australia, it is realized as N. The category V is a popular categorial realization of the (b)-type; and in some languages, N realizes this type. We are aware that there is regularity here, and that there are generalizations to be made. Nevertheless, we will assume that morphosyntactic category and structural type are independent variables in the grammar of lexical projections.

We turn now to a consideration of lexical items that involve the process of "conflation," producing "synthetic" forms of the type represented by English transitive *turn*, as in (22), and various denominal verbs, such as *calve*, *sneeze*, *shelve*, *bottle*, *saddle*, and *blindfold*.

1.3 Synthetic Verbs

An unusually large number of English verbs give the appearance of being related to nouns—for example, *dance* is both a noun and a verb, as are *laugh*, *bottle*, and *saddle*; and *shelve*, *sheathe*, *sheave*, *enslave*, and *imprison* are verbs that are clearly related to nouns, in one way or another. Verbs of this sort are quite generally held to be "denominal"—they are "verbs derived from nouns."

Let us consider first the denominal verbs belonging to the class represented in (25).

(25) belch, burp, cough, crawl, cry, dance, gallop, gleam, glitter, glow, hop, jump, laugh, leap, limp, nap, run, scream, shout, skip, sleep, sneeze, sob, somersault, sparkle, speak, stagger, sweat, talk, trot, twinkle, walk, yell

These verbs share an important lexical and syntactic property with analytic verbal expressions like *make trouble* and *raise Cain*: they do not enter into the transitivity alternation that characterizes verbs like *turn* and *split*, exemplified in (19).

(26) a. i.   The cowboys made trouble.
         ii. *The beer made the cowboys trouble.
              (i.e., the cowboys made trouble because of the beer)
      b. i.   The children laughed.
         ii. *The clown laughed the children.
              (i.e., the children laughed because of the clown)

We account for this shared property, as well as the denominal character of the verbs of (25), by assigning these verbs the monadic structure (27), representing the lexical structure of *laugh*.

(27)

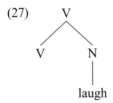

laugh

The impossibility of *laugh the child, cough the colt, cry the baby, sleep the dog,* in the sense of *make the child laugh, make the colt cough,* and so on, follows from the fact that the lexical head of each of these verbs, and of those in (25) generally, belongs to the monadic type (24a), exemplified by (27). This configuration lacks a specifier and therefore cannot transitivize in the *simple* manner.

Simple transitivization of a verb involves its insertion into the complement position of a matrix verb, for example, a verb of type (24a). This is a "free" option within the present conception of argument structure; in fact, this cannot be avoided. Suppose, then, that (27) is embedded as a complement in another verb of type (24a), giving the structure in (28).

(28)

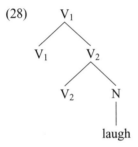

laugh

Whether a verb of this structure actually exists or not, or whether it *could* exist, is an issue that must eventually be addressed. But putting this question aside, it is clear that (28) cannot give rise to the transitive verb of *The clown laughed the children.* And this is a good thing, of course, since such a verb is impossible. This follows straightforwardly from the fact that the verbal head of the lexical structure of *laugh* projects no specifier, nor is its complement (the noun *laugh*) the type of element that forces the appearance of a specifier in the projection of the host verb (as in (24c)). Hence, there is no place in the lexical structure for the surface object *the children* in the hypothetical transitive clause *The clown laughed the children.* These observations apply generally to the verbs of (25) and to the class of verbs known as "unergatives."

By contrast, insertion of the composite dyadic ((b)-type) configuration (20) into a monadic ((a)-type) structure, giving (21), yields an acceptable transitive structure. The specifier of the dyadic complement *the leaves turn green* functions as object in the derived verbal construction. This is simple, and successful, transitivization, a free option in this framework. This option accounts as well for the large number of "fully synthetic" (often, but not exclusively, deadjectival) verbs of English, including those listed in (29), which exhibit the familiar transitivity alternation exemplified in (30).

(29) break, broaden, cool, crack, darken, deepen, enlarge, freeze, grow, harden, lengthen, loosen, lower, melt, narrow, redden, shorten, shrink, sink, soften, split, thicken, thin, tighten, widen

(30) a. The screen cleared.
     b. I cleared the screen.

The lexical item *clear* has the dual properties of the (c)-type head (i.e., the head shown in the complement position of (c)): it requires a specifier and does not take a complement. Consequently, it must appear in the composite dyadic structure, like *green* of *turn green*. It appears, therefore, as the complement of a host that projects the required specifier. Here, however, the host—unlike *turn* of *turn green*—is a phonologically empty verb, as depicted in (31), the idealized abstract structure corresponding to (19a).

(31)

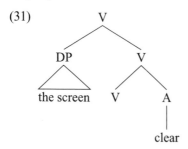

The actual verb, as seen in (30a), is derived by conflation, which introduces the phonological matrix of the adjective into the empty matrix of the verb. The verbs in (29) are of the same general type and are derived in the same way, although many of the deadjectival members of the type involve phonologically overt morphology associated with the derived verb. We assume that the host verb in these cases is bipartite, consisting of an empty phonological matrix together with a following overt matrix. The empty matrix is given phonological substance (and thereby eliminated) through conflation, resulting here in a derived verb made up of an adjectival root followed by a suffix, as in *short-en, thick-en*. Among the languages of the world, this pattern, according to which the derivation of verbs is signaled morphologically, is probably more common than zero derivation of the type represented by English *clear*. The fundamental process is the same, however.

The structure depicted in (31) corresponds, of course, to the intransitive variant of *clear*. In sentential syntax, the argument occupying its specifier will be licensed in one way or another, in the simplest case by raising to an appropriate functional category where, as subject, it will satisfy the Extended Projection Principle (EPP), a sentential syntactic condition. Transitivization, as noted, is a free and inescapable possibility, given by virtue of the fact that a verbal projection may appear as complement in the (a)-type argument structure configuration, as in (32).

(32)

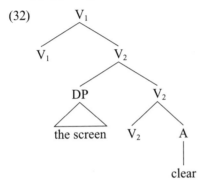

Transitivization is successful here, since *clear* forces the appearance of a specifier in the (c)-type structure and accordingly presents an object for the derived transitive verb. The derived verb itself is the result of conflation, first of A with V_2 and then of V_2 with V_1, and its derived position ensures that it will assign Case to the DP that it locally c-commands (i.e., the specifier of its complement), in accordance with the principles of Case assignment that hold in English and other accusative languages.

As an aside, we should mention that representations like (31) and (32) do not exist at any stage in the syntactic representations of sentences. Rather, they are used here simply to register the properties of the heads that comprise the lexical item involved (e.g., the specifier requirement of *clear*, the complement requirement of V_2, and the complement requirement of V_1). The actual derivation of argument structure configurations, like the derivation of syntactic structures generally, proceeds according to the principles of bare phrase structure (Chomsky 1995). We take conflation to be a concomitant of Merge. Thus, when (phonologically null) V and the adjective *clear* are merged to form the derived verbal projection [v V A], conflation "happens immediately." That is to say, in addition to the standard head-complement configuration that results from Merge, we assume that it is a property of heads that are phonologically empty, whether wholly or partially, that they attract the phonological matrix of their complement, conflating with it (but see chapter 3 for further developments). This has certain consequences for the theory of argument structure, as we will show presently.

Conflation is also involved in the derivation of English "location" and "locatum" verbs ((33a) and (33b), respectively; see Clark and Clark 1979).

(33) a. bag, bank, bottle, box, cage, can, corral, crate, floor (opponent), garage, jail, kennel, package, pasture, pen, photograph, pocket, pot, shelve, ship (the oars), shoulder, tree

       b. bandage, bar, bell, blindfold, bread, butter, clothe, curtain, dress, fund, gas, grease, harness, hook, house, ink, oil, paint, paper, powder, saddle, salt, seed, shoe, spice, water, word

These verbs are synthetic counterparts of the verb *put*, whose argument structure is depicted in (18). Thus, they involve the dyadic (b)-type structure appearing as the complement of the (a)-type, as shown in (34).

(34)

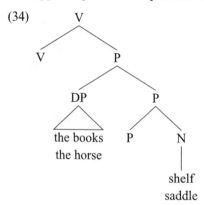

Here again, we interpret the diagram in (34) as a depiction of the properties of the heads that make up the lexical item. The inner head, belonging to the category P, has the syntactic property that it takes a complement and projects a specifier (a DP: e.g., *the books*, *the horse*). In addition, it has the morphological property that it is empty and therefore must conflate with its complement. The upper head, V, is also empty and thus necessarily conflates with its complement (i.e., with the head of its complement) P, itself the product of conflation. These processes give phonological constituency to the verbal head in (34), as required, and as exemplified in the sentences of (35).

(35) a. I shelved the books.
     b. She saddled the horse.

The recognized and real distinction between location and locatum verbs is not solely structural. It resides in the fundamental semantic properties of the prepositions involved. While the prepositions in (35a,b) are tacit, they correspond respectively to overt locational *at, in, on*, on the one hand, and overt "possessional" *with*, on the other. Thus, the preposition of (35b) corresponds to *with* in *She fitted the horse with a saddle* or *She brought it about that the horse came to be "with saddle."*[8] In *The book is on the table*, it is appropriate to identify *the book* as the "theme" and *the table* as the "location" (see Gruber 1965). And in *I saw John with a new car*, the relation between *John* and *a new car* is one of temporary possession, in which the "theme" of the possessive relation is *a new car*, and *John* names the possessor. It is a fundamental property of *at* (likewise *on, in*) that its complement is understood as the "location," while the "theme" role is associated with the argument that satisfies the specifier requirement of the preposition (i.e., *the book* in *The book is on the table*). In the case of *with*, in its (temporary) possessive sense, these relations are reversed: the object of the preposition (i.e., *a new car* in ... *John with a new car*) is understood as the "theme" of the possessive relation, while the specifier (*John*) is understood as the (temporary) possessor.

Structures of the type represented by (35) raise a question in relation to the theory of argument structure. Suppose, for example, the inner head P in (35a) were not empty, but contained an overt preposition—say, *on, onto,* or *with*. English does not permit incorporation of a noun into these prepositions, nor does it permit incorporation of bare prepositions into an empty verb. These are local facts of English, not necessarily of languages generally. So no conflation will occur from the P or its complement. The latter cannot "skip" the preposition, of course, by virtue of the Head Movement Constraint. But suppose the specifier of P were a simple noun, rather than a DP. Could that noun conflate with the verb? That is to say, could N conflate with V in (36)?

(36)

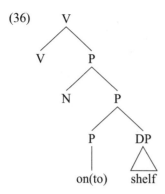

By hypothesis, conflation of nouns into verbs is possible, straightforwardly giving unergatives like *laugh, sleep,* and so on, as we have shown. But conflation from a specifier would give rise to a class of location verbs like those exemplified in (37a,b) and locatum verbs like those in (37c,d).

(37) a. *He booked on the shelf.
          (cf. He put books on the shelf/shelved books.)
     b. *We appled in the box.
          (cf. We put apples in the box/boxed apples.)
     c. *They housed with a roof.
          (cf. They fitted a house with a roof/roofed a house.)
     d. *They water with poison.
          (cf. They contaminate water with poison/poison water.)

So far as we can tell, these are impossible in any language, a fact that follows, we believe, from the view of conflation as a concomitant of Merge and a relation holding strictly between a head and its complement. In (36), for example, the head-complement relation holds between P and V. The former is (the head of) the complement of the latter. Accordingly, P can conflate with V—depending on language-specific factors, to be sure (thus, in English, only with prior conflation of empty P and its N complement). By contrast, N, the specifier of P in (36), bears no relation whatsoever to V in lexical argument structure, where the only "visible" relations are specifier-head and head-complement (see chapter 3).

   The same principle might also explain the impossibility of verbs of the type represented in the "serial" constructions of (38).

(38) a. *He speared straighten.
          (cf. He straightened a spear. The spear straightened.)

  b. *She cinched tighten.
     (cf. She tightened the cinch. The cinch tightened.)

The starred sentences are derived by hypothetical conflation of the specifier of a composite dyadic—(c)-type—verb into the higher empty verb of the transitive alternate. That is to say, N of (39) conflates with V_1, an impossibility if conflation is a relation, established at Merge, between a head and its complement.[9]

(39)

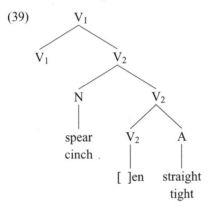

1.4 Interaction

In subsequent chapters, we will examine certain cases in which argument structure, as defined above, interacts with other linguistic systems, including the following (repeated from (14)):

(40) a. conflation and selection (chapter 3),
     b. merge and obviation (chapter 2),
     c. active and stative (chapter 7).

In this section, we merely introduce these topics, leaving a fuller treatment for the chapters noted in (40).

1.4.1 Conflation and Selection

Conflation is a term we use to refer to the phonological instantiation of light verbs in denominal verb constructions. Specifically, conflation has to do with the problem of how the verb ends up carrying the phonological matrix of its nominal complement, as in examples like (2) and (10a), the relevant structures for which are repeated in (41).

(41) a.

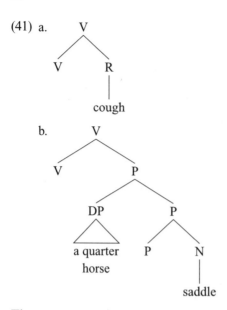

These representations give the impression that the basic structures locate the phonological matrix of the noun in the noun itself—that is, in the complement of V in the case of (41a), of P in the case of (41b). On this view of the matter, which for many years we held to be self-evident, the spell-out of the verb (*cough, saddle,* in these examples) required a kind of movement, resulting ultimately in the acquisition by the V of the phonological matrix of the relevant noun. It seemed reasonable to propose that the movement operation involved in these derivations was incorporation, in the technical sense invoked by Baker (1988). This idea was abandoned, however, because incorporation overgenerates, incorrectly sanctioning incorporation from the position of the internal specifier (e.g., from the position of DP in (41b)). Unconstrained, incorporation permits forms like those in (42).

(42) a. *They salted in the box.
          (cf. They boxed the salt.)
     b. *They tiled with grout.
          (cf. They grouted the tile.)

A properly constrained conflation operation must be strictly local, relating a head (say, V) and the head of its complement (e.g., V, P, N). The relations expressed in (41) are local in the required sense. Thus, in (41a), the noun *cough* heads the complement of V. In (41b), there are two relevant local relations to consider: P and its complement *saddle*, and V and its complement P. This chain of local relations permits the conflation of V with *saddle*. Importantly, the specifier DP in (41b) is completely "out of the loop."

A slightly different way to think about the structural relation that is relevant for conflation is in terms of selection. Strict locality holds for conflation if the governing head (V) *selects* the target X^0 in its complement. This guarantees locality and precludes conflation of a specifier, which bears no structural relation to the governing head. In (43b), the noun *box* is selected by P, and P is selected by V, but *salt* is not selected by V or any other head.

(43) a. They boxed salt.
      b.

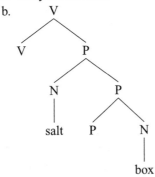

The correct structural relation for conflation can be guaranteed in a number of ways. As just suggested, selection itself guarantees the correct structural relation: a head X^0 may enter into the conflation relation with the head of its complement C if X^0 selects C. In (43b), P conflates with *box*, and V conflates with P. Conflation of V and *salt* is impossible. In (41a), V conflates with R.

1.4.2 Merge and Obviation

The previous discussion has brought out the special role of root elements. For present purposes, we maintain that a verb like *dance*, for example, has two components: (i) the categorial signature V and (ii) the root component *dance*, a core lexical item comprising the correct phonological matrix (or matrices) and the correct semantic structure. The phonological matrix determines the spelling of the verb.

In this section, we consider certain aspects of the meanings of root elements, with the expectation that what we will find will be some sort of interface relation between semantics and argument structure, with no fundamental effect on our conception of the latter. In this connection, consider the following pair, illustrating a common transitivity alternation in English:

(44) a. The kids splashed mud on the wall.
    b. Mud splashed on the wall.

The transitive alternant results from "immediate gratification" of the specifier requirement of P, as shown in (45a); and the intransitive variant results from "delayed gratification" of that requirement, as shown in (45b).

(45) a.   b.

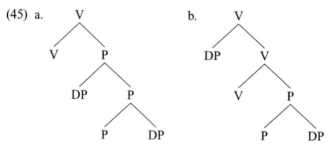

The two alternants are defined straightforwardly and automatically by the operation Merge (Chomsky 1995). Other things being equal, the alternation seen here should always be available. It is not always available, of course, as shown by (46), where the intransitive alternant is ungrammatical. The structure of the two alternants is depicted in (47).

(46) a.   The kids smeared mud on the wall.
     b.   *Mud smeared on the wall.

(47) a.   b.

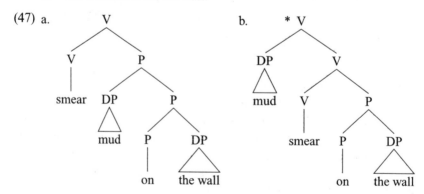

The difference between these two verbs lies in the semantic components of their root elements. Specifically, the difference is to be found in what might be termed the "manner factor" inherent in the semantics of the root. The verb *splash* in (44) involves a manner feature that is in a clear sense "linked" to the internal argument *mud*. It represents the motion and dispersal of particulate matter associated with *mud*, not with the external argument. This relation is preserved in both the transitive and the intransitive alternants. By contrast, the verb *smear* in (46) is characterized by a "manner feature" linked externally—that is, embodying a gesture or motion associated with the external argument. This relation is, of course, disrupted in the intransitive alternant depicted in (47b). The *smear* factor cannot be linked to the external argument in this case, since that position will be taken by the internal argument, raised there in sentential syntax. Accordingly, the sentence is ungrammatical.

Examples of this sort will be taken up again in chapter 2, and the analysis adopted for them there will be extended to verbs of impact and concussion (like *dent* and *kick*) and to the well-known distinction between subject-experiencer and object-experiencer psych verbs (like *love* and *anger*, respectively).

1.4.3 Active and Stative

This section is much more speculative than the previous two, however speculative those may also be. We begin with a discussion of adjectives.

Adjectives pose an immediate problem for the framework assumed in Hale and Keyser 1993. This is the case, in particular, for adjectival nuclei whose fundamental property is that they take just one argument—specifically, an argument that stands in the relation of specifier, not complement. The problem resides in the fact that the appropriate cooccurrence of the adjective and the specifier it requires cannot be effected by Merge. The creation of a syntactic constituent by merging DP and A(djective) results in the complementation configuration, putting the DP in the wrong relation to the adjectival nucleus. What is required is a configuration in which the DP occupies a position in which the adjective will be attributed, or predicated, of the DP—a relation that can be expressed notationally by coindexing DP and an appropriate projection of A. This is the essential adjectival requirement, and it can be satisfied in a configuration in which the DP is suitably close to the A-projection but is not a sister to the A-head. By *suitably close*, we mean that the specifier DP locally c-commands the relevant (whether maximum or intermediate) projection of the adjective and the latter is c-subjacent to the former (see Williams 1980).

The problem is resolved in the argument structure configurations of deadjectival verbs like *clear, narrow, redden, darken.* These are assumed here to have a structure like (48) in which a verbal head serves not only to project the verbal category (i.e., to "verbalize" the adjective) but also to host the specifier required by A (here a maximal projection, trivially).

(48)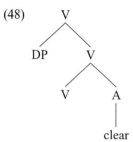

As usual, this diagram represents the properties of the heads involved. It is the "virtual" structure, not the actual "output": Merge applied to V and A results immediately in conflation, giving the verb *clear,* as in *The sky cleared.*

But what of the adjective when it appears to lack a host for the specifier it requires? Consider, for example, the structure of an adjectival small clause, of the type illustrated in (49).

(49) a. We found [the sky clear].
     b. We consider [our students brilliant].
     c. With [the sky clear], we can fly today.
     d. With [my clothes wet], Mom wouldn't let me in the house.

If *the sky* in (49a) is in a specifier position, what head projects that position? We have assumed that A itself does not merge directly with the phrase that satisfies its specifier requirement, since the resulting relation would be indistinguishable from that holding between a head and its complement, not the required relation here. And in (49) there is no other obvious candidate to host the specifier—a problem, on the face of it.

This problem, among others, will be taken up in chapter 7, where we are concerned in large part with the question of stativity and its "source" and proper representation in the grammar. In relation to its source, that chapter considers a number of possibilities, including (i) the possibility that stativity is a matter of category (e.g., with P, N, and A identified as "stative" and V identified as "active"), (ii) the related possibility that stativity is rooted in a simple feature opposition (e.g., in which "stative" versus "active" corresponds, respectively, to the opposition "central" versus "terminal" coincidence; see Hale 1986); and finally, (iii) the possibility that stativity is derived from a purely configurational relation in the syntax of argument structure. If the last possibility were correct, then the opposition would be expected to be, to some extent, independent of category. The well-known distinction between the prepositional elements in (50a–d) might be understood in terms of this opposition (see Jackendoff 1983, where a structure for the complex preposition *into* is suggested).

(50) a. The parrot flew in its cage. (i.e., flew around in its cage)
     b. The parrot flew into its cage.
     c. With the parrot in its cage, we can all breathe a sigh of relief.
     d. *With the parrot into its cage, we can all breathe a sigh of relief.

1.5   Other Topics

While the three issues briefly described in the foregoing section have to do with questions of interface, the other chapters of this book deal with questions variously related to argument structure as defined at the outset. Chapter 4 briefly visits four languages superficially quite different from English with a view to gaining some modest crosslinguistic perspective on at least one aspect of argument structure, namely, the standard transitivity alternation of so-called labile (freely alternating) verbs, like English *break, sink, clear*. The choice of four Native American languages for this purpose is purely a matter of convenience, these being languages about which we have something relevant to say.

Chapter 5 is a tentative and highly preliminary discussion of the double object construction of English, a favorite topic in treatments of argument structure. Chapter 6 is in large part our reaction to the idea that verbs like *arrive* are the true unaccusatives. From our perspective, the inchoative member of labile verbs is the true unaccusative. Something special has to be said about verbs like *arrive, exist, arise, appear*. We hasten to mention that chapters 5–7 are highly tentative and only partially integrated into the general discussion. They are in the nature of notes to ourselves and have been left more or less in the form in which they were first set down.

Chapter 8 is somewhat more carefully considered, having to do with a problem in computation. Specifically, it deals with a timing issue, or traffic problem, in relation to the operation Merge and the satisfaction of a certain requirement (the "specifier requirement") inherent to individual lexical items.

Chapter 2

Bound Features, Merge, and Transitivity Alternations

2.1 Introduction

With certain exceptions, denominal verbs in English do not participate in the standard transitivity alternation readily enjoyed by deadjectival verbs. Thus, while verbs like *clear*, *narrow*, and *widen* have both transitive and intransitive uses, location and locatum verbs, like *bag* and *harness*, have only the transitive use, and denominal unergatives, like *sneeze* and *foal*, have only the use traditionally called "intransitive" (setting aside the cognate object and small clause complementation constructions, *sneeze a raucous sneeze* and *sneeze one's head off*). All this can be explained quite easily in a variety of frameworks, including those that, like ours, attempt to explain such phenomena in structural, or configurational, terms. In our framework, unergatives fail to transitivize because they project no specifier; location and locatum verbs fail to "detransitivize" because omission of the upper verb leaves a P(repositional)-projection, not a verbal projection. These features are often mirrored by corresponding analytic constructions. Thus, for example, the location verb phrase *put the loot in the bag* and the locatum verb phrase *fit the mule with hobbles* have no intransitive counterparts. Likewise, *make trouble*, an analytic unergative, so to speak, has neither an intransitive counterpart nor a further transitivization of the relevant sort—*make him trouble* does not mean 'cause him to make trouble'. These are explained in the same way as the synthetic (denominal) constructions above. Finally, the transitive denominal verbs of the location and locatum type share the property that they can participate in the middle construction, like the transitive deadjectival verbs; thus, *These apples bag easily*, *This colt saddles easily*, and *This paint thins easily* are all well formed. The middle is possible here, we maintain, because the argument that advances to subject is a specifier. The object of an analytic unergative is not a specifier, by hypothesis; hence, *Trouble makes easily* is ill formed.

In this chapter, we attempt to explain certain counterexamples to these proposals. Consider, for example, the use of English *get* in the analytic location construction *get the books on the shelf*, in the sense of 'put the books on the shelf'. This has an intransitive counterpart, *The books got on the shelf (mysteriously)*, not accounted for in the manner suggested in the previous paragraph. According to what is implied there, this should be transitive only. The same observation can be made about *splash* and *smear*, as in *splash/smear mud on the wall*. While *smear* behaves "as it should" in having only a transitive use, *splash* has an intransitive use as well, as in *Mud splashed on the wall (when the car passed)*. Similarly, the analytic locatum construction *load the truck with hay* is transitive only, while *fill the room with smoke* has an intransitive counterpart, as in *The room filled with smoke*. In explaining these examples, we will consider the nature of the Merge operation responsible for the composition of lexical argument structure configurations. We will also refer to what we term "manner" features inherent in the overt lexical nuclei heading verbal predicates of the type just adduced. These features lead us to propose an extension of our framework beyond our core program of explaining lexical argument structure solely in terms of the structural relations head-complement and specifier-head.

Certain verbs to which we impute the structure of location and locatum denominals fail to participate in the middle construction. The verb *dent*, for example, does form middles, as in *This kind of fender dents easily*. But the verb *kick*, for example, does not: *This kind of tire kicks easily*. Here we will refer again to inherent manner features distinguishing the two classes and accounting for the "affectedness" or "change of state" associations of one as opposed to the other. We will extend this analysis to subject-experiencer and object-experiencer psych verbs; the former resist the middle (*Leecil Bewd respects easily*), while the latter do not (*Leecil Bewd angers easily*).

2.2 Merge

We turn first to verbs like *splash* and *get*, which take P-projection complements and, unlike *put* and *smear*, nonetheless participate in the transitivity alternation.

(1) a. The pigs splashed mud on the wall.
    b. Mud splashed on the wall (when the pigs ran past).

(2) a. The pigs got mud on the wall.
    b. Mud got on the wall.

(3) a. We put spurs on Leecil.
    b. *Spurs put on Leecil.

(4) a. Leecil smeared saddle soap on my chaps.
    b. *Saddle soap smeared on my chaps.

In the past, we accounted for verbs of the type represented by (3) and (4), which we assumed to be the "normal" location verb type, under the assumption that the overt verbal head (*put*, *smear*) took as its complement an "entire" P-projection, as does the phonologically null verbal head of a denominal location verb like *shelve*, whose structure is depicted in (5).

(5)

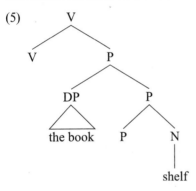

Removal of the matrix verbal projection leaves a P-projection, not an intransitive verbal projection. This is in contrast to deadjectival verbs, whose inner and outer heads are both verbs. Absence of the outer verb leaves the standard (unaccusative) intransitive verbal projection, as exemplified by *clear* in (6).

(6)

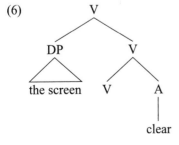

If this is correct, then something additional must be said about verbs like *splash, drip, dribble, spill*, and many others, which take P-based complements and nevertheless participate in the transitivity alternation exemplified in (1) and (2).

Although many possibilities exist, the simplest is one that, so far as we can tell, stems directly from the principles inherent in Merge (Chomsky 1995, 2000), deriving the basic structures upon which the relations head-complement and specifier-head are defined. Accordingly, let us suppose, contrary to what we have suggested in the past, that a constituent consisting of a preposition and its complement (e.g., *on the wall*, a syntactic object previously defined by Merge) can itself be merged, not with its required specifier, but with a verb (e.g., *splash*), giving the structure portrayed in (7).

(7)

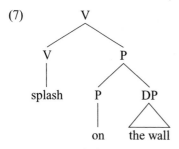

There is nothing to prevent this; in fact, it is an unavoidable possibility, so far as we can see. We must assume, however, that this structure is ill formed unless the specifier requirement of P-projections is met, in the same manner in which it is met in deadjectival verbs: to wit, the verb necessarily projects a specifier, giving the structure in (8).

(8)

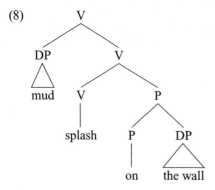

In essence, this is the structure associated with the intransitive alternant of the standard transitivity alternation for deadjectivals, extended here to P-complemented alternating verbs of the type represented by *splash* in (1), the transitive alternant being derived now in the usual way (by further application of Merge with a nonovert V), as in (9).

(9)

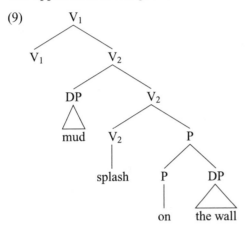

On the assumption that the structure shown in (9) cannot be avoided within the conception of argument structure we have adopted throughout, we have a solution to one-half of the problem of P-complemented verbs: the alternating-type verbs are basically like verbs with adjectival complements. But this analytical decision creates another problem: what about the nonalternating P-complemented verbs, like *smear* and *daub*? Why do these *not* alternate?

This is the topic of the next section. But before taking up that question, we would like to remark briefly on denominal location and locatum verbs in this connection. With occasional exceptions (among them verbs of "moving to an edge, surface, or point," such as *land, center, back, front*), these verbs systematically fail to participate in the transitivity alternation (e.g., *The books shelved*, *The horse saddled*). We feel that this follows, to some extent at least, from the fact that the verbal component is of the nonovert variety, which has just the features of a verb, nothing else, and by its very nature therefore does not project a specifier, necessarily taking the entire P-projection as its complement (the required specifier being projected by P itself).[1] It is the essential, unmarked property of verbs that they take complements but do not project specifiers, exceptions being those cases in which the complement forces projection. Denominal location and locatum verbs represent the unmarked, or regular, case, in contrast to deadjectival verbs, where a bare adjective cannot project its required specifier autonomously.

2.3 Bound Features

We must now account for the "normal case"—that represented by verbs like *put* and *smear* in (3) and (4). Specifically, we must somehow ensure that *smear*, for example, is excluded from the configuration associated with the intransitive variant of alternating verbs like *splash*. In other words, we must ensure that the verb phrase of (4b), depicted in (10), is excluded.

(10)

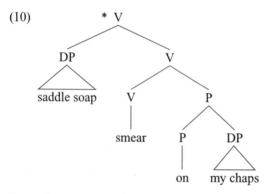

Instead, we assume the verb *smear*, and its like, enters directly into construction with the maximal projection of P, including its specifier, of course, as in (11).

(11)

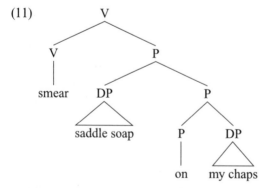

If (11), but not (10), is the correct configuration for *smear*, then the data of (4) are accounted for. But how can we ensure this? One possibility is that (11) is simply the regular case, (10) being ruled out by preemption. On this view, the alternating type (i.e., the *splash* type) would represent the marked case and would have to be specially learned, implying that the whole matter might simply be unsystematic.

There is another possibility, one that requires us to depart somewhat from our program of focusing primarily on the role of syntactic configuration in the study of argument structure. It is generally agreed that certain aspects of the meanings of lexical items are relevant to their functioning in syntactic structures. We are referring here not to meanings that stem from the configurations in which they appear (e.g., the so-called θ-roles, and the various eventuality relations such as causation, coincidence, affectedness, change of state, and result) but to features of the lexical semantics of individual items, often of an "encyclopedic" character (in the sense of Marantz 1997). We believe that the contrast between *smear*-type and *splash*-type verbs is to be found in this realm, though it has clear syntactic correlates (namely, the ones we are concerned with).

Consider again the contrast involved here. The verbs of (12) can be termed *patient-manner* verbs because they include, perhaps in their lexical-encyclopedic entries, an adverbial semantic "feature" that identifies the physical motion, distribution, dispersal, or attitude of the entity denoted by the argument (the "patient") occupying the specifier position in the P-projection that functions as their complement.

(12) a. Mud splashed on the wall.
         (cf. The cars splashed mud on the wall.)
     b. Ice cream dripped on the sidewalk.
         (cf. The child dripped ice cream on the sidewalk.)
     c. Water spilled on the floor.
         (cf. The puppy spilled water on the floor.)

Patient-manner verbs belong to the alternating type, of course, the lexical semantic adverbial feature being associated with an *internal* argument. By contrast, P-complemented verbs of the steadfastly transitive type might be termed *agent-manner* verbs.

(13) a. *Mud smeared on the wall.
         (cf. They smeared mud on the wall.)
     b. *White pipeclay daubed on the dancers' bodies.
         (cf. The kurdungurlu daubed white pipeclay on the dancers' bodies.)

   c. *Quarter moons stamped on the leather.

     (cf. The saddle maker stamped quarter moons on the leather.)

These can be said to include an adverbial feature that describes the actions of entities denoted by their *external* arguments: to "smear X on Y" requires an "agent" who executes the gestures that, in accordance with the lexical-encyclopedic entry, are necessary in performing the action so named (and similarly for "daub X on Y," etc.).

We propose that it is the circumstance just described that prevents the nonalternating verbs from appearing in the otherwise freely available intransitive configuration (10). Briefly, that configuration obfuscates the correct association of the "agent-manner" adverbial feature with the external argument, there being no truly external argument in the intransitive configuration. On the other hand, the alternating verbs will permit the correct adverbial feature association in both transitive and intransitive configurations, the relevant internal argument being present in both.

There are complications associated with this idea, but we would nevertheless like to pursue it somewhat in the final portion of this discussion. Before proceeding, however, we suggest a notation (a notation, not a true formalism) analogous to indices of the type used in expressing coreference and anaphoric binding. We will represent the adverbial feature associated with a lexical item by means of a (curly) bracketed index, for example, $\{i\}$. This index must be "bound" (by an argument subscripted with an identical alphabetic subscript); otherwise, the structure fails. The configuration shown in (14), in a sentential syntactic context in which an external argument is locally available, is well formed, since $\{i\}$ will be properly bound.

(14)

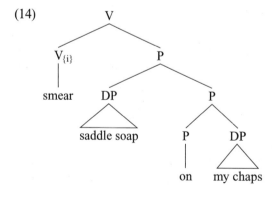

In (15), however, assuming just the argument structure configuration shown, the adverbial index is not bound, assuming it to require an external binder, and the structure fails.[2]

(15)

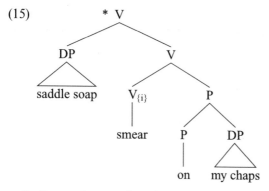

So far, we have assigned bracketed indices only to items bearing externally bound adverbial features, as if internally associated features were simply bound to the "closest" argument and needed no special notation. In the best situation, this would be true in general, we suppose—the proper association would be decided by the configuration in which heads and arguments appeared, returning us nicely to our original expectations of argument structure relations. But we have not been able to achieve this. Instead, we are led to believe that, at the very least, a distinction between obviative and proximate adverbial features must be recognized. In the following section, we examine a somewhat different case.

2.4   *Respect* and *Impact*

The problem we will take up here has to do with the behavior of certain verbs in relation to the renowned and much-studied middle construction of English (see, e.g., Ackema and Schoorlemmer 1995; Condoravdi 1989; Fagan 1988, 1992; Kemmer 1993; Keyser and Roeper 1984; Levin 1993; Rapoport 1997). As is well known, many transitive verbs cannot participate in that construction. Among these are certain subject-experiencer psych verbs of the type represented in (16).

(16) a. *The truth respects easily.
          (cf. We respect the truth.)
     b. *John's talent envies easily.
          (cf. Everyone envies John's talent.)

    c. *French films love easily.
       (cf. My kids love French films.)
    d. *The Misumalpan languages know easily.
       (cf. Most Sumus know at least two Misumalpan languages.)

Many object-experiencer verbs, by contrast, form middles straightforwardly.

(17) a. Politicians anger easily.
       (cf. The truth angers politicians.)
    b. This colt frightens easily.
       (cf. Loud noises frighten this colt.)
    c. I worry easily.
       (cf. Economic downturns worry me.)
    d. Children bore easily.
       (cf. Adult talk bores children.)

This asymmetry is a problem for the view that the two types of experiencer predicates share the same essential argument structure—the theme
being a complement and the experiencer a specifier in the internal P-
projection complement of the verbal head. This arrangement is shown in
(18a,b), the assumed lexical configurations for *respect the truth* and *anger
politicians* (abstracting away from conflation, as usual).

(18) a.

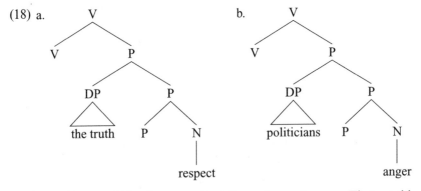

The problem could be these structures themselves, of course. That would
be a serious problem for our conception of predicate argument structure,
since these structures are virtually forced on us by our conception of
conflation as (i) a concomitant of Merge and (ii) a relation between
heads—and not, say, a relation between a head and a specifier it locally
c-commands (the latter being invisible for conflation, by hypothesis).

The usual account here is that object-experiencer verbs form middles because they conform to the requirement that the relevant argument (the experiencer in this case) is "affected" by the action denoted by the verb, while the relevant argument of subject-experiencer verbs is unaffected, in some sense, and therefore fails to meet the Affectedness Requirement. This is descriptively true, to be sure, but what does it mean, exactly, in relation to the grammar? What is behind the notion that the object of a subject-experiencer verb is unaffected? We think this is probably true, though it is hard to argue for it in some cases—does loving someone leave that person unaffected? The issue becomes a philosophical question rather than a grammatical one. However, if we look at the problem from a different point of view, there is perhaps something that can be said of a grammatical nature.

Consider not whether the object of a subject-experiencer verb is affected or unaffected, but rather the semantic connection between the inner complement (the conflating "theme": e.g., *respect, anger*) and the internal and external arguments of the transitive verb. And consider as well the expressions cited in (19) and (20), which bear a quasi-paraphrastic semantic relation to corresponding subject-experiencer verbs.

(19) a. Mary has my respect.
     (cf. I respect Mary.)
  b. She has the boss's esteem.
     (cf. The boss esteems her.)
  c. He has his children's love.
     (cf. His children love him.)

(20) a. I give my respect to Mary.
  b. The boss gives her his esteem.
  c. His children give him their love.

These have in common that the phrase corresponding to the "emotion" (i.e., the "psych nominal": here, *my respect, the boss's esteem, their love*), contains overt material (a genitive nominal or pronominal) representing the experiencer. Without this (e.g., in *Mary has respect, He has love*), the character of these expressions is greatly altered; for all intents and purposes, the experiencer disappears (except to the extent that it can be imagined somehow and variably attributed).

Importantly, morphology referring to the experiencer in sentences of the type represented by (19) and (20) is *obviative*, in the sense that it cannot refer to the entity corresponding to the "closest" argument (compare the similar effect of the interesting and quite separate semantic principle embodied in Wechsler's (1995) Notion-Rule).[3] Thus, for example, the genitive pronouns in (21) cannot be linked to the subject.

(21) a. John$_i$ has his$_j$ respect.
     b. Mary$_i$ has her$_j$ esteem.

Likewise, in (22), the genitive pronouns cannot be linked to the indirect object; instead, they are linked to the subject (i.e., the more distant argument).

(22) a. Mary$_j$ gives her$_i$ all her$_j$ love.
     b. John$_j$ gives him$_i$ his$_j$ respect.

Thus, the psych nominals in such sentences as these contain a genitive that

(23) a. refers to an experiencer,
     b. is obviative, and
     c. is anaphoric, in the sense that it is necessarily linked to a
        c-commanding antecedent if there is one.

Of course, these characteristics do not hold of genitives in structurally similar constructions of a different type.

(24) a. John has his foibles.
     b. Mary has her customs.
     c. Mary gives her all her money.
     d. John gives him his money.

Here, it seems to us, only the general binding theory limits the range of coreference possibilities.

   The properties enumerated in (23) essentially boil down to two: the genitive in psych nominal expressions is *obviative* and *anaphoric*. We believe that this is the key to the problem of the middle construction illustrated in (16). Notice first that in a sentence like (25a), the psych noun *love*, which we assume to give rise to the corresponding verb (through Merge and conflation), has semantic properties identical to those of the psych nominal phrase in (25b).

(25) a. Mary loves her children.
     b. Mary$_i$ gives her children$_j$ her$_i$ love.

That is to say, the emotion "love" is attributed to Mary, the experiencer, in both cases. That emotion is not attributed to the children, whatever the real-world situation might be. This pattern is true of all subject-experiencer verbs we have considered: the conflated noun "acts as if" it contained a genitive specifier conforming to the principles of (23). We will assume that something of this nature is in fact true.

It cannot be "literally" true that the conflating noun in subject-experiencer verbs has a genitive specifier, since that would entail that it heads a phrase (nontrivially) and hence would not conflate with the verb. We will assume instead that the psych noun (*love, respect, envy*, etc.) is to be understood as a bare noun that bears the "part" relation to some entity (the "whole") and, as in many languages, is related to the latter by means of a relation akin to, perhaps identical to, secondary predication (as suggested for part-whole relations in Warlpiri, for instance, in Hale 1981). We will employ the bracketed subscript to represent this informally, and we will speak informally as if the subscript assigned to the psych noun, in addition to signaling its relation to its antecedent (bearing the corresponding plain subscript), were an actual item having the properties set out in (23), specifically the properties of being obviative and anaphoric. That is to say, technically, it corresponds to a variable and hence must be bound (obviatively in these constructions). Accordingly, the abstract structural configuration given in (18a), corresponding to (16a), would have the representation in (26), where, in accordance with (23), the bracketed subscript is necessarily disjoint from the specifier, the closest argument, but it is necessarily bound by the next closest argument, the external argument, corresponding to the subject-experiencer (not shown).

(26)

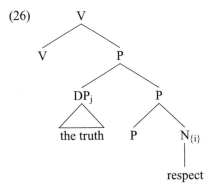

Correspondingly, in (25), the subscript is not bound by *her children*, by virtue of (23b). Instead, it is bound by the external argument *Mary*—it is Mary's emotion, not her children's.

(27)

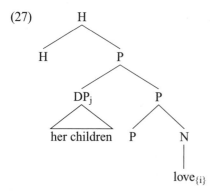

Not shown here is the external argument, the subject-experiencer, which by hypothesis must bear the i-subscript in accordance with the anaphoric nature of the bracketed subscript assigned to the psych noun *love*.

It is the anaphoric property of the bracketed subscript, or rather of its real linguistic correlate (i.e., necessary attribution of the psych noun to the external argument), that is most relevant to our account of the failure of subject-experiencer psych verbs to form middles. We assume with a number of other writers (see Ackema and Schoorlemmer 1995; Rapoport 1997) that the middle lacks an external argument.

Consider again verbs like *shelve* or *saddle*, which freely enter into the middle construction. The structure is essentially that shown in (28), abstracting away from conflation.

(28)

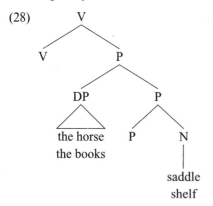

Under "ordinary" circumstances, a verb with this structure will form a predicate in sentential syntax and will take an external argument, its subject. The bare noun will have conflated with the empty P at Merge, P will have conflated with V at Merge, and the DP in the internal specifier position will be Case-licensed by the locally c-commanding V.

We maintain that the essential circumstance driving middle formation is the need to Case-license the DP in specifier position (*the horse, the books*, in (28)). In the middle, the verb has the property that it is unable to assign Case. From this, it follows, other things being equal, that the verb will not take an external argument; it cannot, since the DP in internal specifier position must raise to sentential syntactic subject position (for a formal proposal on the verbal property correlating with the ability or inability to assign Case, see Bittner 1994 and Bittner and Hale 1996a,b). From this, it follows in turn that subject-experiencer verbs cannot form middles; otherwise, the principles in (23) would be violated. In particular, the requirement that the bracketed subscript be appropriately bound cannot be satisfied in the middle, inasmuch as the hallmark of the middle is its lack of an external argument. The internal argument, the specifier DP, cannot satisfy the binding requirement, because the bracketed subscript is obviative.

Location and locatum verbs, types that freely form middles, have the property, we assume, that the nominal in the complement position is not assigned a bracketed subscript—nouns like *saddle* and *shelf* do not represent the part member of a part-whole relation (i.e., they are not inalienably possessed, so to speak). Consequently, middle formation with location and locatum verbs does not violate the principles in (23).

But the relevance of (23) is not limited to the psych verbs we have looked at here. Consider, for example, the behavior of certain verbs of "impact," as in (29).[4]

(29) a. i.   I kicked the wall.
           (cf. give the wall a kick)
      ii. *This wall kicks easily.
     b. i.   He punched the bag.
           (cf. give the bag a punch)
      ii. *This bag punches easily.
     c. i.   She slapped the fender.
           (cf. give the fender a slap)
      ii. *This fender slaps easily.

We assume that these verbs have the relevant structure (i.e., V with P-projection complement) and that the complement of P is a noun (the "impact noun": e.g., *kick, punch, slap, jab, poke, knee, elbow*) that must be linked to its source, the external argument (i.e., the sentential syntactic subject in cases like the (i)-sentences in (29a–c), identified here as the "agent," rather than the "experiencer" as in the case of the psych verbs). Notationally, the impact noun is supplied with a bracketed subscript like the one in (26), representing a variable that must be bound obviatively. The suggested middle counterparts therefore violate the principles in (23).

By contrast with verbs of impact, verbs of material separation like *cut, split,* and *crack* and object-experiencer verbs like *anger* and *frighten* are based on nouns that, although anaphoric, are "proximate" rather than obviative and are accordingly linked to the closest c-commanding argument, namely, the DP in specifier position, as shown in (30), the abstract structure corresponding to the verb of (31ai).

(30)

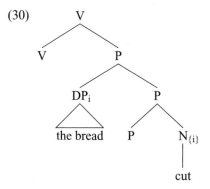

It follows that these verbs form middles readily, since the binding requirements of the "result nouns" (*cut, slice, dent,* etc.) and nouns of "induced emotion" (*anger, fright,* etc.) are met internally. In (31ai), for example, the separation in material integrity entailed by a successful instance of cutting is an acquired property of the internal argument (DP_i), not of the external argument; similarly, for object-experiencer verbs, the induced emotion (*anger, fright*) is linked to the internal argument.

(31) a. i. I cut the bread.
          ii. This bread cuts easily.
      b. i. He sliced the salami.
          ii. Salami slices easily.
      c. i. She dented the fender.
          ii. This fender dents easily.

    d. i. That angered me.
      ii. I anger easily.
    e. i. The dog frightened the chicken.
      ii. Chickens frighten easily.

2.5   Final Remarks

Our purpose here has been to address certain apparent shortcomings in the theory according to which argument structure is defined solely in terms of complement and specifier relations. We maintain that these short-comings are not, properly speaking, failings in our conception of argument structure. Rather, they derive from our failure to understand fully certain implications of the system. The first problem is that we failed to understand the possibilities inherent in the Merge process and, therefore, to understand that P-complemented verbs naturally fall into two classes, an inevitable outgrowth of the basic structural relations. The second problem dealt with here is just one of many similar problems that will have to be confronted, since it has to do with the interaction of subsystems, not with the basic argument structure relations themselves. The observed asymmetries in this case relate to the connection between features of lexical meaning and the arguments of the verb—internal on the one hand, external on the other.

Chapter 3

Conflation

3.1 Introduction

The process we have been calling "conflation," extending a term introduced by Talmy (1985) for a related phenomenon, has figured importantly in our discussions of argument structure. We use this term to refer to the "fusion of syntactic nuclei" that accounts for derivations in which the phonological matrix of the head of a complement (say, N) is inserted into the head, empty or affixal, that governs it, giving rise to a single word (a denominal verb, where the conflating head is N; a deadjectival verb, where the conflating head is A; and so on). For example, the verb *laugh*, we contend, is fundamentally transitive, having the structure portrayed in (1).

(1)

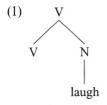

The actual pronunciation, however, has the phonological matrix (abbreviated here by means of the standard spelling *laugh*) under V, not under N, the item with which it is associated in the lexicon.

(2)

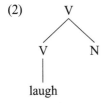

The result of conflation is the single verbal word *laugh* that functions, in sentential syntax, as a standard intransitive verb of the type currently termed "unergative," retaining, however, the canonical transitive characteristic of not projecting a specifier.

Conflation accounts as well for an impressive store of English deadjectival verbs and transitive denominal verbs of the location and locatum category. Deadjectival verbs often implicate overt verbal morphology, typically the suffix *-en*, as in (3) and (4), the basic and conflated representations of the unaccusative verb *redden* (as in *The sky reddened*).

(3)

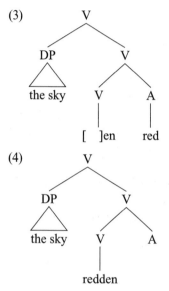

(4)

The transitive alternant of *redden* involves two conflations, the first being that depicted in (4), the second being the further conflation of the primary derived verb *redden* into a matrix empty verb, as in (5), the verb of *The sunset reddened the sky*.

(5)

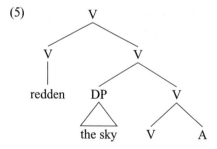

Location and locatum verbs are similarly "complex," involving conflation of N with P and of the result of this with the matrix V. An example is *bag* in *bag the apples*, derived as shown in (6) and (7).

(6)

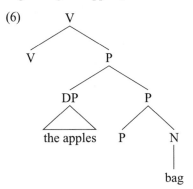

(7)

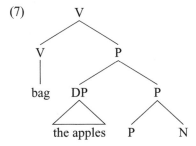

Our portrayals of conflation are purposely informal, since our concern here is with the very questions that must be answered before any formal representation of conflation can possibly be given. Our questions are the following, among others. What is the precise nature of conflation? Is it a form of incorporation observing the Head Movement Constraint (Travis 1984) and the Empty Category Principle (Baker 1988)? What motivates conflation? Does conflation leave a trace in the position corresponding to the conflated item? What is the nature of the trace, if there is one? Is conflation a strictly phonological matter? Or is it visible at LF?

In effect, all this amounts to just one large question, regarding the grammatical nature of conflation. There is another rather large question, however—namely, what is the proper analysis of so-called cognate argument constructions of the type represented in (8)?[1]

(8) a. They are dancing a Sligo jig.
   b. He shelved the books on the windowsill.
   c. Leecil saddled old Gotch with his new Schowalter.

This is a problem, presumably, because each of the verbs here is evidently the product of conflation. The sentential syntactic object in (8a), *a Sligo jig*, cooccurs with the presumably conflated N *dance*. Unless something else is involved here, this should be impossible. It would be impossible, other things being equal, if conflation were movement leaving a trace in complement position, under the standard assumption (perhaps incorrect) that lexical insertion cannot take place into a position occupied by a syntactic object (whether that is an empty category or not). Similarly, the location and locatum verbs of (8b,c) are the product of conflation, by hypothesis. In (8b), for example, *shelf* has conflated first with P and then with V, giving the derived verb *shelve*. Here again, under standard assumptions this structure should be impossible, because the conflated element (the complex P resulting from the conflation of *shelf* with the empty preposition) cooccurs with a projection of P located in the position of the presumed trace of the conflated P itself. In short, we must develop a theory of cognate arguments.

3.2 Some Preliminary Observations on Conflation

In this discussion, we will be concerned with the nature and function of conflation in the derivation of denominal verbs. The derivation of deadjectival verbs will be considered briefly near the end of the discussion. In addition, in our informal use of the term *conflation*, we include the process according to which, by initial hypothesis, an empty verb acquires phonological constituency from an overt verb that it selects; this process corresponds to the head movement operation often called "verb raising." The nature of this process will also be considered briefly toward the end of this discussion. For now, however, we are concerned primarily with denominal verb formation alone, that is, with conflation of the lexical category N.

Incorporation comes to mind as the syntactic process most like conflation, sharing with it the property of conforming to the Head Movement Constraint and the Empty Category Principle, as well as the property of forming a word by attaching the head of a complement to the head of its syntactic governor.

It is possible, despite the obvious similarity, that conflation is different from syntactic incorporation. The difference, if it exists, resides in the matter of government, a relation that plays a role in constraining both processes. In the case of conflation, it is evident that government, while certainly implied by it, is not sufficient to constrain it. This can be appreciated through a consideration of location and locatum verbs. While (9a,b) are possible, (10a,b) are not.

(9) a. Leecil corralled the calves.
        (cf. put the calves in the corral)
     b. Myrtis rosined the rope.
        (cf. treated the rope with rosin)

(10) a. *Leecil calved in the corral.
     b. *Myrtis roped with rosin.

The structural configuration involved in (9) is that associated with location and locatum verbs, and conflation proceeds as in (7). In the case of (10), the structure is the same, as shown in (11), which corresponds to (10a) (abstracting away from conflation).[2]

(11)

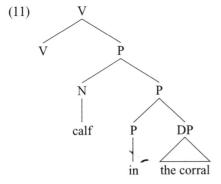

The ill-formedness of the hypothetical location construction (10a) results from the fact that conflation stems from the specifier of the P-projection, not from the head of that projection. This is what we contend, at least. Conflation of a specifier is evidently impossible, although incorporation under government would presumably permit this—the bare noun *calf* is governed by V in (11), but this is evidently insufficient for conflation. Our account of the hypothetical locatum construction (10b) is parallel—*rope* is a specifier and hence cannot conflate with V.

The special character of conflation in this regard is questionable, in fact, since it might be the case that syntactic incorporation is also subject to this constraint. Putative examples of incorporation of a specifier are not fully convincing. The Uto-Aztecan language Hopi has a number of "incorporating verbs" that permit the adjunction of a bare nominal to a governing verb. Examples of the type represented by (12) are unproblematic, presumably, since the bare noun (N) is the complement, hence structural sister, of the verb. Incorporation is always permissible in cases such as this, for languages that have incorporation at all. In (12), the verbal head is the dependent morpheme *-ta* (underlyingly *-toya*, glossed -TOYA); in this use, it functions as the verb of "making" or "manufacture."

(12) Ita-na   kii-ta-ni.
     our-father house-TOYA-FUT
     'Father will build a house.'

This is canonical incorporation and so far does not contrast with what is possible in conflation. However, given our assumptions, many examples of incorporation in the language must involve incorporation from the specifier of the complement of an incorporating verb. Consider in this connection the (a)-examples of (13) and (14) (the (b)-examples illustrate the case in which the nominal object remains unincorporated).

(13) a. Itam tap-wari-k-na. (cf. tapwarikna; Hopi Dictionary Project
        1p   cottontail-run-K-NA   (HDP) 1998, 578)
        'We flushed a cottontail rabbit out (of hiding).'
     b. Itam pu-t   taavo-t   wari-k-na. (cf. warikna.2; HDP
        1p   that-ACC cottontail-ACC run-K-NA   1998, 729)
        'We flushed that cottontail rabbit out (of hiding).'

(14) a. Pam inu-ngem kaway-kwakwha-Ø-ta. (HDP 1998, 136)
        3sg 1s-for   horse-tame-Ø-TOYA:PERF
        'He broke a horse for me.'
     b. Nu' pay naap   itàa-kawayo-y kwakwha-Ø-ta. (HDP 1998,
        1s   now unaided our-horse-ACC tame-Ø-TOYA:PERF   169)
        'I tamed our horse on my own.'

In Jeanne and Hale 2000, a large number of intransitive verbs are analyzed as having a bipartite structure consisting of a verbal thematic element, functioning as the nucleus (V), and a root element (R), often of indeterminate category, functioning as the complement of V. The root element in most (possibly all) cases has the lexical property that it requires the projection of a specifier (regardless of whether the resulting verb "translates"—to English, say—as an unaccusative or an unergative). For example, the underlying verb of (13), *wari-k-* 'run', includes the basic head-complement configuration augmented by a specifier—in this particular case, *taavo* (with compound form *tap-*) 'cottontail rabbit'. Such a nominal must appear in the projection defined by the verbal head *-k-* in order to satisfy the specifier requirement of the root *wari* 'run'. These features of the verb are displayed in (15), where the linear order of elements (itself theoretically immaterial for present purposes) mimics the Hopi surface arrangement.

(15) *Intransitive*

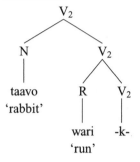

If this is correct, then transitivization of this structure takes advantage of the virtually inescapable possibility of embedding (15) as the complement of the transitivizing (so-called causative) verbal formative *-na*, giving *wari-k-na* 'make run, flush out', whose structure is diagrammed in (16).

(16) *Transitive*

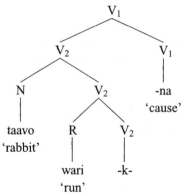

The pair (15)–(16) represent the prototypical transitivity alternation, possible when the inner V projects a specifier (functioning as the derived object in the transitive alternant).

In the derived verb form of (13a)—that is, *tap-wari-k-na*, with incorporated object (in the shortened compound form *tap-*)—the incorporated nominal is, by hypothesis, a specifier. Although it is governed by V_1 (*-na*), it bears no grammatical relation to that verb. This is precisely the kind of development that is impossible in conflation, accounting for the ill-formedness of such verb phrases as *apple in the box* (beside *put apples in the box, box the apples*), *calf in the corral* (beside *put calves in the corral, corral the calves*), and *house with a roof* (beside *fit/provide the house with a roof, roof the house*) (see chapter 1, where location and locatum verbs are discussed in some detail).[3]

The sentences in (14) exemplify the Hopi class of adjectives, which, in their predicative use, are assumed to involve a root element of indeterminate category (often arguably nominal), combined with a nuclear element functioning as predicator (itself often nominal in inflectional category, glossed *PRED* below). The latter is purely hypothetical (Ø) in the adjectival component of the derived transitive verbs of (14), and for many other adjectives as well, but it is overt in some adjectival predicates, as in (17b). The following sentences exemplify adjectives in their simple predicative function:

(17) a. I'   kawayo pas paas   kwakwha. (HDP 1998, 169)
        this horse   very completely tame:PRED
        'This horse is completely tamed.'
     b. I'   muuna paala-ngpu. (HDP 1998, 370)
        this flow   red-PRED
        'This runoff water is red.'

Hopi adjectives, like their English counterparts, are fundamentally attributive and must appear in a configuration that includes a nominal of which they can be attributed, whether as a modifier in expressions like *pala'omaw* 'red cloud' and *pala'anu* 'red ant', or in the predicative use seen in (17).

We assume that the predicative projections of (17) have the form shown in (18), in which the specifier DP satisfies the essential requirement of the adjectival component.

(18)

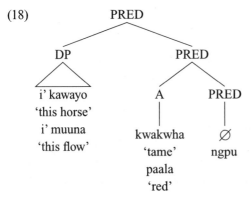

This is precisely the configuration that, by our principles, can freely transitivize. By hypothesis, then, the derived transitive of (14b) has the structure shown in (19).

(19)

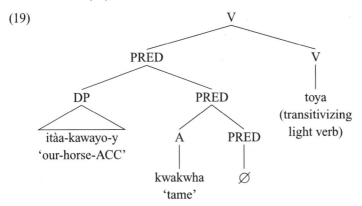

This abstracts away from the effects of conflation, a concomitant of Merge. In actuality, conflation will have fused A *kwakwha* 'tame' and the head that selects it (PRED), and this derived PRED (containing A) will have conflated with the higher head (V *toya*), resulting ultimately (by processes of phonology) in the surface verb form *kwakwhata* 'tame, make tame'.

By hypothesis as well, the verb of (14a) is derived by incorporation, from specifier position. Abstracting away from these processes (i.e., conflation and incorporation), we have the configuration in (20).

(20)

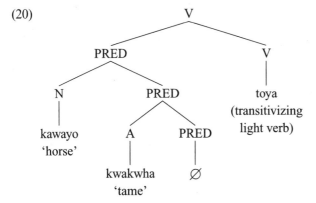

We assume that the specifier *kawayo* 'horse' is incorporated into the derived higher verb *kwakwhata* (<*kwakwha-Ø-toya*) and not first into the inner predicate *kwakwha* (<*kwakwha-Ø*), on the basis of the independent impossibility of a predication of the form **kaway-kwakwha* (<*kawayo-kwakwha-Ø*), leading to a violation of the EPP. This could be wrong, of course, since transitivization would "rescue" a hypothetical intermediate incorporation of the form just cited. In any event, the well-formed incorporation of (14a) involves a process, incorporation, that cannot be duplicated by the process we have called "conflation." At least, it is true of our conception of the argument structures of location and locatum verbs that conflation cannot effect a derivation of the type we must posit for the verb form *kaway-kwakwha-ta* 'tame a horse, tame horses'.

Another feature of Hopi incorporation, and of incorporation quite widely among the languages of the world, is seen in constructions where an incorporated nominal is "construed" with elements (determiners, modifiers) outside the verb word, as in (21), where an adjectival modifier is construed with an incorporated noun *angvu* 'cornhusk(s)' (compound form *angap-*). The Hopi adjective, being nominal in morphological category, must be assigned Case when it appears as a separated modifier, as here. Clearly, Case is assigned by the incorporating verb, so incorporation of a nominal evidently does not remove this capability.

(21) Pas wuuwupa-t   angap-soma. (HDP 1998, 880)
     very long:PL-ACC husk-tie:PERF
     'She bundled up really long cornhusks.'

The morphological form of the adjective here is that found in predicative function, that is, *wuuwupa* 'long:PL'. By contrast, as an attributive modifier, the adjective would appear in its shorter compounding form *wupa-* (neutral for number, as expected). It is possible, therefore, that the incorporated noun (*angvu* 'cornhusk(s)') originates in specifier position in relation to the adjective, the latter being the predicate of a so-called internally headed relative clause (a construction known to exist in Hopi; see Jeanne 1978). If so, then this Hopi construction may be an additional example of syntactic incorporation of a specifier, and the hypothetical configuration underlying the verb of (21) is as depicted in (22), abstracting away from conflation and incorporation, as usual.

(22)

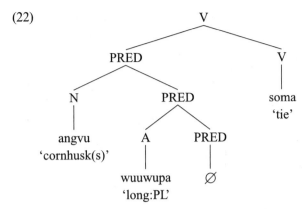

We are arbitrarily setting aside the alternative according to which the nominal is indeed incorporated from the modifier-head construction (corresponding to surface *wupa'angvu* 'long cornhusk(s)'). In either situation, however, the construction exemplified by the derived verb in (21) is most probably beyond the capability of conflation (but see below).

We are claiming that derivations in which, so to speak, a residue remains as an autonomous phrase outside the verb word is beyond the capability of conflation not only in the case of English location and locatum constructions—accounting for (10)—but also in the case of deadjectival predicates, as in (23), more closely resembling the Hopi example just considered.

(23) a. *Japanangka spears straight.
         (cf. Japanangka straightens spears.)
     b. *The north wind skies clear.
         (cf. The north wind clears the sky.)

The verbal projection of (23a) has the structure shown in (24), abstractly the same configuration as the well-formed *Japanangka straightens spears.*[4]

(24)

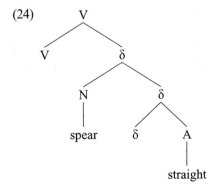

The ill-formedness of (23a), on the intended reading, is due to the illegitimacy of conflation from specifier position, on our assumptions.

It does not really matter whether our analysis of the Hopi construction in (21) is exactly correct. Whatever turns out to be the correct analysis, the essential fact is that alleged incorporation of the Hopi type is distinguishable from conflation in certain important respects. It could be, for example, that Hopi constructions of the type represented by (21) are simply instances of the general phenomenon in that language of "leaving a residue" in an argument position from which incorporation (head movement) takes place. This is enough to distinguish the two operations. Conflation never "leaves a residue" of the sort seen in (25), for example.

(25) a. Umu-na   kaway-mu-y   kuk-hep-ma. (HDP 1998, 880)
        2pl-father horse-PL-GEN track-seek-GO:PERF
        'Your father has been to search for horses' tracks.'
    b. Nu' pu-t   ki-'yta.
        I   that-ACC house-HAVE
        'I have that as a home.'

If these are also cases of incorporation, we suppose that (25a) involves incorporation of the nominal head (*kùuku* 'tracks', *kuk-*) of a possessive construction, leaving the possessor behind. As usual, the residue is assigned Case, glossed as genitive in this instance, though it is indistinguishable from the accusative morphophonologically (see Jeanne 1978).

The type exemplified by (25b) is reasonably common in languages with noun incorporation. It is subject to various analyses, however. On the analysis according to which it is derived through incorporation, the residue of that process is the determiner *pu-t* 'that-ACC'. This remains in the position corresponding to the grammatical object of the verb (and is accordingly assigned accusative Case).[5]

To be sure, conflation, as we conceive it, can leave a residue. It does so necessarily in the derivation of location and locatum denominal verbs, as, for example, in the derivation of (9a), giving the denominal location verb *corral* by conflation of *corral* with empty P and conflation of P with the upper head V in the structure given in (26). The latter step introduces the derived item *corral*—that is, P conflated with its complement N (*corral*)—into the phonological matrix of V.

(26)

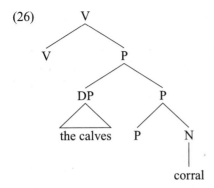

It is the conflation of P with V that leaves a residue: namely, the structure dominated by P in (27), containing the overt specifier *the calves*.

(27)

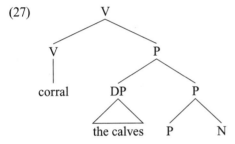

There is a difference between the English conflation examples and the Hopi cases of supposed incorporation. In conflation, the syntactic relation between the nuclei involved is one we will refer to here as *strict complementation*.

(28) *Strict complementation*

A head X is the strict complement of a head Y iff Y is in a mutual c-command (i.e., sister) relation with the maximal categorial projection of X.

The categorial projections of N are N′ and NP; of P, P′ and PP; and so on—although this is not always reflected in the notation, the bare categorial labels (N, V, etc.) being used for any level of projection. The maximal categorial projection is a node that does not project further. DP is not a categorial projection of N, nor is TP a categorial projection of VP, and so on, though these functional projections may be significantly related as extended projections (Grimshaw 1991) to the categories they select.

Conflation in (27) conforms to the strict complementation requirement, since the maximal projection of P (also symbolized *P*) is a sister to V, the "target" or "host" of the conflating head *corral*. All cases of conflation that we know of conform to this requirement, which incidentally also accounts for the fact that specifiers do not conflate, since the categorial projection of a specifier never stands in the sister relation to a potential target. For example, *spear* in (24) is not a sister of V, though *spear* is surely governed by V, demonstrating that local c-command and government are not enough.

Incorporation of the type we have attributed to Hopi is not subject to the strict complementation requirement, assuming that it does indeed permit the kinds of "stranding" exemplified in (21) and (25). Consider, for example, the structure of the verbal projection in (25b), shown in (29).

(29)

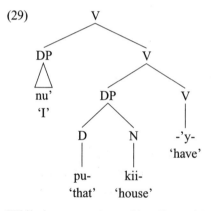

While incorporation of *kii-* 'house' is possible, giving the denominal possessive verb *ki-'y-* 'have house' and stranding the determiner *pu-* (ultimately the accusative form *pu-t*) 'that', conflation is impossible in this case because N is not a sister of the matrix verb, as would be required of conflation in conformity with the strict complementation requirement.

Our task now is to determine why conflation, unlike incorporation, is subject to this requirement.

3.3   On the Nature of Conflation

We would like to take seriously the idea that conflation is a concomitant of Merge, the operation that is fundamental in defining the projection of syntax from the lexicon. We expect that a proper understanding of conflation's relationship to Merge will lead automatically to an explanation of the constraints that govern it.

To say that conflation is a concomitant of Merge is to say that it is in some intimate manner *bound up* with Merge, that it is a *part* of Merge in some sense. To pursue this idea, let us consider the simplest case—for example, the verbal projection *make trouble*. This is formed by selecting each of the items *make* and *trouble*, and combining them by means of the Merge operation, as shown in (30).

(30) a. Select [make]
     b. Select [trouble]
     c. Merge([make], [trouble]) = {[make], [trouble]}

This defines a syntactic configuration in which the two items, *make* and *trouble*, are sisters—they are Merge-partners. These parts are customarily represented by means of a "general" categorial label (e.g., *V* for *make*, *N* for *trouble*), but this is no more valid a convention than using the spellings of the words themselves, the intent in any case being to abbreviate the set of features inherent in each of the constituents. But here we touch on an issue that is central to our investigation, namely, the labels of lexical items and other syntactic objects. We say that *V* is the label for *make*, or alternatively that "make" itself is the label, but in either event this is clearly an abbreviation for something; presumably it is an abbreviation for the features of the item, as suggested. Parallel remarks apply for the noun *trouble*, of course.

But it is not only terminal nodes that have labels; all syntactic objects do. In particular, syntactic objects defined by Merge have labels. For example, the expression {[make], [trouble]}—whether abbreviated in this manner or by means of the customary categorial abbreviations, {V, N}— must be associated with a label, traditionally *V'* or *VP*, in this case. The label of the phrase is determined by one or the other of the two constituents, and that constituent is therefore the head of the construction. If V determines the label, then V is the head; if N determines the label, then N is the head; the choice of category labels or standard spellings is arbitrary in customary usage, and there is no need to distinguish phrasal levels.[6]

(31) a. {V {V, N}}
     b. {[make] {[make], [trouble]}}

What is a label, precisely? Standard arboreal representations of syntactic configurations like (32) give the impression, almost certainly misleading, that nodes corresponding to nontrivial projections of terminal nodes are somehow "simpler," less encumbered with features, than the terminal nodes themselves.

(32)
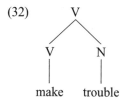

For example, while the terminal nodes presumably have phonological features associated with them, the same is certainly not true of higher projections of those nodes. This is at least a popular working assumption. It could be wrong, of course; it may belong rather to the category of unexamined initial impressions unsupported by any real linguistic considerations. In fact, this assumption is almost certainly wrong if, as is probably the case, the labeling of syntactic objects is automatic and simple (see Chomsky 1995).

Let us consider the simplest possibility, namely, that the label of a syntactic configuration is a copy of the features of the head.

(33) *Label*

The label of a syntactic object X is the feature set [F, H], where [F, H] is the entire complement of phonological, morphological, syntactic, and semantic features of H, the head of X.

This is actually quite natural, given that it is trivially true in any event: it is true where X is only trivially a maximal projection (i.e., where it is unprojected X^0). The principle formulated in (33) simply extends the automatic labeling to all nodes that are projections of X.

For present purposes, we are holding in abeyance the question of what exactly is meant by *features* in (33). We are assuming, however, that one of the implications of this principle is that the label of a syntactic object includes information germane to its PF interpretation, that is, to the spell-out operation(s) affecting it. Without specifying too precisely the form in which this information is registered in the label, we will refer to it by the expression *p-signature*, representing a phonological feature set of some sort, possibly a set of feature matrices.[7] It is the p-signature that is directly relevant to the theory of conflation. For a given item, the p-signature will be symbolized by means of the standard orthographic representation of the item; thus, *make* symbolizes the p-signature of the verb in (32), and *trouble* that of the nominal complement. This is merely a notational convention, of course.

If conflation is a concomitant of Merge, as we claim, then, in theory at least, conflation has access to the same linguistic elements that Merge itself has access to. In particular, conflation has reference to labels, perhaps *only* to labels.

We propose that conflation is in fact an operation on labels.

(34) *Conflation*

Conflation consists in the process of copying the p-signature of the complement into the p-signature of the head, where the latter is "defective."

There are two cases in which a p-signature is "defective." The first and most obvious is the case where the p-signature is entirely empty, containing no phonological features. This is the situation involved in zero derivation, so common in English. The second is the case where the head is an affix. Here we assume that the p-signature is partially defective, being bipartite, with one part consisting of a set of phonological features (the affix) and the other consisting of an empty root.

English denominal verbs, like unergative *laugh* and *sneeze*, exemplify the simplest case. The head has a defective p-signature, lacking phonological features entirely; the complement, on the other hand, has a "substantial" (as opposed to "empty") p-signature. (P-signatures are cited in square brackets.)

(35) *Head*   *Complement*
     {V, [Ø]}   {N, [laugh]}

The symbols *V* and *N* stand for the lexical and syntactic features associated with these syntactic objects. The notations [Ø] and [*laugh*] correspond to the p-signatures of the two items, the first being the empty p-signature, the second the phonologically substantial one.

When these items are selected and undergo Merge, the label of the head—that is, the feature set {V, [Ø]}—is projected to define the features of the construction as a whole. Simultaneously, we propose, the substantial p-signature of the complement is copied as in (36) into the empty p-signature of the head, substantiating the latter.

(36)   {V, [laugh]}

     {V, [laugh]} {N, [laugh]}

When this is spelled out, the p-signature of the complement will be deleted (i.e., it will not be pronounced), a circumstance we will represent notationally by eliminating the p-signature of the complement entirely, as in (37).

(37)   {V, [laugh]}

        {V, [laugh]}   {N}

In subsequent portrayals of conflation, we will use this more reduced representation, notationally eliminating the p-signatures of complements where those are copied into the head.

The affixal case can be illustrated by means of a deadjectival verb involving the common derivational affix *-en*, which we take to be the head verb, combined with an empty root [Ø]. Consider *thicken*, consisting of the following items:

(38) *Head*   *Complement*
       {V, [[Ø]en]}   {A, [thick]}

As a result of Merge and concomitant conflation, the empty root is replaced by the p-signature of the complement, as represented in (39).

(39)   {V, [[thick]en]}

        {V, [[thick]en]}   {A}

Deadjectival verbs project a specifier, corresponding to the sentential syntactic subject of the transitive and the object of the transitive. The addition of a specifier (e.g., the DP *the broth*), through Merge, results in (40), in which the p-signature of the head projects to determine the label of the construction, a verbal projection headed by the verb *thicken*.

(40)   {V, [[thick]en]}

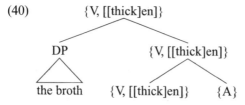

       DP   {V, [[thick]en]}

    the broth   {V, [[thick]en]}   {A}

This is the intransitive, or unaccusative, alternant, as in *The broth thickened*. The transitive, sometimes called "causative," alternant is the result of Merge combining (40) and a verb, a verb whose p-signature is defective and, hence, supplied by conflation, replacing the defective p-signature with the substantial p-signature of the complement (i.e., the p-signature of (40)), as in (41), the argument structure representation of *thicken the broth*.

(41)

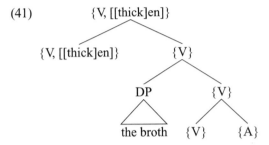

The derivation of a denominal verb of the so-called location type proceeds in parallel fashion. Consider the verb *bottle*, as in *bottle the wine*. According to our view of the matter, the inner projection is headed by an empty P. Its complement is the bare noun *bottle*.

(42)   *Head*   *Complement*
      {P, [Ø]}   {N, [bottle]}

These items are selected and subjected to Merge and concomitant conflation, giving (43).

(43)   {P, [bottle]}

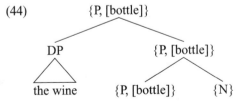

Since the category P forces the projection of a specifier, (43) must enter into the Merge relation with some appropriate expression, such as the DP *the wine*.

(44)   {P, [bottle]}

In and of itself, (44) will not succeed in English, inasmuch as P-headed small clauses need further lexical support in that language.[8] This is remedied by Merge, combining (44) with a verb. If the latter is an empty verb, conflation will supply it with a substantial p-signature in accordance with the principle embodied in (34), resulting in (45) headed by the verb *bottle*.

(45)

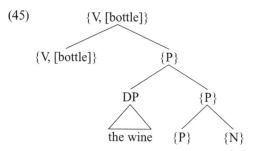

If this is the correct view of conflation, it is clear why conflation is impossible from specifier position. The only p-signature that is, so to speak, visible to a head at Merge is that of the complement, a Merge-partner. Conflation is strictly a relation between the labels of two items combined through Merge. It is also clear why conflation cannot strand a determiner, for instance. A determiner heads a D-projection, that is, a DP. A noun internal to a DP cannot conflate with a verbal head sister to DP. This follows directly within the view being courted here, because the p-signature of the noun is inaccessible to the verb. It does not stand in the Merge relation to the verb; only DP does.[9]

It follows from these considerations that the denominal verb formation process involved in the Hopi verb of (25b), with corresponding structure (29), cannot be conflation. That is to say, it cannot be conflation if the determiner is indeed a "stranded" residue of DP, resulting from the extraction from DP of the lexical head N *kii* 'house' in the formation of the derived verb *ki-'y-* 'have house'. The lexical head N is not the strict complement of V; rather, DP is the strict complement of V, in accordance with (28) and the Merge operation. The same is true of putative cases of adjectival modifier stranding (e.g., (21) 'long . . . husk-tie') and possessor stranding (e.g., (25a) 'horses' . . . track-seek'), if the stranded elements (in their base positions) are contained in categories that "intervene" between the maximal projection of the noun and the target verb. And this would seem to be the case, as we will show.

If these examples, as well as countless others that Hopi offers, involve moving a noun into an appropriately situated V, then this movement is not effected by conflation, since it greatly exceeds the constraints on that process. Rather, if syntactic movement is involved in the Hopi cases, as seems impressionistically to be correct, then the process that effects it should probably be classed with noun incorporation as studied in detail by Baker (1988).[10] Consider again the structure depicted in (29), corresponding to sentence (25b). The noun *kii* 'house' is internal to DP; hence, D "intervenes" between the noun and the target verb -'*y*- 'have'. Thus, the derived N-V compound *ki-'y-* 'have house' must be brought into existence by means of incorporation (i.e., by head movement), extracting the noun from DP and adjoining it to the governing verb, as shown in (46).

(46)

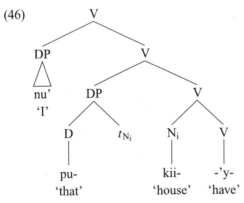

As expected in incorporation, nuclear relations are not affected: the target (V, in this case) remains the head of the construction. It is a property of this particular verb that it projects a specifier, having this in common with members of the category P and with possessional verbs in many languages. It also has the morphophonological property that it is dependent: it is a suffix and must attach to an incorporated (i.e., adjoined) nominal root.[11]

Now consider the stranding of an adjective, as in the Hopi sentence (21). The adjective is the lexical head of a small clause (in our sense of the term: that is, a structure projected either by a head that must itself project a specifier or by a head that is forced to project a specifier by virtue of a property of its complement). In Hopi, by hypothesis, the adjective stands in the complement relation to a nuclear element PRED, the true head of the small clause.[12] The PRED-projection is itself the complement of the verb *soma* 'tie', the target of incorporation; and it is the specifier of the PRED-projection that is extracted in this case, as shown in (47) (abstracting away from the conflation of PRED with V).

(47)

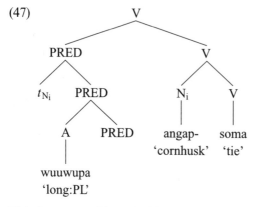

This is presumably a legitimate instance of incorporation, inasmuch as the specifier of the PRED-projection is governed by the target verb, according to an accepted conception of government. But this would not be a possible conflation, since the specifier of the PRED-projection is not the strict complement of V. It is not a Merge-partner of V. Rather, the PRED-projection itself is the strict complement, and Merge-partner, of the target V.

The Hopi sentence (25a) illustrates possessor stranding. Here again, the compound verb (*kuk-hepma* 'go seek track') arises as a result of incorporation, not conflation. This follows, by hypothesis at least, since the noun (*kùuku*, *kuk-* 'track(s)') is extracted from a category that is not the strict complement of the target V (*hepma* 'go seek').[13] We assume that the functional head of the possessive construction is D, as shown in (48). The stranded possessor is the specifier in the D-projection, and the incorporating nominal (represented by a trace in (48)) stands in the complement relation to D.[14]

(48)

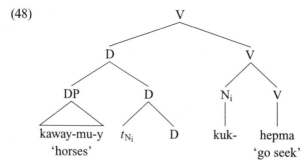

Our assertions about incorporation depend rather crucially upon a conception of phrase structure according to which extended nominal projections and adjectival small clauses are headed by functional categories, not by the lexical items that evidently undergo the process. And incorporation, unlike conflation, is permitted to occur between a head and an item *properly contained* within its complement. An item M is properly contained in a phrase XP if it is dominated by the maximal projection XP and the latter is not the label of M. Thus, while N is the lexical head of DP, its label is distinct from that of DP, and N is therefore properly contained in DP. Similarly, A is the lexical head of its extended projection, δP (or PREDP); its label is distinct from δP (PREDP), and A is therefore properly contained in δP (PREDP). Under this assumption, Conflation could not implicate the lexical heads in these constructions because a functional projection intervenes. But it should be said, as an aside at least, that these assumptions about phrase structure are highly theoretical and could, of course, be wrong. For one thing, in the DP examples considered here, for instance, it could well be that the label (and hence the p-signature) of the relevant lexical head does indeed appear at the node that dominates the strict complement and Merge-partner of the target verb. This would be true, for example, if the phrases harboring the nouns at issue here were in fact NPs projected by those very nominal heads (as assumed in Baker 1988, following a respected traditional view, contra the DP hypothesis of Abney 1987). And the small clause structure attributed to the complement in (21), as diagrammed in (22), may not be the proper source of the putative incorporation. The proper source might instead be the modification construction, in which the noun, not the adjective, is the lexical head. In that case, the noun would project its label to the phrase as a whole. Under these revised assumptions, incorporation and conflation would be identically subject to the strict complementation requirement.

For our purposes, the outcome of these considerations does not change our conception of conflation, which we will continue to assume is a relation between Merge-partners, according to which the p-signature of a complement replaces and thereby substantiates the defective p-signature of a head. If incorporation turns out to conform to the same strict complementation requirement, then incorporation might actually turn out to be conflation. This is immaterial to the nature of conflation itself.

3.4 Consequences of Conflation

In the proposal we are considering now, conflation is strictly a matter of labels, in particular, of the p-signature component of labels. Importantly, it has no effect whatsoever on what we might call the *s-signature*, that is, the syntactic and semantic features of a syntactic node. Consider, for example, the verb phrase *bottle the wine*, whose structure (45) is repeated here in (49).

(49)

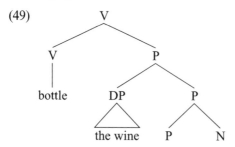

We return here to the more reduced graphic representation in which the conflated p-signature is written just once, beneath the head where it is ultimately spelled out. The essential point we wish to make here is that the syntactic structure of the verb phrase is left intact. All information necessary for the purposes of syntax and logical form is fully present in the structure (with the understanding, of course, that *P* and *N* are abbreviations of the full sets of syntactic and semantic features pertaining to those nodes). We can assume that the p-signatures of all nodes are irrelevant, and invisible, to syntax and LF.

This answers the question concerning the traces of conflation, posed in section 3.1. Does conflation leave a trace? In one sense, the question is beside the point, since conflation is not a movement rule, but the substantiation of a defective p-signature at Merge. In another sense, however, the answer is yes, trivially. Conflation leaves the entire structure intact, unchanged, with respect to syntax and semantic structure.

This has consequences for another question asked in section 3.1—namely, the question of cognate and hyponymous arguments. We must reject the idea we once advanced that the trace of conflation (then taken to be a movement process) could, countercyclically, be "replaced" by lexical insertion (Hale and Keyser 1997c), effecting a hyponymous relation between an incorporated nominal and the trace-displacing inserted material (as exemplified by *dance a jig*, where conflated *dance* classifies the referent of the S-Structure object *a jig* as a type of dance, rather than a fiddle tune, whistle tune, musical score, or the like).

We must now make a distinction between true cognate object constructions, like that exemplified in (50a,b), and another construction, exemplified in (50c,d), more aptly labeled the *hyponymous* argument construction, in which the relevant argument (direct object in the first instance, prepositional object in the second) is not root-identical to the nominal component of the associated denominal verb.

(50) a. She slept the sleep of the just.
   b. He laughed his last laugh.
   c. He danced a jig.
   d. He bagged the potatoes in a gunnysack.

For present purposes, we will set the hyponymous argument construction aside and deal with the cognate object construction. The examples we have provided in (50a,b) might ultimately prove not to be genuine examples of this construction, but we will take them to be such.

Whatever the outcome in this case, we take it to be a fact that there is such a phenomenon—that is to say, a transitive verbal construction headed by a denominal verb whose object is headed by a noun that is root-identical to the verb, as in the examples cited. Further, in the true cognate object construction, the object can only be headed by a root-identical noun, not some random distinct noun, even a hyponym. Thus, if (50a,b) are true examples, as we will assume, then the following are predicted to be ill formed.

(51) a. *She slept her last nap/a long winter slumber.
   b. *He laughed a surreptitious giggle/chuckle.

These verbs can, of course, occur in other transitive constructions, with a range of S-Structure objects (e.g., *sleep one's life away, laugh them off the stage*), but these are not relevant to the issue at hand.

If verbs of the type represented by *sleep* and *laugh* are strict cognate object verbs, as we are suggesting, then not only do they not permit hyponymous objects, but they also reject pronominal versions of their cognate objects.

(52) a. *John slept the sleep of the just and Bill slept it too.
   b. *John laughed the last laugh and Bill laughed it too.[15]
   c. *Robin laughed the laughs of the Rat Pack, and Jonathan laughed them too.

By contrast, verbs like *dance* and *sing* readily accept pronominal objects.

(53) a. John danced the tango and Bill danced it too.
   b. Robin sang the songs of the 60s and Bill sang them too.

We must admit that sentences like (52a–c) sound better and better with repetition. However, sentences like (53a,b) need no repetition. They sound perfectly well formed immediately. We take this difference to lend at least some credibility to the idea that strict cognate object constructions are to be distinguished from the hyponymous argument construction exemplified by (53a,b). If so, we must account for this difference.

To begin, we will attempt to develop an account of the strict cognate object construction. There are at least two possibilities: (i) strict cognate object verbs arise through incorporation (in the technical sense of Baker 1988); (ii) strict cognate object verbs arise through conflation (in the sense suggested here, i.e., label copying).

The incorporation hypothesis would account for the "strict cognate" relation under the reasonable assumption that incorporation—that is, head movement—is a copying operation. In English, the argument would go, both the head and the tail of the movement chain would be spelled out, as seen in (54), an informal representation of the verb phrase of (50a).

(54)

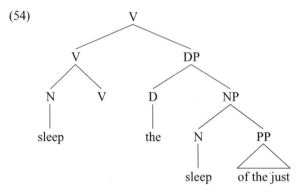

The key to this account would be that the tail of the chain (the inner N here) would be spelled out, presumably because English does not allow stranding of determiners, modifiers, and the like. English differs in this regard from languages like Mohawk and Hopi that allegedly permit the trace of head movement to appear within the "residue" of a DP, for instance.

We must assume that this extraction is possible in the first place—in other words, either that DP does not constitute a barrier to extraction, or that the Empty Category Principle is simply not involved here because the trace is spelled out. There is a problem here, technically, since the determiner (D) is a head that intervenes between the noun and the verb; extraction across DP therefore violates the Head Movement Constraint. This is a general problem, and determiner stranding, if it actually occurs, flies in the face of it (though it does not do so in Baker's (1988) analysis of the constructions).

If the strict cognate object construction arises through head movement, as suggested in (54), it is to be expected that the point of origin (i.e., the tail of the chain) could be a specifier. Thus, for example, the noun *sleep* appears in the specifier position of the small clause complement of the verb *turn* in (55).

(55) She can turn sleep into dreams.

The structure of the verb phrase here is essentially as in (56).

(56)

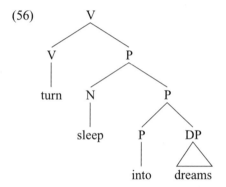

Now consider the same structure with empty V. On the assumption that the specifier can incorporate, we might assume that (57) is derived in that manner.

(57) She can sleep sleep into dreams.

We cannot rule this sentence out. While it may be somewhat strange, it is perfectly grammatical; if someone could actually turn sleep into dreams by sleeping, then (57) would describe that ability. However, this does not come about by incorporation—at least, it would be very difficult to argue that it does. Rather, this is the resultative construction quite generally available with transitive manner verbs based on unergatives, as exemplified by the following sentences:

(58) a. He slept the hours away.
     b. She laughed her way through life.
     c. I sneezed my head off.

So, if (57) means anything, it means something along the lines of what was just suggested, for example, 'bring it about by sleeping that sleep becomes dreams'. This is not the strict cognate object relation. Specifically, as sentences like (58a) show, there is no strict dependency between the nominal component of the verb and the nominal head in the specifier position of the small clause complement.

In the final analysis, so far as we can see, the true cognate object relation cannot be shown to have a range of instantiations much greater than that of the canonical conflation relation seen in earlier sections. In canonical conflation, the conflating element is consistently the head of a lexical projection sister to the target verb. Thus, in the case of the denominal verb *laugh*, for example, the noun that contributes its p-signature to the verb is not only the sister of the verb, but also maximally a lexical projection, not an extended projection. Similarly, in the case of *bottle*, as in *bottle the wine* (see (45)), the p-signature ultimately passed on to the verb is from a lexical projection, P (itself phonologically substantiated by the p-signature of its own complement *bottle*).

By contrast, the strict cognate object relation generally holds between the verb and an *extended* projection sister to it. That is to say, the nominal component of the verb is identical to the p-signature of the lexical head of the extended projection (DP) of the complement of the verb. This is portrayed in (54), the structure that results under the assumption that the cognate object relation is established by incorporation. But suppose that this relation is in fact brought about by conflation. This would involve copying the p-signature of the N into the defective p-signature of the V. This would conform with the general sisterhood limitation on conflation under the assumption that certain features of the label of a lexical head project to the maximal projection of the *extended projection* of the lexical head, not just to the maximal projection of the lexical head itself. If the features that project to these heights include the p-signature, in the manner shown in (59), there is a point in the structure at which the defective verb is a structural sister to a node (D in this case) bearing the p-signature of the lexical head. The nominal p-signature [*sleep*] is therefore copied into the defective label of V.[16]

(59)

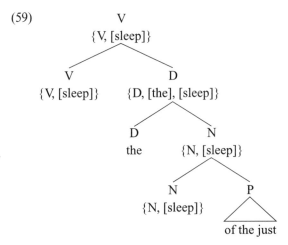

We believe that the limitations on the strict cognate object relation correspond to the limitations implicated by the notion that the phenomenon is in fact conflation, with the provision that the critical structural node is the extended projection of the conflating noun. The strict cognate object relation can be no more distant than this. It is not necessary, however, to be committed to the idea that the p-signature of a lexical category actually projects to the dominating node of the extended projection, as it is shown to do in (59). Perhaps it projects only to the maximal projection of the lexical head. If so, the sisterhood requirement is relaxed and it is necessary only that the conflating element be the lexical head of an extended projection that is the complement, and therefore the sister, of the target head. In the example at hand, N and V can enter into the conflation relation because D, the extended projection of N, is complement, and sister, to V. Thus, in the particular circumstance of the cognate object, conflation operates at "long distance," but only in the sense that it bypasses the functional category superstructure of an extended projection—it is still restricted to the head-complement relation.

In English, stranding of determiners is not allowed. This is why the cognate object construction has the name that it has: the conflating element is necessarily represented by a copy, its "cognate," in the source head position, as shown in (60), a modified version of (59).

(60)

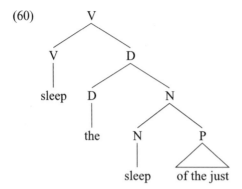

If this is conflation, then it is clear from such examples that conflation is a copying process. Under certain conditions, copies are realized overtly in both positions, that is, target and source. This will be so where the source position is dominated, within its extended projection, by certain functional categories, for example, D. Otherwise, the copy is deleted in the source position, as in the canonical conflation relation, exemplified diagrammatically by the location verb of (49), repeated here as (61).

(61)

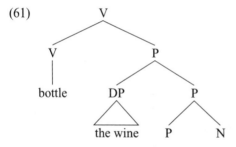

Here, there are two instances of conflation, and accordingly two source positions, N and P. In neither case is the source head contained in an extended projection dominated by a functional category. This circumstance is prominent among those in which the source copy is covert—that is, deleted or, perhaps, simply not spelled out at PF. Descriptively, for the cases considered here, the source copy of a conflating head is covert if the shortest "path" (of connected nodes) leading from the source lexical head to the target head passes through lexical category nodes exclusively, as is the case in (61). This probably does not constitute the actual principle involved in determining the occurrence of overt and covert copies of conflated heads, because it sidesteps the issue of stranding, which is responsible for the basic intuition at work here: namely, the source copy is spelled out when a determiner (and perhaps other elements as well) would otherwise be "stranded" (i.e., would be unsupported by a phonologically overt lexical head).[17]

Major questions remain concerning the nature and status of verbal predicates involving the relation we have referred to as "hyponymous," as in *He danced a jig* and *She hobbled the mule with clothesline*. Do these involve conflation (of *dance* and *hobble*, in these cases)? And, in general, how do we account for the presence of the nominal component in this populous class of verbs? Before taking up these questions, however, we want to consider the nature of the so-called p-signature that now plays a central role in our conception of conflation.

3.5 The P-Signature

As yet, we have said little about the exact character of the p-signature and its occurrence in the nodes of the configurational structures projected from lexical items. There are two questions, essentially, one having to do with the relation of p-signatures to the phonological representation of terminal nodes, the other with their presence or absence in particular nodes.

The first question can be addressed in part by asking whether the p-signature of a head H is a complete phonological matrix of H as it appears at PF. The evidence is against this. Arguments for "late insertion" of vocabulary items, in the sense of Halle and Marantz's (1993) theory of Distributed Morphology, are extraordinarily compelling. For one thing, syntactic processes of movement and morphological processes of fusion and fission, among others, define the morphosyntactic structures, or "slots," into which vocabulary items are inserted. And these structures are of course not present in the argument structure configurations defined by lexical items. Suppletion is a clear case. The English form [*went*], for example, cannot be inserted before the syntax has brought the verb together with the past tense, for it is the latter process that creates the environment for the suppletive element [*wen*]; the elements involved here are in distinct nuclear positions in the basic syntactic representations of sentences containing the form. Similarly, the insertion of Hopi *yu'tu* 'run (plural)', as opposed to *wari* 'run (nonplural)', requires information unavailable at D-Structure; in other words, it requires information that is present in the structure only after the verb joins with the higher inflectional heads (tense/aspect and number agreement), heads that are demonstrably separate from and higher than the verb in the base structure of clauses. Assuming that arguments of this type are persuasive, we must at least reject the idea that the p-signature of a nuclear element is the phonological matrix corresponding to its actual form at PF.

The p-signature of a head H must contain information that will permit H to be properly associated in syntax with the appropriate forms of vocabulary items drawn from the lexicon. We are assuming, of course, that the p-signature is present in H at all levels of syntax; this is necessarily the case in our conception of conflation. The p-signature can be copied, we have argued, so that the p-signature of the noun *laugh*, when copied into the defective p-signature of a verb, is in an intuitively common and ordinary sense "the same" as the "original" nominal p-signature. When it is "spelled out," through lexical insertion, we require that it appear in the appropriate place, for example, in the verb if conflation has applied there. And, of course, we want the right spellings to appear in the right places, that is, in the right slots in terminal nodes. There must be some way, therefore, to relate a p-signature to the correct vocabulary item.

One possibility is that the p-signature of a head H consists of the entire set of phonological matrices of H—that is to say, the entire register of the allomorphs of H and their contextual frames. Lexical insertion would amount to discarding all allomorphs that do not satisfy the particular environment in which H appears at S-Structure, that is, at the syntactic level relevant to PF. In this conception of the matter, the vocabulary is ever-present in the syntax, being carried around through the syntactic derivation, to be partially discarded, or "trimmed," at PF. This model is probably not correct, because of fission, fusion, and the well-known phenomenon of portmanteau morphemes, whose phonological matrices are simply not available before S-Structure.

Another possibility is that the vocabulary is entirely autonomous, consulted only at PF. Items are inserted if they can be, in accordance with their allomorphy and contextual requirements; portmanteau morphemes exist as vocabulary items and are appropriately inserted into "fused" positions available at S-Structure. This, as we understand it, is "late insertion." Although this is what we will assume, it is not clear in this model that there is any place for the p-signature that we have taken to be essential to our conception of conflation. We will therefore assume that some mechanism exists to keep track of p-signature copies so that they can be "found" and properly spelled out when vocabulary items are inserted. Our proposal is tentative, provisional, and somewhat clumsy at this point; we adopt it as a temporary convenience. We will simply assume that p-signatures are indices and that vocabulary items bear indices as well. The index of a particular vocabulary item must match that of the morpheme, or terminal node, into which it is inserted. So the spelling [*laugh*]$_i$ will appear at the terminal V-node substantiated by the p-signature (index) PS$_i$, copied from the N *laugh* in the position of its syntactic complement.

The second question posed above can be restated as follows. Do all nonempty heads in syntax bear a p-signature? Are there categories that do not have a p-signature? We are not referring here to the question of zero morphemes, since zero or null is itself a possible p-signature; some alternant of an affix, a noun root, or a verb root, could have the null p-signature (e.g., the root component arguably has the null p-signature in Spanish *ir, ido* 'go, gone'; in Miskitu, the verb root has the null p-signature in *ai-k-* 'give me' and *mai-k-* 'give you', consisting solely of the dative person agreement and the transitive conjugation marker *-k-*, while the verb root is overt in *yâb-* 'give him'). Rather, what we are asking here is whether the p-signature could be entirely and systematically missing from some head or category of heads.

Bittner (1994) gives a detailed argument, further developed by Bittner and Hale (1996a), that the marked structural Cases (e.g., ergative, accusative) belong to a functional category K and, moreover, that these categories are "empty" at D-Structure. The argument that structural K is empty revolves around the idea that its licensing can be accounted for within the independently supported theory that empty categories must be "bound," in order to satisfy the Empty Category Principle (ECP). At S-Structure and PF, a properly bound K is "realized" as a specific Case, ergative or accusative, for example. If the language realizes these overtly at PF, they will acquire phonological substance in the course of Vocabulary Insertion. In this case, presumably, we can assume that at least a part of what it means to say the relevant heads are "empty" is that they are phonologically defective, lacking a p-signature, like the empty heads that, by hypothesis, are targets of conflation.[18]

Case is a functional category, not a lexical category. And it is not unreasonable to expect other functional categories to lack p-signatures, acquiring their phonological substance through Vocabulary Insertion (possibly mediated by conflation). We must assume also that at least one member of each of the lexical categories V and P (and perhaps one each of the other lexical categories as well) lacks a p-signature, since the entire edifice of conflation is constructed upon that premise. We would like to go a step further, however, and propose that (in English) the "closed class" lexical category P has this property generally, a characteristic it therefore shares with the functional category K (to which it has some affinity, as is well known, P being the historical source of K in many language families).[19] If this is correct, then P acquires its phonological index in two ways: (i) through conflation (of nominal heads), as we have shown in the derivation of location and locatum verbs (like *shelve*, *saddle*), and (ii) through Vocabulary Insertion directly (as in the standard PP construction: e.g., *in the house, on the table, at the movies*).

On this assumption, we can explain the failure of P to conflate in English.[20]

(62) a. *We inned the calves the milkpen.
         (cf. We got the calves in the milkpen.)
     b. *On the bandage here.
         (cf. Put the bandage on here.)
     c. *She will in the horse there.
         (cf. She will put the horse in there.)
     d. *She onned the horse.
         (cf. She got on/mounted the horse.)
     e. *Jurgen inned the room.
         (cf. Jurgen got in/entered the room.)

Since a preposition has no p-signature, it cannot pass a p-signature on to the defective V; hence the impossibility of the starred forms of (62). The overt prepositions (*in, on*) in the parenthetical examples of (62) arise directly from Vocabulary Insertion, independently of any p-signature. This possibility, we assume, derives in part from the fact that prepositions belong to a relatively small list of items, each identifiable through its syntactic and semantic features. Insertion can proceed without reference to phonological features—although, of course, a morphophonological register will be carried along, if one is present in the vocabulary item.

In the derivation of (61), the preposition acquires a p-signature from its complement N, *bottle*, and passes it on to the verb, giving the derived verb *bottle*. By contrast, in (63b), no conflation takes place.

(63) a. Put the wine in the bottle.

b.

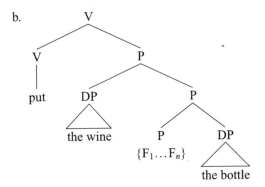

Instead, Vocabulary Insertion applies, inserting the preposition P, whose s-signature matches the feature set $\{F_1 \ldots F_n\}$ associated with the terminal node P in (63b). The inserted P has the p-signature and phonological matrix corresponding to the actual preposition *in*, as part of its entry in the vocabulary, accounting for the preposition in (63a). The p-signature of the inserted preposition presumably appears at all projections of P, though with no effect in this case. Since the verb is not defective, the p-signature of its complement will not be passed on to it. Thus, in the end, we have the structure shown in (64) (simplified in the usual manner).

(64)

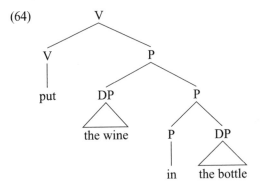

In an alternative fate for (63b), *bottle* would conflate into P, giving the "cognate object" construction in (65).

(65) *Put the wine [P bottle] [DP the bottle].

Here, the p-signature of the noun *bottle* is copied into the defective P, leaving its own copy behind in the DP complement, in accordance with the putative principles of cognate object formation. This possibility must be ruled out, perhaps by a principle according to which Vocabulary Insertion is preferred over conflation (for some reason). In (61), and the like, Vocabulary Insertion of P is impossible, because if it applied, the bare, phonologically realized noun *bottle* would be "stranded" in object position. Hence, in that structure conflation must apply. Failure of conflation in deference to Vocabulary Insertion in (63) might be quite natural if the cognate object construction were "more costly" than Vocabulary Insertion. This might be the case, for example, if surmounting the D functional projection required a special provision, say, an operation akin to Move—extraction out of the D-projection and copying into V. This combination is reminiscent of the pair "Move and Merge," naturally more costly than Merge alone. On this analogy, the cognate object construction, involving "Move" and conflation, would be more costly than Vocabulary Insertion, the latter being essentially costless.

Cognate object formation is arguably more costly than Vocabulary Insertion, as suggested, but it could simply be that conflation is *in general* more costly than Vocabulary Insertion, a possibility arising from the relatively special nature of conflation (e.g., the requirement that it be stipulated to apply to a restricted set of heads, differing from construction to construction, from category to category, and from language to language). If so, then the following ill-formed sentence type might also be explained in this manner:

(66) *Put the wine [$_{PP}$[$_P$ bottle] [$_N$ Ø]].

Here, the bare noun complement of P conflates with the latter (deleting the source copy, as usual). This is also impossible—(66) is not a way to say *Put the wine in a bottle* or *Put the wine in bottles*. Instead, Vocabulary Insertion applies to introduce the appropriate preposition, blocking (66).

When Vocabulary Insertion blocks conflation in (64), precluding (65), the result is the desired one. As mentioned earlier, however, when the same scenario is played out in relation to (66), yielding (67), the result is ill formed, since it "strands" a bare N.

(67) *Put the wine in [$_N$ bottle].

We assume that the principle involved here has to do with the licensing of an overt argument, in an argument position. Presumably, an overt argument must be a phrase, in the traditional sense; that is, it must be an extended projection, not a bare root or stem. An overt nominal extended projection, DP, is licensed by Case and agreement; an overt bare noun, on the other hand, is licensed by incorporation. The bare noun *bottle* in (67) is not properly licensed. By contrast, the bare N in (61), repeated

here as (68), does not face these licensing difficulties, by virtue of being a
nonovert complement linked to an antecedent p-signature in V.

(68)

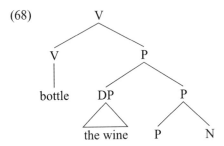

There is a problem here, however. As matters stand, (68) will be blocked,
since Vocabulary Insertion will preempt conflation, giving (69), ill formed
on two grounds, the defective V and the overt bare N.

(69)

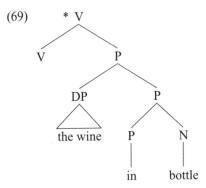

Clearly, Vocabulary Insertion cannot preempt conflation in this case.
There are two possibilities, at least: (i) the processes apply freely in any
order within the relevant domain (this being the cycle defined by the
highest implicated node, e.g., defective V in (69)); (ii) conflation is
ordered before Vocabulary Insertion, and the latter is ordered before
"complex conflation," that is, the process involved in forming cognate
objects.

In addition to an eccentric interpretation of the principle of cyclic rule
application, the first possibility will require independent principles ruling
out derivations that fail to converge (in the sense of Chomsky 1995). Such
derivations are ruled out already in the case of bare overt noun complements. This possibility will not account for (66), however. The second
possibility also fails to account for (66), and it has the added feature of
divorcing cognate object formation from conflation. This may or may not
be desirable.

We do not have a solution to this problem, though we suspect the first possibility is the more likely to be correct. Quite apart from this question, the type represented by (66) is a problem for any analysis of the conflation phenomenon. It probably involves a local stipulation—in English, a noun can conflate into P only if the latter conflates into V. There are some exceptions, like *home* (as in *She is home* or *Take it home with you*), which evidently involves the conflation of a noun into a defective preposition; other possible examples are the locatives and directionals in *a-* (*adrift, aloft, aboard*, etc.).[21]

In concluding this section, we mention that independent evidence exists that some prepositions, and perhaps the category as a whole, occupy a special position among lexical items. We have attributed to them the special feature that they lack a p-signature and hence do not conflate into V, unless they "acquire" a p-signature through conflation of a complement. At Vocabulary Insertion, of course, prepositions acquire phonological substance. As terminal nodes in syntax, however, they are phonologically undetermined. Suppose this lack of a p-signature is true of functional categories as well—categories like tense, Case, articles, and agreement, that is, elements whose phonological constituency is often highly dependent upon morphological context. If this is so, then, while prepositions constitute a lexical category, they share an important characteristic of the other closed class items (i.e., the functional categories).

Possible evidence that at least some prepositions belong with the functional categories comes from several quarters. It is well known that in many languages, elements that correspond most closely to the more caselike prepositions of English, or to the caselike postpositions of canonical head-final languages, are affixal and exhibit the same sorts of phonological dependencies that acknowledged inflectional categories do. So far as we know, these are never treated as "full" lexical items, for example, in auxiliary languages whose proper use involves the replacement of lexical items (N, V, A, say) by items from a special vocabulary. Thus, for example, in Linngithigh and Wik Me'nh of Cape York Peninsula, North Queensland, the instrumental, elative, and allative postpositions are suffixal and entirely inflection-like in their morphophonological behavior, and, unsurprisingly, they are not implicated in the vocabulary replacement process entailed in the special avoidance lexicon used in speaking to or about certain in-laws (also see Dixon's (1972) extensive study of this linguistic practice in another North Queensland language, Dyirbal). Similarly, in Damin, the advanced initiates' language of the Lardil people of

Mornington Island, North Queensland, Lardil lexical items in general must be replaced by items drawn from a special set of vocables of extraordinary phonological and semantic character. Again, this process does not implicate the suffixal categories instrumental, comitative, or locative. These are not replaced and instead remain in standard Lardil, like all inflectional elements.

It is also well known that adpositions often fuse with adjacent functional heads in nominal extended projections, typically with D, often in a manner that eliminates any vestige of the original, unfused shapes of the individual components. Thus, the French preposition *à* fuses with the masculine articles to give *au* and *aux*, strongly supporting the idea that these entities owe their phonological realization to Vocabulary Insertion and that the notion of p-signature plays no role in this matter. In Ulwa, a Misumalpan language of eastern Nicaragua, the locative and allative case postposition *kau* fuses with the definite article *ya* to give *yau*—not as extreme a case as the French one, to be sure, but nonetheless illustrative of a widespread and amply documented phenomenon in morphology.

The study of certain language impairments also provides evidence that P can be viewed as a functional category. Agrammatism, for example, is characterized by the "widespread omission of function words and affixes and the greater retention of content words"; specifically, "studies of the production of prepositions by agrammatic patients indicate that different types of prepositions show greater or lesser susceptibility to omission" (Kaplan 1992). Kaplan also notes that "Friederici (1982) reported that 12 agrammatic aphasic patients were better at supplying prepositions with lexical content (such as *under* in *The dog is under the table*) than prepositions that are entirely determined by the verb of a sentence and play little semantic role (such as *for* in *He hopes for a nice present*) in a sentence completion task." And he concludes that "these results are broadly consistent with the view that some agrammatic patients have difficulty with the production of syntactic structures, and that the omission of function words is related to that problem: prepositions with greater semantic similarity to open class words are better produced than those that play a more syntactic role."

Among the properties shared by some functional heads and some P-heads are

(70) a. contextually dependent phonological realization,
     b. tendency toward atonicity,

    c. membership in a closed class, and

    d. relational semantics.

The first two of these are self-explanatory and well documented; the third is also clear in the abstract, but not so clear in practice. We will assume that P is a closed class, but it is not obviously so—particularly in the many languages in which the full inventory of "relational" heads, having traditional P-like function, is filled out by so-called relational nouns (in the manner of English *on top of, at the side of, at the rear of,* etc.). It is nevertheless arguably true that caselike adpositions form a restricted and closed class, even in languages with a large and potentially extendable inventory of nominal adpositions (like those of the Athabaskan language Navajo, its relatives, and the Misumalpan languages Miskitu and Sumu, for example). The fourth property, relational semantics, is intended to reflect the often-cited "semantic poverty" of caselike adpositions. This is very subjective, it seems to us, but there is perhaps some reality to the notion that the semantics of these elements differs from the semantics of lexical items that name eventualities (V, A) or entities (N). Adpositions are relational, expressing, for example, the motional or locational relation between some entity (a "figure") and another entity (a "place"). There is, therefore, an element of contextual dependency in their semantics. An adposition is interpreted by virtue of the construction in which it appears and, in that respect, it shares a feature with the functional category Case. While particular adpositions have "semantic content" (like *under, above,* etc.), the class as a whole, like Case, includes members that are essentially empty semantically, expressing a relation pure and simple (e.g., *of* in most of its functions, and *to, at, for* in many of their functions).

    Some subset of the properties listed in (70) could well render the p-signature at least redundant, or even impossible, for functional categories and adpositions. But adpositions do not possess these characteristics uniformly. They do, however, steadfastly and uniformly resist conflation in English, departing sharply in this respect from the other lexical categories (V, N, and A), all of which participate productively in the process. The property that might be attributed to English prepositions as a group is (70c), membership in a closed class. Although the class of prepositions is rather large in English, exceeding in number the inventory of true verbs in some languages of the world (e.g., the non-Pama-Nyungan Australian language Jingulu, as reported in Pensalfini 1997), it is nevertheless arguably a closed class in the generally accepted sense. Let us assume that it is indeed a closed class, sharing this characteristic with the functional categories, like Case, Tense, Agreement, and so on. It is reasonable to suppose, it seems to us, that the members of a closed class would lack p-signatures. These would be redundant, essentially, since Vocabulary Insertion would entail locating items in a finite list of items, each identified by means of grammatical, not phonological, features. If p-signatures are redundant, then they are impossible, we would argue, explaining their failure to conflate in English.

It is possible as well that (65) and (66) are to be explained in relation to these considerations. The idea would be that Vocabulary Insertion is necessary in the P-position in these cases, and it fails because the p-signature of the P-node in syntax (i.e., the p-signature copied into P from N) and the principles of insertion for P amount to contrary instructions for Vocabulary Insertion: both *in* and *bottle* are identified for insertion at P, an impossibility. Vocabulary Insertion would be necessary, presumably, because P is otherwise not properly licensed in syntax. While it contains a p-signature, the latter is not "bound" (it is not "p-bound") by an antecedent p-signature in a c-commanding head (i.e., in V). We are making the ancillary assumption here that p-binding is a requirement for closed class items in a conflation chain, like that represented by the well-formed terminal sequence V-P-N in (68), in which the p-signature of V antecedes and binds that of P, and the p-signature of P binds that of N. While P can, and often does, appear in a conflation chain, P cannot *head* one; (65) and (66) fail the p-binding requirement, and Vocabulary Insertion is also blocked, as we have shown. In (64), of course, P is licensed by Vocabulary Insertion.

In summary, in a structure like (63b), repeated here as (71), only Vocabulary Insertion can apply, giving *put the wine in the bottle* (= (64)), assuming the relevant features of P to coincide appropriately with those of the vocabulary item *in*.

(71)

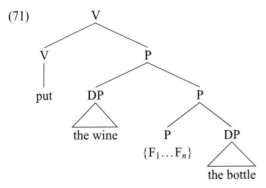

If conflation applied here, the derivation would fail, since P would not be p-bound and Vocabulary Insertion would result in a terminal that is uninterpretable at PF.

3.6 Hyponymous Arguments and a Revision of the Theory of Conflation

Having suggested a general theory of conflation, together with a treatment of cognate objects, we are left with the class of linguistic expressions that, for better or for worse, we have termed "hyponymous argument constructions," as illustrated by (8), repeated here as (72).

(72) a. They are dancing a Sligo jig.
     b. He shelved the books on the windowsill.
     c. Leecil saddled old Gotch with his new Schowalter.

We will not reconsider here the analysis suggested in Hale and Keyser 1997c, according to which hyponymous arguments and cognate objects alike were the result of "reinsertion" into the trace position created by conflation. This is an impossible notion, not only for general theoretical reasons. It is also impossible, within the theory considered in previous sections, because conflation is not head movement and hence does not leave a trace in any conventional sense.

In fact, any serious consideration of cognate and hyponymous arguments leads directly to the conclusion that matters would be greatly simplified if conflation did not exist in any of the forms so far suggested. In relation to these specific constructions, the grammar would involve virtually no machinery at all beyond what is already present in any theory of syntax. The derivation of sentences like those in (72) would not differ in nature from that of ordinary sentences like those in (73), apart from the individual lexical items appearing at the terminal nodes.

(73) a. She is playing a jig.
     b. He put the books on the windowsill.
     c. Leecil fit the mule with a new harness.

Here, of course, there is no talk of conflation. For our purposes, Vocabulary Insertion is the relevant operation, applying to the verbal projection contained in (73a), for example, to give the structure in (74).

(74)

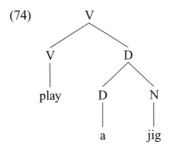

The idea that there might be a difference between the examples in (72) and those in (73) has support, so far as we can tell, only from two considerations: (i) the denominal character of the verbs in the former, as opposed to the putative "pure" verbal character of the verbs in (74); and (ii) the semantic relation of hyponymy, which, we have claimed, holds between the verb and the assumed nominal source (e.g., the "classificatory" relation between *dance* and *jig* in (72a)). If there is in fact no difference between (72) and (74), then there is of course nothing that would force us to treat the hyponymous argument construction as in any way different from the simple, run-of-the-mill outcome of Vocabulary Insertion.

Suppose then that *dance a jig* involves just two essential processes, Merge of V and [DP D N], giving (75),

(75)

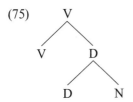

and Vocabulary Insertion, giving (76).

(76)

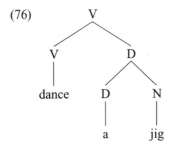

If this is correct, the item inserted in the terminal position labeled V is already supplied with a phonological matrix, as part of its lexical entry.

The notion "p-signature" plays no role here; that is, it plays no substantive role beyond what is already implied in the phonological matrix of the vocabulary item.

This raises the question of the reality of the p-signature in general and, more importantly, the reality of conflation altogether. Let us consider the superficially intransitive *dance*, as in *watch her dance*. Heretofore, we have maintained that this involved conflation, in order to express the evident fact that this is a "denominal verb," representing the abstract V-complement structure shown in (77).

(77)

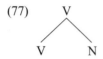

Conflation, in our most recent conception, transfers the p-signature of the noun to the verb. But if the lexicon contains a verb *dance*, complete with phonological matrix, what prevents us from saying that that item itself is inserted in the V-position, giving (78)?

(78)

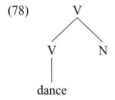

If this were the situation in general, conflation would be entirely redundant.

Conflation was motivated originally by two considerations: (i) the denominal character of verbs like *laugh* and *dance*, as mentioned above, and (ii) the idea that such verbs project an abstract transitive structure. The first of these considerations must be expressible without resort to conflation in any event. The phonological matrices that give the verbs in question their alleged denominal appearance must already be present in the lexicon, as seen in the case of (75) and (76). The second consideration is independent of the issue of conflation. It has to do with the syntactic properties of these verbs, the claim being that they have a central property associated with canonical transitive verbs—namely, they do not project a specifier. It follows that they take an external subject and consequently cannot transitivize in the simple manner of inchoative or unaccusative verbs of the type represented by *break* and *clear*.

We can retain the account of the syntactic property of simple denominal verbs, by assuming the structure verb-complement [V N] for them, as in (77), and at the same time we can rid ourselves of the machinery of conflation (under any of its incarnations). The association of a particular phonological matrix with the terminal V-node would result from insertion of a vocabulary item already supplied with a phonological matrix, as is necessary in (76). We might simply generalize it to all cases, including (76).

Let us pursue this possibility, ridding ourselves of conflation and its trappings, where possible. In the original, incorporation-like conception of conflation, the empty verb needed to be licensed. This was effected by conflation, which gave the empty verb phonological constituency; the empty N left behind was licensed as a trace, as expected in a movement theory of the phenomenon. In our more recent, label-copying conception of the process, the empty heads are presumably licensed through the connection established between a complement and its governing host by label copying itself. But if we give these things up, and assume that the structure of *dance* is as in (78), derived by Merge and Vocabulary Insertion, and not by conflation (in any version), some other principle must be involved in licensing the empty heads. The verb is presumably licensed by Vocabulary Insertion. It is the empty nominal complement (N) that is now at issue.

Is it generally true that an empty N complement must be licensed? If so, then N in (78) must be licensed.[22] Consider the following cases, by comparison:

(79) a. *He made.
      (cf. He made trouble/fishtraps/mistakes.)
    b. *She did.
      (cf. She did a jig/pirouettes/the MCATs.)

Evidently, transitive light verbs cannot take an empty object. Another class of verbs that resist "object drop" of this type is exemplified in (80), where the verbs are to be understood as the transitive variants of the verbs exemplified parenthetically in their grammatical uses.[23]

(80) a. *He cleared.
      (cf. The screen cleared. He cleared the screen.)
    b. *Leecil tightened.
      (cf. The cinch tightened. Leecil tightened the cinch.)

   c. *She split.
       (cf. The log split. She split the log.)

Consider (79) first. Intuitively, what is wrong here is that there is not enough information around to posit an object. The object is, so to speak, invisible, unidentified. By contrast, in a standard unergative construction, of the type central to the question of conflation, the verb itself gives information relevant to the interpretation of the verb in conjunction with its nonovert complement: the verb identifies the complement to some sufficient extent.

(81) a. The baby slept.
     b. Isadora danced.
     c. The colt sneezed.

What these considerations show, we think, is that the "nominal" component of these verbs is in fact real and serves to license the nonovert complement. In the movement theory of conflation, this followed straightforwardly, since the nominal component of the verb originated in the complement. But we have evidence, from many sides, that the nominal component is in the verb in any event—movement is redundant, and arguably impossible.

Suppose we say, then, that the relevant ingredients here are these:

(82) a. the relations expressed in the argument structure configuration, and
     b. a "classificatory" relation between certain semantic features of the head and a designated argument.

The second of these is in a sense nothing more than classical semantic selection. It is the relation involved in what we have called "hyponymy," as in (72a) and (75), where the verb itself encourages us to understand *jig* in the sense 'kind of dance'—by comparison with, say, *whistle a jig*, where the verb instead suggests 'kind of tune'. In the case of the unergatives illustrated in (81), the verbs identify the nonovert complements in an intuitively more or less obvious manner, as eventualities or entities corresponding to the English nouns *sleep, dance, sneeze*. It is this identification that licenses the nonovert complement. We might represent this special "classificatory" selectional relation by means of braced indices, linking the verb to its complement, as in (83).

(83)

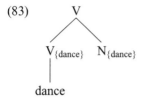

This represents the structure for the verb *dance*; the braced index is notated with the standard spelling of the English noun, rather than the more usual arbitrary letter index. This notation is no less arbitrary, of course; it is chosen to suggest what is intended, namely, a semantic relation between the verb and its object—a selectional relation, or classificatory binding relation—above and beyond the purely structural relation expressed by the verb-complement configuration alone.

With this background, we can say something now about the verbs of (79). We propose that their inability to take a nonovert object follows from the fact that they are "light verbs"—in other words, verbs without any semantic component that could enter into a classificatory binding relation capable of licensing an empty complement. At the risk of being redundant, the difference between (79) and (81) thus resides in the *lexical semantics* of the verb. The two types share the *structural semantics* of "production" generally associated with the verb-complement configuration of unergatives. But the verbs of (79) lack the lexical semantic component present in the verbs of (81); it is this component, represented by the braced index in (83), that licenses the nonovert nominal complement.

Here we have appealed to the second part of (82), on the assumption that semantic features of lexical items are relevant to the licensing of nonovert complements. The first part of (82) has to do with structure. As a first approximation, we propose that the licensing function expressed in the indexing relation shown in (83) and the like can only hold between a head and an argument selected by it, the clearest case being that of a head and its complement. This structural consideration is the most likely factor involved in the verbs of (80). These verbs are certainly not lacking in lexical semantic content; they are not "light verbs" in any sense. But the hypothetical nonovert nominal—the argument omitted in the ill-formed sentences—is not selected by the verb and hence does not enter into the right structural relation with it. The hypothetical nonovert argument in (80) is the specifier of the inner V-projection. As we have maintained in other contexts (see (9)–(11) et passim), the specifier of the inner projection bears no direct argumental relation to the upper verb. Thus, it is not eligible to be linked to the upper verb in the manner expressed informally by means of the brace coindexation; hence, that position must be overt, as it is in the parenthetical examples cited in (80).

Another contrast we must deal with is found in the domain of location and locatum verbs, as in (84) and (85).

(84) a. *John put the books.
        (cf. John put the books on the top shelf.)
     b. *Leecil fit the horse.
        (cf. Leecil fit the horse with a new Schowalter.)

(85) a. John shelved the books.
        (cf. John shelved the books on the top shelf.)
     b. Leecil saddled the horse.
        (cf. Leecil saddled the horse with a new Schowalter.)

The verbs of (84) are too "light" to license a nonovert argument. The sole semantics associated with *put* and *fit*, in these uses, are those of the construction itself, the meaning corresponding approximately to the idea of effecting a relation between two entities: one (the internal specifier) functioning as a "figure," the other (the complement of P) as a "place or end point." This is the meaning sometimes described in terms of bringing about a change of location (in the case of *put*) or of possession (in the case of *fit*)—and it is the canonical "meaning" of argument structure configurations of the form [V PP].

The much-cited fact that *put* has both an object (DP) and a prepositional phrase (PP) in its "subcategorization frame" is, in our conception of the matter, the same as the fact that *do* and *make* must have overt complements. The verb *put* simply does not "have what it takes" to license a nonovert argument in the syntactic position corresponding to the "place or end point," that is, the prepositional complement position. And similarly for *fit*.

By contrast, the verbs of (85) freely permit omission of this constituent. In fact, its omission is the normal state of affairs for these verbs. Sentences in which this item is overt (exemplified parenthetically in (85)) are somewhat contrived, though perfectly grammatical. Evidently, then, verbs like *shelve* and *saddle*, and other members of the location and locatum types, have the lexical semantic features required to license a nonovert [P N] that our hypothesis assumes to be structurally present in the sentences of (85). Thus, by hypothesis, the verb *shelve* must be brace-coindexed with the nominal complement of the preposition, as shown in (86).

(86)

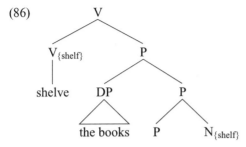

This is intended to capture the idea expressed in conventional and successful uses of the verb *shelve*, namely, that it is brought about by some agent (person or machine) in some appropriate manner that books come to be on a shelf or shelves in a manner satisfying the definition of "shelving." The verb alone does not express all of this; the structural configuration is also implicated. The lexical semantic features of the verb "make visible" certain properties of the nonovert nominal with which it is coindexed, and for this reason, the nominal is licensed in its nonovert form.

Assuming that something of this sort is correct, or at least reasonable, there is an additional detail that must be dealt with. Strictly speaking, the verb in (86) does not bear a direct relation to the object of the preposition. The preposition intervenes—from the structural point of view, it is P that selects N in (86). So how is it that the verb can license the nonovert N? The answer probably has to do with the fact that the verb selects the preposition (structurally, and probably semantically as well, where that is relevant) and the observation widely made, and discussed briefly in the previous section, that P belongs to the functional system, as much as, or more than, to the lexical inventory. Thus, there is a chain of selection extending from the verb to the object of the preposition, and one of the links, the P, might be especially porous in relation to semantic selection.

Be this as it may, there *is* a special semantic relation between V and the object of the preposition in configurations of the type represented by (86). It can be seen in sentences like those in (87) and (88).

(87) a. I corralled the calves in the milkpen.
    b. He boxed the apples in a gunnysack.
    c. They armed the trap with teeth.
    d. They saddled us with responsibilities.

(88) a. We armed the priest with a lawyer.
    b. We armed the lawyer with a priest.

In (87a), there is a coherence between the verb and the object of the preposition: a milkpen qualifies as something that could be used to contain calves in the manner of a corral. This congruity is lacking in (87b); at least, it is lacking in the ordinary understanding of the meanings of the verb *box* and the noun *gunnysack*. While *bag apples in a gunnysack* is congruent, *box apples in a gunnysack* is not, and the congruence, or lack of it, is a matter having to do with the verb and the object of the preposition, bypassing the linearly adjacent specifier *apples*. We understand (87c) as figuratively "classifying" teeth, not the trap, as a kind of armament. In parallel fashion, the verb *saddle* in (87d) attributes to responsibilities the property of being a burden; again, the special semantic relation holds between the verb and the object of the preposition, bypassing the inner specifier. And in (88), the quality of being something like supportive armament is attributed to the lawyer or to the priest, depending upon the appearance of the corresponding nominal argument as the object of the preposition; this attribute is not attached to either referent when the corresponding nominal is in the specifier position projected by the preposition.

We conclude from this that a location or locatum verb bears a selectional relation to the nominal object of its prepositional complement. If the latter is nonovert, it must be licensed; it will be licensed if it can be brace-coindexed with the verb (as in (86)). The verbs of (84) stand in the proper structural relation to the nominal at issue, but the required coindexing cannot take place, because the verb is semantically empty in the relevant sense.

This system is not quite right, however. Licensing of an empty argument evidently requires something more. If the verb can "semantically select" the object of its prepositional complement, and if this were enough to license an empty nominal in that position, then the following sentences might be expected to be grammatical, contrary to fact:

(89) a. *We shelved the books on.
     b. *She saddled Gotch with.

The preposition must be "neutralized," by itself being empty. In this respect, the relation between the semantic features of the verb and the empty nominal made visible by them has the character of a strictly local binding relation. In the simplest case, that of a verb and its nominal complement (e.g., in the structures attributed to *laugh, dance*, etc.), the structural relation is absolutely local. In the more complex case of a verb and the object of its prepositional complement, the relation is not local if an actual P intervenes, in the sense that it is closer to V than N is (i.e., PP contains N but not V). This is the effect seen in (89), where P blocks the required "binding" relation between V and N. This blocking effect, we suggest, is absent if P is sufficiently empty. The blocking effect requires that certain features be present in P; only then is it visible as an intervening head.

Let us suppose that the relation holding between the coindexed verb and noun in (83) is antecedent government, continuing the thought that this is a binding relation and that an empty N must be antecedent-governed. In (86), let us assume, the relation between the verb and the empty noun is also antecedent government. If so, the structure projected by an empty preposition is not a barrier for this relation. In (89), however, a contentful preposition evidently projects a barrier to antecedent government; hence, the empty N is not licensed. In (87) and (88), however, the post-prepositional overt nominal projection is licensed, since it does not need to be antecedent-governed. The binding requirement of an empty nominal complement is reminiscent of the requirement that an anaphor must be locally bound. A contentful preposition sets up a barrier for binding of an empty nominal complement, in much the way that a "specified subject" defines a barrier for unproblematic anaphoric binding (see Chomsky 1981, 1986).

Our conclusion is this. So-called conflation, where that involves a nominal argument, is simply the situation in which a verb, endowed with certain semantic content, is coindexed with a nominal argument standing in a structural relation that permits the verb to "antecedent-bind" it. The noun can therefore be nonovert (i.e., an empty category), by virtue of antecedent government.

Observationally, it is not enough to say that a verb capable of antecedent-binding a nonovert noun has certain semantic content. The original motivation for conflation, especially in its earlier incarnation as incorporation, derived from the idea that verbs like *laugh*, *dance*, and *saddle* are "denominal" verbs. This idea comes, no doubt, from the fact that most of the verbs at issue here are morphologically related to nouns, typically, but not always, to the extent of being phonologically identical to them: *dance* (V), *dance* (N); *laugh* (V), *laugh* (N); and so on. Moreover, this relationship, to a greater or lesser extent, carries over to the meaning: modulo the meanings of *perform* and *produce*, it seems to us correct to say that *John danced* entails *John performed a dance*, and that *Mary laughed* entails *Mary produced a laugh*.

What, then, is the relation between the noun and the verb, in those cases where the two are clearly "related"? At this point, we suggest that the question is not one of a noun being related to a verb; rather, it is one of an indeterminate item, a root, as it were, which is not inherently either a noun or a verb. That is, its alleged categorial affiliation is contextual: it is a verb if it heads a "verbal" extended projection and therefore enters into inflectional relations conventionally associated with the category V, such as tense and mood; it is a noun if it heads a "nominal" extended projection and, depending on the details of the language, takes on case, inflection, and the like.[24] Thus, it is not correct, on this view, to say that *dance*, whether in the simple unergative construction or in the phrase *dance a jig*, is a "denominal verb." Rather, the element at issue is simply the categorially indeterminate vocabulary item *dance*, with its phonology, selectional features, and (encyclopedic) meaning. By means of the process of Vocabulary Insertion it assumes the "verbal" position in these cases, that is to say, the position corresponding to the head of a verbal extended projection, in accordance with local requirements (e.g., principles of allomorphy). As a verb with appropriately classificatory semantic content, *dance* imposes a selectional claim on its object, licensing the empty N in the first case and establishing the hyponymous relation (a *jig* is a *dance*) with the overt complement in the second.

The essential features of conflation, in relation to so-called denominal verb formation at least, appear to us to have evaporated. The special relation that holds between a verb like *dance* and its nonovert object N, or between *shelve* and the nonovert object of its PP complement, is properly subsumed in the general relation of semantic selection and hence does not provide evidence for conflation. And the alleged cross-categorial relation, accounting for such terms as *denominal* and *deverbal*, is simply an appearance, a consequence of categorial indeterminacy. Therefore, we take the position now that conflation, as we have been using the term, is not a part of the theory of argument structure. There is, however, one issue that remains to be discussed.

3.7   Incorporation

The foregoing remarks relate to constructions involving verbs that suggest that they might be derived, by zero morphology, from nouns. We have dismissed this idea for English, eliminating both incorporation and conflation from consideration in the theory of these verbs' structure and origins.

But there is another verbal type that must be considered in this discussion. This is the class of deadjectival verbs of the type represented by *clear*, as in (90).

(90) a. The sky cleared.
     b. The wind cleared the sky.

The question here is whether these verbs should also be analyzed as cases of selection and coindexation, like the denominal verbs we have been considering so far. The alternative would be to say that verbal *clear* is derived by incorporation or conflation. This has been our position on the matter up to now, in fact—and in this context, furthermore, the supposed distinction between incorporation and conflation is baseless, and we can assume that the question at hand is whether or not *clear* and other deadjectival verbs are derived by incorporation.

The selection alternative would maintain that, in the case of *clear*, there is a root element in the vocabulary that, in addition to appearing in the head position of an adjectional (A) projection, also appears in the position heading a verbal extended projection. As a verbal head, it selects a complement, as depicted in (91).

(91)
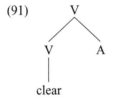

In parallel with our analysis of denominal verbs like *dance*, we assume that the complement is an empty category A linked by selection with the verb, in the same way the verb *dance* is linked to the empty N complement in (83). Thus:

(92)
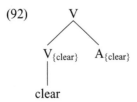

By virtue of the properties inherent in its complement A, the verb would necessarily project a specifier—for example, *the sky* in (93).

(93)

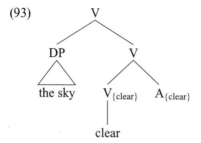

By general rules of interpretation, the verb projects a structure corresponding to the semantic relation "change of state" and the adjective denotes the state; the entity denoted by the specifier corresponds to the "theme."

It is necessary, in our framework, to maintain that verbal *clear* involves a structure of the form [$_V$ V A]. It must have the V component, because it enters into a verbal extended projection; and it must have a complement (A) that forces the projection of a specifier. This follows, because of the transitivity alternation that it freely enters into, namely, the one in (90).

There are at least two reasons to doubt that the account just sketched is correct. One of these is, so to speak, a negative reason. Denominal verbs of the type represented by *dance*, and denominal location and locatum verbs like *shelve* and *saddle* likewise, enter productively into cognate object and hyponymous argument relations, discussed in section 3.4 and exemplified by such constructions as *dance a wild dance*, *shelve it on the top shelf*, and *saddle the colt with an English saddle*. By contrast, deadjectival verbs do not enter into this relation productively. Thus, *clear it very clear, redden the cloth bright red, lengthen the road two miles long*, and the like, do not seem to us to be grammatical. If this is true, then it is a fact that does not follow from the selection theory sketched above and embodied in the structure modeled by (93).

The unacceptability of cognate and hyponymous complements in the case of deadjectival verbs might be explained, on the other hand, by a theory in which the process involved in their derivation is in fact incorporation, the very process ruled out for denominal verbs. According to the incorporation theory of deadjectival verbs, the adjectival complement would move from its base position into the verb (adjoining to it) in accordance with the principles constraining head movement. The process would create a chain relation between the base position of the adjective (the tail of the chain) and its landing site, that is, the adjunction site at V (the head of the chain). Two additional and generally accepted assumptions will account now for the failure of the cognate object construction with deadjectival verbs: (i) the trace of head movement, like movement traces generally, blocks reinsertion at the position of the trace (this in turn follows from the cycle), and (ii) a chain is spelled out at its head alone.

Another observation that casts doubt on the selection theory of deadjectival verbs is the manifestly composite morphological makeup of most of them, for example, the type represented by *redden, widen, lengthen, strengthen, tighten,* and *darken.* So far as we can see, there is no natural account of these in which the composite verb (e.g., *redden*) appears in the V-position of a structure corresponding to (93) and selects an adjectival complement (A), as in the hypothetical (94). Without additional machinery, the features associated with *red* in *redden* cannot antecedent-bind the adjective, since *red* in *redden* does not c-command the empty A in complement position, assuming *redden* to be in fact composite.

(94)

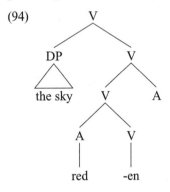

On the other hand, the incorporation theory of deadjectival verbs accounts for the composite verbs straightforwardly. The adjectival complement moves to V in conformity with the Head Movement Constraint, adjoining to the left of V, in conformity with the prevailing word-internal headedness arrangement of the languages of the world. Accordingly, (94) is the correct structure for *the sky redden,* if empty A is the trace of head movement and *-en* is the verb hosting the incorporated adjective. According to this scenario, *red* in V antecedent-governs and binds the empty A, being the head of the chain defined by incorporation. The zero derivation cases, like *clear, narrow,* and *thin,* differ from the *redden* type only in that the V component is empty.

Deadjectival verb formation is part of a more general process of predicate raising, of course. Simple transitivization, as exemplified in (95), is likewise defined by incorporation.

(95) a. The setting sun reddened the sky.
　　 b. The fall in prices narrows our options.

According to our general assumptions, the verb phrase of (95a) is abstractly as depicted in (96).

(96)

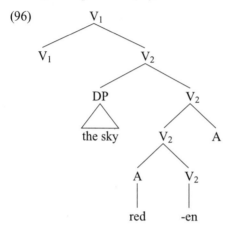

Verb raising and incorporation, forming the final transitive construction, raise the complex derived head V_2 and adjoin it to V_1, giving the configuration in (97), corresponding to the verb phrase of (95a).

(97)

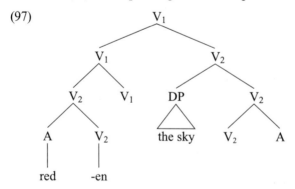

The empty categories V_2 and A are the traces of the two applications of incorporation, each properly governed by a head: A by V_2 and V_2 by V_1. In the derived structure, the DP *the sky* is governed and Case-marked by the complex verbal head V_1 *redden*.

3.8 Concluding Remarks

Our purpose in this chapter has been to explain why conflation, as opposed to incorporation, fails to access the specifier position—in other words, why a verb cannot "conflate" with the specifier of its complement.

Our explanation is this. Conflation is not a "process," that is, not a movement operation. Rather, the phenomenon we have been calling by that name is in reality merely the binding relation that holds between the semantic features of a verb (phonologically overt now) and features of the nominal head of its complement. This in turn is a result of the selectional relation between the verb and its complement. Selection holds between the verb and the *head* of its complement; selection is *not* a relation that holds between the verb and a specifier that might be present in the complement of the verb. We have had the intuition throughout that conflation is closely associated with Merge and have sought to identify it more and more closely with that process. Since conflation is a matter having to do with selection and, therefore, the relation between a head and its complement, it is, in effect, to be identified with Merge, the desired result of this inquiry.

By contrast, incorporation is constrained by government, a relation that subsumes selection but is not confined to it. Since a head governs the specifier of its complement, there is no barrier to incorporating from that position.[25]

Chapter 4
A Native American Perspective

4.1 Introduction

In this chapter, we look briefly at our elementary theory of argument structure from the point of view of four Native American linguistic traditions. Our purpose here is merely to lend a certain degree of cross-linguistic perspective to this work. For the most part, we limit our discussion of the four Native American traditions to the transitivity alternation commonly referred to as causative-inchoative, or in a different but relevant terminological usage, the alternation of so-called labile verbs such as English *break*, *sink*, *clear*, and *redden*. From our perspective, this is the alternation that is in a clear sense "inevitable," involving as it does the free embedding, by Merge, of a dyadic verbal projection into the complement position of a monadic verbal projection. The crucial ingredient here is the dyadic verbal projection, which, by nature, expresses the specifier relation as a function, generally, of the essential lexical property of the root element (i.e., complement) in the innermost verbal projection, as in the English deadjectival verb *clear*, whose adjectival component has the fundamental property that it forces its verbal host to project a specifier (see chapter 1 for details). The configurational diagram corresponding to English intransitive *clear* (abstracting away from conflation; see chapter 3) is given in (1) (linear ordering arbitrary).

(1)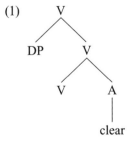

The adjectival component is responsible for the appearance in (1) of a DP in the specifier position of the verbal projection, being an element that, so to speak, must be attributed of something, inducing a relation akin to that of predication. The DP (e.g., *the sky*, as in *The sky cleared*) fulfills this fundamental requirement.

The transitive alternant results (as an automatic, inevitable option, in our view) through Merge of (1) with a monadic verb, implicating an external subject, as depicted in (2), again abstracting away from conflation.

(2)

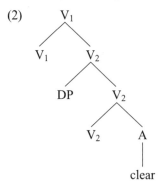

The external argument is not shown, inasmuch as it is not part of the verbal projection, being introduced (by Merge) at a higher specifier position.

In the intransitive alternant (1), the internal DP functions as the subject in sentential syntax, while in the transitive alternant (2), the internal specifier functions as sentential syntactic object (barring the intervention of other processes such as middle formation or passive).

This scenario for English is familiar from chapter 1. In this chapter, a similar scenario emerges in the Native American examples, which could have been chosen arbitrarily from any number of other languages of the world. The four languages we discuss are

- the Southern Athabaskan language Navajo (section 4.2);
- a member of the Misumalpan family of eastern Nicaragua and Honduras, specifically, Ulwa, confined primarily to the town of Karawala on the Atlantic coast of Nicaragua (section 4.3);
- (Tohono) O'odham, a Uto-Aztecan language, formerly known as Papago, spoken in southern Arizona and northern Sonora (section 4.4); and
- Hopi, also Uto-Aztecan, spoken in northern Arizona (section 4.5).

The material is modified from published papers (Hale and Platero 1996; Hale and Salamanca 2001; Hale 2000b; Jeanne and Hale 2000). Although some modifications have been made in excerpting these materials, we do not integrate them fully into a smooth and consistent text. In particular, our use of the terms *incorporation* and *conflation* lacks complete consistency and has not been adjusted fully to our conception of these notions in chapter 3. However, this failing should not interfere in any way with the principal points of data and theory inherent in this chapter.

4.2   Athabaskan: Navajo

In this section, we confront our basic theory of argument structure with certain aspects of the grammar of the Navajo verb, limiting our discussion primarily to the simple transitivity alternation reviewed in section 4.1. Consider the following sentence pairs (*Y&M* = Young and Morgan 1980):

(3) a. Tóshjeeh si-ts'il. (Y&M 80.804)
       barrel   SPF:3-shatter:PERF
       'The barrel shattered, broke to pieces.'
    b. Łeets'aa' sé-ł-ts'il. (Y&M 80.798)
       dish   3:SPF:1s-ł-shatter:PERF
       'I shattered the dish.'

(4) a. Tin yíyį́į́'. (< -ghį́į́') (Y&M 80.794)
       ice   YPF:3-melt:PERF
       'The ice melted.'
    b. Yas yí-ł-hį́į́'. (< -ghį́į́') (Y&M 80.782)
       snow 3:YPF:1s-ł-melt:PERF
       'I melted the snow.'

(5) a. Kǫ' n-eez-tsiz. (Y&M 80.664)
       fire n-SPF:3-extinguish:PERF
       'The fire went out.'
    b. Kǫ' n-é-ł-tsiz. (Y&M 80.657)
       fire 3:n-SPF:1s-ł-extinguish:PERF
       'I put the fire out.'

(6) a. Tł'óół k'í-ní-dláád. (Y&M 80.502)
       rope k'í-NPF:3-break:PERF
       'The rope broke.'

b. Tł'óół k'í-i-ní-ł-dláád. (Y&M 80.510)
   rope k'í-3o-NPF:3-ł-break:PERF
   'He broke the rope.'

These pairs represent the simple transitivity alternation of Navajo. Its principal morphological reflection is the presence of the classifier -*ł*- in the transitive member of the pair, the intransitive member being associated with the so-called zero classifier -Ø-, omitted from the glosses in (3)–(6). We take this morphological reflection as being nothing more than that, a simple marking of the transitivity alternation. Categorially, however, it is a light verb, symbolized *v*, suggesting *voice* or *valence* (see Rice 2000). There is no "meaning" attached to this light verb, such as 'causative'; it is, at most, a voice or valence marker, as indicated. Where the *l*-classifier is involved productively in the transitivity alternation, it is, so to speak, the exponent of transitivity. It is also found in a purely "lexical" function, where it is simply an inherent part of particular lexical verb themes, independent of transitivity. Here we are concerned with its productive use as a light verb with the value transitive, capable of assigning abstract Case to the object of a verb.

We contrast the situation just described—the simple or automatic transitivity alternation of "labile" verbs, such as those of (3)–(6)—with what can be called *complex* transitivization, such as the causative, which implicates extra morphological material—prefixal—in addition to the *l*-classifier. The causative is exemplified by the following pairs:

(7) a. 'Awéé' naa-gh-á.
      baby   na-IMPF:3-walk:sg:CI
      'The baby is walking around.'
   b. 'Awéé' na-b-ii-sh-ł-á. (Y&M 80.525)
      baby   na-3-y-IMPF:1s-ł-walk:sg:CI
      'I am walking the baby around (i.e., making it walk).'

(8) a. 'Awéé' d-ee-za'.
      baby   d-SPF:3-belch:PERF
      'The baby burped.'
   b. 'Awéé' bi-di-y-é-sa'. (< ... -ł-za') (Y&M 80.184)
      baby   3-d-y-SPF:1s-ł-belch:PERF
      'I burped the baby.'

(9) a. 'Awéé' yi-dloh.
      baby   PROG:3-d:laugh:PROG
      'The baby is laughing.'

b. 'Awéé' bi-y-eesh-dloh. (Y&M 80.259)
   baby 3-y-PROG:1s-ł-d:laugh:PROG
   'I am making the baby laugh.'

These causative formations share two features that distinguish them from
the simple transitives of (3)–(6), in addition to the *l*-classifier shared by
both simple and complex transitives. These two features are the appearance of a position VI prefix -*y*- and a set of object markers representing
the "causee" (logical subject of the basic verb); the latter precede (not
necessarily immediately) the "causative" prefix, and they differ from ordinary position IV object markers in that the third person is overt (underlying *b*-) in the presence of a first or second person subject, as if attached
to an incorporated postposition. We will refer to these as *oblique* object
pronominals.

Returning to the simple transitivity alternation, it is a fact that the set
of Navajo verbs participating in it is rather large. The following list is
a sample, in addition to the verbs illustrated in (3)–(6), extracted from
Young, Morgan, and Midgette 1992; page numbers are cited in brackets
(see that source for details):

(10) 'i-(ł-)'eeł   'float away' [177–183]
     ii-(ł-)gááh   'whiten' [195]
     (ł-)gan   'dry up' [199]
     'i-(ł-)geeh   'fall away' [as person, animal; 214,6]
     ii-(ł-)kíísh   'become spotted, put spots on' [329]
     ii-(ł-)k'is   'crack' [351]
     (ł-)lląąh   'increase' [369]
     'i-(ł-)lį́   'flow away' [376,7]
     di-(ł-)lid   'be burning' [371]
     'i-(ł-)máás   'roll away' [397,8]
     ii-(ł-)táás   'bend over, double' [493]
     (ł-)t'ees   'cook, roast, etc.' [536]
     'i-(ł-)t'ééh   'extend away' [line, fence; 546,7]
     ii-(ł-)tłíísh   'darken, turn brown' [571]
     (ł-)tł'is   'harden' [as mud, dough; 580]
     ii-(ł-)tsóóh   'yellow' [614]
     di-(ł-)ts'ǫǫd   'stretch' [643,4]
     di-(ł-)zháásh   'begin to wear away, down' [767]
     (ł-)zhǫǫh   'become gentle, make gentle' [796]

However, many verbs do *not* participate in this alternation. Setting aside verbs that are obviously transitive, verbs of dubious transitivity lacking a simple transitive counterpart are probably as numerous as those that enter into the simple transitivity alternation. We will refer to these as *unergatives*, following current linguistic usage (cf. the unergatives of chapter 1). The verbs upon which the causatives of (7)–(9) are based represent this type. Additional examples are cited in (11).

(11) na-bé   'swim, bathe' [69]
      -cha   'cry' [70]
      di-lish   'spurt urine' [as of dog; 375]
      na-né   'play' [423]
      ho-taał   'sing' [490]
      di-zheeh   'spit' [771]
      'i-zhííł   'gasp, inhale sharply' [773]
      di-yih   'pant, puff' [702]
      'i-yóół   'inhale' [723]

The verbs of (11) are selected from among nonalternating verbs having the zero classifier. Many verbs carry overt classifiers, -ł- as well as -l- and -d-. It is not known whether this, in and of itself, inhibits those verbs from participating in the transitivity alternation. The use of a nonzero classifier is not, in principle, a barrier to transitivization, since the causative, for example, can be built upon a verb theme, even a basically transitive one, that contains an inherent classifier: for example, *OBJ-'-y-ł-dlą́* 'make OBJ drink something' [154] (the underlying verb here takes the *d*-classifier, evident in the perfective, for example: *yishdlą́ą́', yoodlą́ą́'*, and so on, not **yídlą́ą́', *yiyíídlą́ą́'*); *ha-OBJ-y-ł-yeed* 'run OBJ up out' [657], based on the *l*-classifier theme *ha-l-yeed* [653]; and *OBJ-'-y-ł-haazh* 'make OBJ sleep' [Y&M 87:215], based on the *l*-classifier theme *'-ii-l-haazh* 'go to sleep'.

The principal point here is that there are verbs that participate in the simple transitivity alternation and there are verbs that do not. The verb of (8) belongs to the class whose members cannot alternate, the class represented by the verbs in (11). Thus, while it is possible to form a causative of that verb, as seen in (8b), the *simple* transitive is not possible.

(12) *'Awéé' d-é-sa'. (< ... -ł-za')
      baby   d-SPF:1s-ł-belch
      'I burped the baby.'

There is no a priori reason why the verb form in (12) should not be possible, since the stem -za' is perfectly possible with the l-classifier, as the causative attests. It is nevertheless a fact that this verb cannot form a simple transitive, of the type represented in (3)–(6). The same can be said of the verbs of (11) and the general class of verbs they represent. Why do they resist simple transitivization? Why is there this asymmetry among the verbs of Navajo?

This asymmetry is not accidental. Even in the absence of a theory, the systematic nature of this asymmetry is evident immediately when the Navajo facts are compared with the corresponding phenomenon in other languages. Consider, for example, the following sample verbs from English, an Indo-European language; Miskitu, a Misumalpan language of eastern Nicaragua and Honduras; and Navajo.

(13) Verbs that alternate

English	Miskitu		Navajo	
	Intransitive	Transitive	Intransitive	Transitive
boil	pya-w-	pya-k-	-béézh	-ł-béézh
break	kri-w-	kri-k-	ii-dlaad	ii-ł-dlaad
shatter	bai-w-	bai-k-	-ii-ts'ił	-ii-ł-ts'ił
dry (up)	lâ-w-	lâ-k-	-gan	-ł-gan
fill	bangh-w-	bangh-k-	ha-di-bin	ha-di-ł-bin
float	â-w-	â-k-	di-'eeł	di-ł-'eeł
melt	slil-w-	slil-k-	-ghį́į́h	-ł-ghį́į́h

(14) Verbs that do not alternate

English	Miskitu	Navajo
cry	in-	-cha
cough	kuhb-	d-l-kos
laugh	kik-	gh-dloh
play	pul-	na-né
shout	win-	d-l-ghosh
sing	aiwan-	hw-taał
sleep	yap-	'-ł-ghosh
snore	krat-w-	'-ł-ghą́ą́'

In an important sense, the alternating and nonalternating classes in these three languages contain *the same verbs*. Morphological details differ, of course, quite apart from the obvious fact that the verbs "sound" different in the three languages. English lacks any special morphology associated with transitivity, while both Miskitu and Navajo overtly distinguish the transitive members of alternating pairs—by means of the *l*-classifier in Navajo and by means of the *k*-increment in Miskitu. In addition, Miskitu marks the intransitive alternants with the *w*-increment, while Navajo uses the zero classifier for the intransitive alternants. These details aside, the verb classes distinguished by these three languages are *identical*, for all intents and purposes. It is virtually impossible for this to be an accident. Something fundamental underlies this coincidence in lexical behavior. This is the question, then: What is behind the asymmetry of the transitivity alternation? What factor *permits* the alternation in the case of the verbs in (3)–(6), (10), and (13), and what factor *blocks* it in the case of the verbs in (7)–(9), (11), and (14)?

We believe that the answer lies in the basic argument structure configurations of the verbs. The difference between the two classes of verbs depends on the basic configurations they realize: alternating verbs realize one structure (the dyadic configuration [Specifier [V Complement]]), while nonalternating verbs realize another (the monadic configuration [V Complement]).

We know that alternating verbs share the feature that the subject of the intransitive alternant appears as the object of the transitive. Thus, in (15), the subject of the (a)-sentence, *leets'aa'* 'dish', functions as object in the (b)-sentence.

(15) a. Łeets'aa' si-ts'il.
      dish   SPF:3-shatter:PERF
      'The dish shattered, broke to pieces.'
   b. Łeets'aa' sé-ł-ts'il.
      dish   3:SPF:1s-ł-shatter:PERF
      'I shattered the dish.'

This argument, sometimes called the "theme" (in the terminology of semantic, or thematic, relations) is constant in the alternation; it is present in both alternants. This suggests that it is *internal* to the lexical structure. And this, if true, leads us to assume that this verb, and other alternating verbs like it, must realize one of the lexical structures that contains a predicate-like subconstituent, and therefore a *subject*, internal to the lexical structure itself—so these verbs must realize the structure depicted in (1).

This is very probably the crucial difference. The nonalternating verbs have only an *external* subject, one appearing in sentential syntax but not in the lexical argument structure itself. These verbs, sometimes called "unergatives," cannot participate in the transitivity alternation, because, lacking an internal subject (i.e., a specifier projected by the lexical head), they provide no source for an object argument in the hypothetical transitive alternant. We will pursue this idea, considering the alternating verbs first. For purposes of the present discussion, we will represent the basic structure of an alternating verb as if it were a realization of (1), with the root of the verb, symbolized *R*, appearing in the complement position, as shown in (16), depicting the basic structure tentatively assumed for the verb of (3), -*ts'ił* 'shatter' (linear order immaterial for present purposes).

(16)

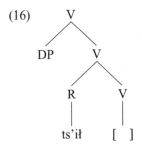

The root R of (16) is a member of the class of basic elements whose essential property is that they are predicate-like, in that they must be attributed or "predicated" of something and therefore force the verb to project a specifier (satisfied by DP in (16)). In effect, the verb "hosts" both the root R itself and, in addition, the specifier (or "inner subject") that is required by R in virtue of its essential properties. The subject is symbolized *DP* in (16), since it will appear in sentential syntax as a full nominal argument. In the surface form of this verb, the phonologically overt root R is conflated with the empty matrix of V, so that V and R form a single terminal node in the overt morphophonological representation of the verb. This sort of "incorporation" represents the same general process that gives rise to English verbs like *dance*, *shelve*, and *saddle*, derived by incorporating the corresponding nouns into the empty phonological matrix of a governing verb, a process that will figure presently in our discussion of the transitivity asymmetry at issue here.

For Navajo, it is not exactly correct to say that the verb (V) is entirely empty phonologically, since it is realized overtly in the system of aspectual and modal inflections, involving processes that modify the syllabic and segmental shape of the root. Some of these involve an element that is clearly a suffix to the root, for example, the future -*l* (see, e.g., Stanley 1969; Hardy 1979). We assume that these "inflections" are in fact the verb (V) (see Rice 2000).

The structure in (16) corresponds to the intransitive use of the verb, that is, the use exemplified in the (a)-sentences of (3)–(6). In that use, the lexically defined "internal" subject, DP, functions as sentential subject as well. We assume it raises in sentential syntax, out of the verbal projection to a higher position (possibly the specifier of v, the zero classifier, in this instance) in which it is appropriately licensed (assigned structural Case and construed with subject agreement).

The transitive alternant of this verb, exemplified in (2), results through a combination of (16) and the simple monadic head-complement structure [V Complement]. The former appears as the complement of the latter. Since the result is a verb, we must assume that the upper head is itself verbal, that is, the typical verbal realization of (2), though, for Navajo, we will assume further that this higher verbal head is in fact v, the classifier. While the upper head, like the lower one, contains a phonologically empty matrix, it contains an overt prefixal element as well, the *l*-classifier, as is generally the case for derived transitives in Navajo.

(17)

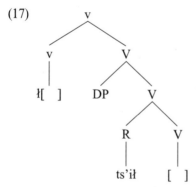

The derivation of the final surface verb proceeds as before (the empty verbal matrices receive their phonological realization through conflation, of governed head with governing head—as a concomitant of Merge, in the manner described in chapter 3), ultimately yielding the transitive verb theme *-l-ts'il*. This appears in the uppermost head position, where it governs the internal subject, DP. This argument will, of course, function now as the sentential syntactic *object*, not the subject. The subject of the transitive is an *external* argument, not present in the lexical structure, in conformity with the fundamental nature of prototypically verbal items (there being no element that would force v to project a specifier). The diagram in (17) reflects the hierarchical organization of the elements involved, and, in general, the structures given in (16) and (17) represent the grammatical relations inherent in the intransitive and transitive alternants of all simple alternating verbs.

If the ability of a verb to participate in the simple transitivity alternation is due to the essential structural property of having an internal specifier, the inability of a nonalternating (or unergative) verb to participate in this alternation is plausibly due to its inherent property as well—that of *not* projecting an internal specifier. And this property would follow straightforwardly, of course, if it were based on a structure whose root element were such that it did not require the projection of a specifier— that is, if it were not fundamentally predicative. The structure portrayed in (18), we claim, has a nonpredicative root (R), therefore giving rise to an unergative, nonalternating verb. Thus, we must assume that the root element *-za'* 'belch' in the verb of (8), and the root elements in the verbs of (11), are nonpredicates. If this is true, then they will neither force nor (by reason of economy) permit the appearance of a subject internal to the lexical structures they define.

(18)

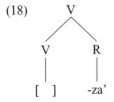

Here again, we assume that the final form of the verb will have the phonological matrix of the R, the complement, incorporated into the empty matrix of the governing V. This cannot be transitivized in the simple manner of an alternating verb (i.e., by freely inserting it as the complement in a verb of the simple head-complement structure, [v [V]]), because V of (18) has no internal specifier (i.e., DP in (19)) that could give rise to the necessary sentential syntactic object.

(19)

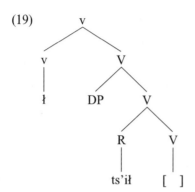

If (18) were embedded as the complement of the light verb v, the structure in (20) would result.

(20)

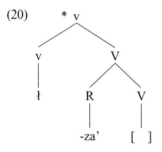

This structure is illegitimate. From the point of view of sentential syntax, one might say it is ill formed because it is "transitive" and has no object, and from the point of view of essentialist structural considerations, one might say it is ill formed because it is not properly economical, being nondistinct in relation to the natural unergative structure (18). Be this as it may, it all follows from the essential properties of the elements involved: R is not predicative, and V itself, in keeping with the general character of full lexical verbs, does not project a specifier (its subject being an external argument—possibly projected by v, though the exact position of external subjects is an issue we will not go into here).

The nature of R in (18) is clear. It has the dual structural properties of (i) not taking a complement and (ii) not forcing the projection of a specifier. This combination of properties is the defining characteristic of the lexical category N, prototypically. It is therefore not surprising, perhaps, that nonalternating verbs in many languages are based on roots belonging morphosyntactically to the category N. To some extent, this is true of Navajo; at least, it is true that some nonalternating verbs in Navajo have stems that are "cognate" with morphosyntactic nouns (page numbers from Young, Morgan, and Midgette 1992).

(21) *V*   *N*
   ghi-dloh   'laugh'   dlo   [156]
   di-yih   'breathe'   -yih (< -ghih)   [702]
   'i-yol   'inhale'   -yol   [723, 728]
   di-za'   'belch'   -za'   [731]
   di-zheeh   'spit'   -zhéé'   [770]

This is obviously a feature of English, leading some linguists to derive a large number of English unergative verbs from structures in which a phonologically empty verb takes a noun as its complement. This idea is supported not only by the syntactic behavior of these verbs but also crosslinguistically by the fact that in many languages, unergatives are verb-noun compounds (i.e., overtly reflecting incorporation) or light verb constructions (overtly reflecting the basic configuration without incorporation). Basque, for example, uses the hypothetical light verb structure [N V(*egin* 'do')] overtly in the sentential syntax projected by many lexical items corresponding to verbs of the nonalternating type.

(22) negar   egin   'cry'
     eztul   egin   'cough'
     barre   egin   'laugh'
     jolas   egin   'play'
     oihu   egin   'shout'
     lo   egin   'sleep'
     zurrunga   egin   'snore'

In Navajo, while many nonalternating verbs appear to be based on nominal roots, the vast majority are simply transitives in which the object is realized as the indefinite third person object prefix '- (glossed *3i* in Young and Morgan 1980 and represented phonologically there as '*a-*). The following verb themes exemplify this type (with bracketed numbers corresponding to Young and Morgan 1980, dictionary section):

(23) '-ł-hosh   'sleep' [126]
     '-ł-háá'   'snore' [126]
     '-yą   'eat' [124]
     '-diz   'spin (yarn)' [123]
     '-d-dlą   'drink' [125]
     '-ł-kǫǫh   'swim' [127]

'-lizh   'urinate' [129]
'-ł-chí   'give birth' [124]
'-d-t'įih   'get rich' [131]
'-tl'iid   'break wind' [131]
'-l-zhish   'dance' [131]

While unergatives cannot enter into the simple transitivity alternation, they can, of course, form causatives, as in (24).

(24) Bi'iishháásh.
     3-3i-y-1s-ł-gháásh
     'I put (am putting) him/her to sleep.'

The causative involves use of the special causative qualifier *y-* together with the *l*-classifier (i.e., the transitivizing light verb *l-*). The lexical verb theme of (24) has an inherent *l*-classifier, as well as the 3i object prefix '-. The causative is built upon the full verbal projection of the unergative and, therefore, includes the subject of the latter. This surfaces as an oblique object (*b-* (glossed *3* above), in this case), held by Athabaskanists to be an incorporated postpositional phrase with null postposition. We assign the abstract structure (25) to the verb of (24) (see Hale 2000a, 2001, for remarks on the causative and the surface ordering of the morphemes internal to the Navajo verb).

(25)

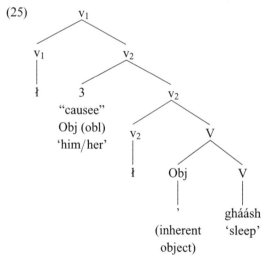

The external subject of the causative (i.e., first person *sh-*) is omitted from this diagram. The subject of the causativized (inner) verb—the "causee"—

appears in an oblique case (see Hale, in progress, for an informal account of the Case marking in this construction; see also Hale 2000a, Bittner 1994, and Bittner and Hale 1996a for a general account of Case assignment). Fundamentally, while the inner object (3i = '-) is Case-licensed by virtue of its D-Structure position relative to the lexical verb V, the outer object is in "Case competition" with the inner object and must be assigned a distinct Structural case from it (hence the oblique case, distinguished from ordinary definite third person objects in that it is overt b-, even when the subject is a local person (first or second), an environment in which ordinary, innermost, definite third person object pronouns are nonovert in Navajo—compare *yishhozh* 'I tickle him/her', with nonovert third person object pronoun, correspondingly *bishhozh*).

In summary, Navajo, like English, possesses a class of labile verbs that enter freely into the simple transitivity alternation, and it possesses as well a class of verbs that do not participate in the simple alternation, requiring use of the true causative construction. The difference, by hypothesis, resides in the nature of the root (R) element. Some roots require the projection of a specifier internal to the projection of the lexical verb V, while others do not require this (nor do they permit it). Roots that do not force the lexical verb to project a specifier are often nominal in character, though it is not always possible to demonstrate this. In addition, many Navajo verbs that exhibit the canonical "unergative" behavior are clearly transitives, built upon the simple monadic configuration in which the complement is the indefinite third person object pronoun '- (3i).

4.3 Misumalpan: Ulwa

A pervasive feature of the Misumalpan languages is the existence of transitivity alternations marked by corresponding alternations in verbal morphology. Most verb themes in Ulwa—all but a handful, in fact—consist of a root and a thematic suffix. This suffix varies with transitivity, for verbs that participate in the standard simple transitivity alternation exemplified above for English and Navajo. Essentially the same is true of the Misumalpan language Miskitu (as exemplified in Hale and Salamanca 2001), although that language possesses a large number of verbs that lack any overt theme marker.

The sentences of (26)–(28) illustrate a common Ulwa transitivity alternation, in which the intransitive alternant is marked by the thematic suffix *-da* (glossed *-DA*) and the transitive alternant by *-pa* (glossed *-PA*).

(26) a. Kuring abuk-d-ida.
      canoe capsize-DA-PST3
      'The canoe turned over.'

    b. Kuring abuk-pa-h.
      canoe capsize-PA-IMPR2
      'Turn the canoe over!'

(27) a. Kuring batirh-da-rang (yataihdaram laih).
      canoe tip-DA-FUT3
      'The canoe will tip (if you lean sideways).'

    b. Turum ya waya batirh-p-am (was ya utuhdangh).
      drum the little tip-PA-OBV2
      'Tip the drum a little (and let the water pour out).'

(28) a. Wâlang bas-ka   sang-da-i.
      savanna foliage-CNSTR green-DA-PRES3
      'The foliage of the savanna is greening up.'

    b. Kahlu âka sang-p-uting.
      shirt this green-PA-IMFUT1
      'I am going to make (dye) this shirt green (or blue).'

As mentioned, Ulwa verbs are typically bipartite in the sense illustrated by these examples. So, for example, the verb *sang-da-* 'become green' (also 'become blue, alive') consists of a root element *sang-* and the intransitive verb formative, or thematic suffix, *-da-*. It is the latter, we must assume, that functions as the head of the lexical projection in which it appears. It is the true verb, so to speak, like the nonovert verbal head postulated for the English deadjectival verb *clear* in (1). It is not surprising—and not an accident, presumably—that the root elements in some of the alternating *da*-themes of Ulwa also enter into the formation of adjectives in the language. The derivation of adjectives involves the use of the construct state morphology, though with syntactic consequences very different from those seen in the syntax of nominals. The root is morphologically nominal, but it functions as a stative predicator in the derived form to which we have applied the term *adjective*. The verbs of (26)–(28) are based on roots that participate in this adjectival use, as shown in (29), where *-ka* is the construct morphology.

(29) abuk-ka   'overturned, capsized, face down'
    batirh-ka   'leaning, tipped'
    sang-ka   'green, blue; alive'

We say that it is not surprising that roots of this type are involved in the formation of Ulwa alternating verbs, because this type quite generally and crosslinguistically has the lexical property that it must appear in a structural configuration that permits it to satisfy its "attributive" or "predicative" character, the fundamental and defining characteristic of adjectives. This requirement is satisfied in the argument structure configuration in (30) assumed for the intransitive verbs of (26)–(28) (as usual, the linear order shown here is chosen arbitrarily).

(30)

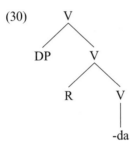

We take the head of the projection to be -da, claiming this to be the verbal nucleus. The root element, R, corresponding here to *abuk-*, *batirh-*, and *sang-*, is perhaps of indeterminate or neutral category. But it has a lexical property of consequence: it must occupy an appropriate structural position in relation to a nominal, to satisfy its attributive character. In (30), this requirement is satisfied by the projection of a DP in specifier position, as shown. We claim that the root element in these structures forces the head V (i.e., -da) to project a specifier. And it is this property that accounts for the transitivity alternation. The root elements force the appearance of a specifier. Verbs in and of themselves do not project a specifier—verbs canonically take external, not internal, subjects.

It is the lexical projection of a specifier, of course, that accounts for the transitivity alternation, the intransitive alternant being the one whose structure is depicted in (30). Like other syntactic "constructions," the transitive arises as the result of Merge, according to which any syntactic object (e.g., (30)) can appear as the complement of another head—say, a verb (e.g., V_1 in (31)).

(31)

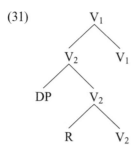

As in the parallel English case (e.g., *clear*), so also in the case of these alternating verbs of Ulwa, this formation is successful as a transitive precisely because of DP, the specifier of V_2. This is appropriately situated in
relation to V_1, its governor and potential Case assigner in sentential syntax. Moreover, this view of the matter correctly expresses the fact that the
subject of the intransitive corresponds to the object of the transitive; in
both cases, the argument functioning in these roles is the DP in the specifier position projected by V_2.

The structures in (30) and (31) are abstractions, representing just the
syntactic relations involved, not the morphology. Conflation applies to
these structures, of course, resulting in the observed affixation of verbal
nuclei to root elements. In (30), the verbal head is realized as the suffix *-da*.
In (31), however, the conflation process is more complex. In accordance
with the strict sisterhood principle of conflation, first the root R conflates
with V_2, then the resulting complex conflates with V_1, and the verbal heads
are realized as the single suffix *-pa*.

The following is a sample listing of Ulwa *da*-theme verbs alternating
with *pa*-theme transitives. The verbs are given in their bare theme forms,
with *-da* in the intransitive, *-pa* in the intransitive.

(32) *Ulwa alternating* da-*theme verbs, with corresponding* pa-*theme
      transitives*

abuk-da	abuk-pa	'capsize, turn face down'
alh-da	alh-pa	'develop a hole; perforate'
asah-da	asah-pa	'spread legs; hold astraddle'
asal-da	asal-pa	'be embarrassed; embarrass, shame'
baras-da	baras-pa	'blacken, darken'
batirh-da	batirh-pa	'tip, lean'
birh-da	birh-pa	'tear, rip, shred'
birik-da	birik-pa	'cover self; cover'
didiu-da	didiu-pa	'stretch, extend'

dim-da	dim-pa	'extend to full length'
kara-da	kara-pa	'melt'
king-da	king-pa	'become clogged; plug up'
kubit-da	kubit-pa	'bend at joint'
kuru-da	kuru-pa	'become unstitched; unstitch'
rî-da	rî-pa	'unfurl, unfold (as sail)'
sang-da	sang-pa	'become green; make green'
sayak-da	sayak-pa	'dislocate (as knee, joint)'
suih-da	suih-pa	'break off (as limb)'
tah-da	tah-pa	'drip, dribble (as water, medicine)'
tak-da	tak-pa	'peel (as skin, paint)'
tarak-da	tarak-pa	'tangle (as fish line, vines)'
tulu-da	tulu-pa	'revolve, turn; make turn, revolve'
turu-da	turu-pa	'flake off (as skin, shell, husk)'
uluh-da	uluh-pa	'come loose, come untied; untie, let loose'
utuh-da	utuh-pa	'spill (liquid)'
warin-da	warin-pa	'bend crooked'
wiri-da	wiri-pa	'swivel, turn around, twist'
wirih-da	wirih-pa	'mix (as medicines)'
wiring-da	wiring-pa	'inflate, bloat (as stomach)'
yaih-da	yaih-pa	'come near; bring near, place near'
yûh-da	yûh-pa	'heighten, lengthen'
yurah-da	yurah-pa	'open (of mouth)'

Given that the verbs of (32) all participate in the transitivity alternation, we assume they have the relevant properties attributed to the verbs of (26)–(28). Accordingly, their intransitive alternant is of the form shown in (30), and their transitive alternant takes the form shown in (31). The key to this is the circumstance that, in each case, the root element (R) has the lexical property of forcing the verbal head to project a specifier, internal to the lexical projection, which functions ultimately as sentential syntactic subject (of the intransitive) or object (of the transitive). While this is a fundamental characteristic of adjectives, given their attributive and predicative functions, the root elements in the verbs of (32) are not always attested independently in an adjectival use. Many are (*sangka* 'green, blue; alive'; *yûhka* 'long, tall'; *baraska* 'black'; *asalka* 'embarrassed'; etc.), but many are not. At this point, we do not know in which cases the missing use is principled and in which cases it is simply a gap in the record. In fact, this illustrates one of the reasons why the sort of theoretical speculation

we are engaging in here is appropriate even at this relatively adolescent
stage of dictionary making. In this instance, our theoretical speculations
tell us that we must, at some point, determine for every verb the full range
of lexical projections in which the root (R) may appear. For example, we
must know whether the root element in all of the verbs of (32) appears
independently in the adjectival form and partakes of the corresponding
adjectival syntax? If not, why not? This sort of question crops up con-
stantly when a particular theoretical perspective is consistently applied,
even if that perspective ultimately proves to be wrong in some respects—
as most theories do, that being the engine which drives the field forward.
The dictionary must, it seems to us, be a resource that, to the extent possible, purports to answer questions of this nature. We will return to this
topic at a later point.

The verbs of (32) share the semantics traditionally referred to as
"change of state," and this is consistent with the fact that they are alternating verbs. Given the generality of the grammatical and lexical principles involved here, it is therefore not surprising that many of these Ulwa
verbs translate into English as verbs that alternate in that language as
well (e.g., *lengthen, blacken, tip, break, tear, capsize, extend, clog, bend,
peel*). In both languages, the root elements share the property of forcing
the verb to project a specifier, the sine qua non of the simple transitivity
alternation at issue here. And we expect the principles observed in Ulwa
to be replicated to a degree in the other Misumalpan languages.

The *da*-theme alternating verbs of Ulwa are not always paired with *pa*-
theme transitives. Some are paired with members of the large *ta*-theme
class instead, as in the sentences of (33), illustrating uses of intransitive
nû-da- and corresponding transitive *nû-ta-* 'hide'.

(33) a. Yang bikiska balna kaupak nû-da-ring.
        I   children PL   from   hide-DA-FUT1
        'I will hide (myself) from the children.'
     b. Yang lih-ki-wan   man kaupak nû-ta-ring.[1]
        I   money-CNSTR1 you from   hide-TA-FUT1
        'I will hide my money from you.'

While *ta*-theme verbs, both transitive and intransitive, are extraordinarily
abundant in Ulwa (and in Northern Sumu as well, where -*ta* has sup-
planted -*pa* altogether), the favored transitive counterpart of Ulwa intransitive *da*-theme verbs is evidently the *pa*-theme verb, themes in -*ta* being
relatively less frequent in this usage. Some of the latter are listed in (34):

(34) *Ulwa alternating* da-*theme verbs, with corresponding* ta-*theme transitives*

dak-da	dak-ta	'snap, break; cut, chop off (as rope, limb)'
mî-da	mî-ta	'stay, dwell; stop, detain'
muh-da	muh-ta	'wake up'
nû-da	nû-ta	'hide; conceal'
pat-da	pat-ta	'pop, burst; puncture (as blister)'
pil-da	pil-ta	'chip (as plate)'
pui-da	pui-ta	'cool (as food)'
pusing-da	pusing-ta	'swell (as lip, hand)'
tap-da	tap-ta	'fall down; lower (as trousers)'
tulup-da	tulup-ta	'peel off whole or in large pieces (as skin)'
yam-da	yam-ta	'become; make, create'

With respect to their essential grammatical properties, these verbs belong to the same category as the verbs of (32). They project the same configurational structures: namely, (30) for the intransitive, (31) for the transitive. A question we will not attempt to answer at this point is whether the choice of -*pa* or -*ta* in the transitive is something significant and regular, as opposed to an "archaic residue" and a mere matter of "spelling" in the synchronic grammar of Ulwa. This is another among many matters that remain to be dealt with properly. In any event, we will assume for present purposes that the verbs of (34) are not fundamentally different from those of (32).

Not all Ulwa labile verbs have intransitive themes based on -*da*. Another prominent intransitive verbal nucleus, defining a significant number of Ulwa intransitive themes, is -*wa* (glossed -*WA*). This element is of some historical interest for Misumalpan, given that it has an apparent cognate in the related language Miskitu (Hale and Salamanca 2001). It is exemplified in (35) by the verb *ala-wa-* 'grow', paired with the transitive *ta*-theme verb *ala-ta-* 'grow, raise'.

(35) a. Baka-ki   itukwâna ala-w-ida.
        child-CNSTR1 large   grow-WA-PST3
        'My child has grown large.'
     b. Alas baka-ka   yam-ka   ala-t-ang.
        she child-CNSTR3 good-CNSTR grow-TA-RPST3
        'She raised her child well.'

Other verbs of this predominantly monosyllabic category are listed in (36).

(36) *Ulwa alternating* wa-*theme verbs, with corresponding* ta-*theme*
     transitives

ala-wa	ala-ta	'grow; raise (as child, plant)'
â-wa	â-ta	'enter, go in; insert, put in'
bah-wa	bah-ta	'break'
dâ-wa	dâ-ta	'burn'
dis-wa	dis-ta	'go out; extinguish, put out (as fire)'
il-wa	il-ta	'go up, ascend; raise, hoist'
î-wa	î-ta	'die; kill'
kah-wa	kah-ta	'smear self, anoint self; smear, anoint'
lah-wa	lah-ta	'boil, cook'
lak-wa	lak-ta	'lower, descend, go down; lower, let down'
lâ-wa	lâ-ta	'pass, go across; move, transfer'
mah-wa	mah-ta	'become sated, full; sate'
pura-wa	pura-ta	'get wet; wet'
râ-wa	râ-ta	'be in the sun to dry; put in the sun to dry'
sah-wa	sah-ta	'split (as wood)'
sing-wa	sing-ta	'heal, get well; heal, cure'

A small number of *wa*-theme verbs are paired with *pa*-theme transitives; these are generally verbs of putting and stance.

(37) *Ulwa alternating* wa-*theme verbs, with corresponding* pa-*theme*
     transitives

balah-wa	balah-pa	'put on self, don (as hat); put on (as hat)'
kut-wa	kut-pa	'lie down; lay down'
lau-wa	lau-pa	'sit down; seat, put in sitting position'
muk-wa	muk-pa	'lie down; lay down'
sak-wa	sak-pa	'stand up; put in standing position'
sih-wa	sih-pa	'move, change location; send'

   Ulwa alternating verbs in -*wa* evidently project the same lexical syntactic structure as those in -*da*. The unifying feature of both types of verbal themes considered here is presumably to be found in the lexical character of the root (R). In both cases, the lexical requirement that the root element be appropriately positioned in relation to a nominal constituent (a "subject" of which it can be predicated) forces the head verb (V) to project a specifier, permitting transitivization, as in (31).

   Part of the theoretical interest in labile, or alternating, verbs lies in the contrast between these and another large class of verbs, namely, the nonalternating verbs. As shown above, many Ulwa intransitives in -*da* have transitive partners. But many do not. The verb *ai-da-* 'cry' does not alternate, for example.

(38) Ai-da-yang   (sûkilu îwida bahangh).
     cry-DA-PRES1
     'I am crying (because my dog died).'

This nonalternating behavior is not random among Ulwa *da*-theme verbs. The following verbs, we suspect, are correctly classified as nonalternating; that is to say, their lack of a transitive partner is almost certainly not a gap in the record but a true linguistic fact:

(39) *Ulwa nonalternating* da-*theme intransitive verbs*

ahdanaka	'moan'
aidanaka	'cry'
amatdanaka	'grieve'
âmhdanaka	'yawn'
âudanaka	'belch'
baladanaka	'rumble, make vibrating sound'
bârhdanaka	'snore'
bilamhdanaka	'blink eyes'
bisakdanaka	'make smacking sound'
bîsdanaka	'make a click or kissing sound'
buihdanaka	'twitch, have muscle spasm'
isamhdanaka	'sneeze'
isdanaka	'play'
nanadanaka	'tremble'
pisitdanaka	'do somersaults'
pitukdanaka	'kick, flail'
rikdanaka	'crawl (as of baby)'
sutdanaka	'jump'
tikahdanaka	'pontificate'
tisdanaka	'spark, sparkle, crackle (as fire)'
tumhdanaka	'swim'
uhdanaka	'cough'
umitdanaka	'dive'
urukdanaka	'breathe'
wamhdanaka	'travel'
wapdanaka	'growl'
wâtdanaka	'walk'

yaradanaka   'stagger, totter, reel'
yuputdanaka   'twitch, stir'

These are basically verbs of sound production, bodily movement, bodily response, and manner of motion. They belong semantically to the category now generally referred to as "unergative," a fact immediately evident from comparing these meanings with David Perlmutter's excellent semantic classification, which predates the use of that term for verbs of this type (Perlmutter 1978). Like these Ulwa verbs, their English translations also fail to alternate, as a rule, permitting only the intransitive use in sentential syntax. For example:

(40) a. *Baka ya ai-t-ikda.
          child the cry-TA-PST1
          *I cried the child.
          (cf. I made the child cry.)
     b. *Aitak ya yâ âmh-t-ida.
          book the me yawn-TA-PST3
          *The book yawned me.
          (cf. The book made me yawn.)
     c. *Sumalting-ka ya bikiska balna is-ta-i.
          teacher-CNST the children PL   play-TA-PRES3
          *The teacher is playing the children.
          (cf. The teacher has the children playing.)

The ideas intended here are perfectly easy to express in Ulwa, using the productive causative construction (e.g., *Baka ya âting aidida* 'I made the child cry'), but they are not expressed using simple transitivization involving the structure depicted in (31). The same is true in English.

What is the reason for this? Given the striking meaning correlation between English and Ulwa, it is tempting to lay the entire business at the feet of semantics. And at some deep, as yet largely inaccessible level of linguistic form this is quite probably where the matter resides. But at the level at which we are now able to operate, semantics is too unreliable, partly because we simply cannot say what the meanings of words are. Good reason for being cautious here comes from crosslinguistic considerations, ironically the very area that inspires optimism much of the time. In Hopi, the verbs that translate many of the unergatives of English and Ulwa do indeed participate in the very transitivity alternation we have been examining here (Jeanne and Hale 2000; and see below). Given our limitations, we cannot simply say that the Hopi roots involved are semantically different from their English and Ulwa counterparts, any more than we can say that they are the same.

We are stuck then with what is observable, namely, the syntactic behavior: some verbs alternate, others do not. And we have an elementary framework within which this difference can be expressed in a manner straightforwardly consistent with general syntactic principles relating to such matters as the argument structure of predicators, (abstract) Case assignment, grammatical and thematic relations, and agreement.

Assuming that we are correct in assigning the structures (30) and (31) to Ulwa alternating verbs, we can express the phenomenon of non-alternation in a simple and straightforward manner. The root elements (R) of nonalternating (i.e., unergative) verbs have the lexical property that they do not force the verbal head to project a specifier. Thus, the argument structures of the verbs of (39) have fundamentally the form shown in (41).

(41)

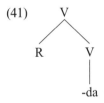

Affixation of -da to R is effected by conflation, as usual, respecting phonological requirements of the language. Transitivization is impossible, of course, since the unergative structure lacks a specifier (and potential sentential syntactic object)—that being the defining characteristic of unergatives. The subject of an unergative, like that of a transitive (e.g., (31)), is an external argument, in keeping with the general default principle according to which a verb does not project a specifier unless its complement, by virtue of its lexical properties, forces it to do so.

We have given a partial account of the alternating and nonalternating verbs of Ulwa. We have not yet looked at the phenomenon of non-alternation from the standpoint of verbs in -ta and -pa (both transitive and intransitive nonalternating verbs are found with these thematic elements), nor have we studied members of the small but rather important class of Ø-theme verbs (tal- 'see', dah- 'hear', wat- 'seize', wâ- 'come', yawa- 'go', kas- 'eat', dî- 'drink', kawara- 'laugh', wasara- 'bathe', îra- 'run', î- 'get', at- 'be', ama- 'sleep', duih- 'carry', kuih- 'achieve'), all non-alternating.[2] We set these matters aside for another occasion.

4.4   Uto-Aztecan: Tohono O'odham (Papago)

This discussion will be a mere beginning in the study of Tohono O'odham (henceforth O'odham) argument structure. As in the previous sections, our primary focus will be the standard transitivity alternation, though some attention will be given to the so-called applicative construction. We will start by considering forms built upon the stative predicators, or "adjectives" (see Mathiot 1974; Hale 1965; Zepeda 1983; Saxton 1982), of the type represented in (42).

(42) a. (s-)wegĭ   'red'
     b. (s-)moik   'soft'
     c. ge'(ej)   'big'
     d. cew(aj)   'long, tall'

These function both as prenominal modifiers and as predicates—as modifiers, (42c,d), and other adjectives of the same class, appear without the characteristic predicative suffix -*Vj*. The category illustrated in (42) is relatively large in O'odham, and its members readily participate in a derivational process that yields a corresponding intransitive verb, of the type sometimes referred to as "inchoative."

(43) a. wegi   'redden, become red'
     b. moika   'soften, become soft'
     c. ge'eda   'increase in size, volume, or amount, become big'
     d. cewda   'lengthen, become long'

The inchoative here is formed by means of a vocalic suffix whose effect is to fully vocalize the underlying final vowel of the root, in the case of (43a,b) and the like, and of the basic predicative theme in the case of (43c,d), altering the predicative suffix from underlying /-di/ to /-da/. Phonologically, the process has been seen sometimes as "lengthening" (see Hale 1965) and sometimes, and perhaps more correctly, as "blocking demoraicization" (see Hill and Zepeda 1992). Our interest here, however, is essentially syntactic.

Derived inchoatives are intransitive verbs, taking a single argument that surfaces as subject in sentential syntax (cited here in the neutral, though textually infrequent, verb-final word order, as used by Albert Alvarez in his examples in the appendix of Hale 1972).

(44) a. 'Iks 'at   wegi.
         cloth AUX.T.3 redden:PERF
         'The cloth became red.'

    b. Hogĭ ’at   moika.
       leather AUX.T.3 soften:PERF
       ‘The leather became soft.’
    c. ’Ali ’at   ge’eda.
       child AUX.T.3 grow:PERF
       ‘The child got big.’
    d. Wijina ’o   ’i   cewda-him.
       rope   AUX.3 INCEP lengthen-PROG
       ‘The rope is getting long(er).’

These verbs have transitive variants, formed by suffixation of the generalized transitivizing element /-(i)da/ directly to the inchoative form just seen, or, in the case of the type represented by (43a,b), by using this as an augment to which the same suffix is added again (giving the sequence /-(i)dida/, phonetically [-jid]).

(45) wegi(ji)d   ‘redden, make red’
     moika(ji)d   ‘soften, make soft’
     ge’edajid   ‘enlarge, increase, make big, much’
     cewdajid   ‘lengthen, make long, tall’

The argument structure of these derived transitives is entirely uniform, and it is related to that of the corresponding inchoatives in a completely straightforward manner. The object of the derived transitive corresponds to the single argument (i.e., the subject) of the inchoative. The subject of the transitive is an external argument, corresponding thematically to the "agent," and is, of course, absent from the argument structure of the inchoative.[3]

(46) a. ’A:ñ ’ant   g   ’iks o   wegij.
       I   AUX.T.1 ART cloth FUT red.TR.PERF
       ‘I will redden the cloth.’
    b. Hogĭ ’ant   moikaj.
       leather AUX.T.1 soft.TR.PERF
       ‘I softened the leather.’
    c. Lial ’att   o   ge’edaj.
       money AUX.T.1p FUT much.TR.PERF
       ‘We will accumulate a lot of money.’
    d. ’A:ñ ’ant   g   ñ-ṣaliw o   cewdaj.
       I   AUX.T.1 ART my-pants FUT long.TR.PERF
       ‘I’m going to lengthen my pants.’

The relationship that holds between the verbs of (43)–(44) and the verbs of (45)–(46) is the same popular diathesis alternation relating intransitives to corresponding transitives; it is often referred to as the "causative/inchoative" alternation (see Levin 1993). The English verbs used to translate the four O'odham verbs themselves illustrate this alternation: *redden, soften, enlarge, increase, accumulate, lengthen*. English expresses this alternation with so-called zero derivation: the transitive and intransitive are morphologically identical; no affix marks transitivity or intransitivity. O'odham, on the other hand, conforms to the more usual pattern whereby the alternation is characterized by overt morphology (of the type commonly termed "derivational"). In that language, the transitive member of the alternation is marked by means of a transitivizing suffix (glossed *TR*), called "causative" or "applicative" in the literature (see Saxton 1982). In this, O'odham is joined by many languages, including Miskitu, Navajo, and Hopi, as illustrated in sections 4.2, 4.3, and 4.5. In Miskitu, the intransitive is also specially marked, by the suffix -*w*-; this is replaced by -*k*- in the transitive, as in *pih-w-/pih-k-* 'whiten', *lâ-w-/lâ-k-* 'dry'. In Navajo, the relevant morphology is embodied in the so-called classifier, the voice-related light verb characteristic of Athabaskan. The intransitive typically shows the zero classifier, while the transitive employs the *l*-classifier: -*gan/-l-gan* 'dry', *ii-gááh/ii-l-gááh* 'whiten'.

The O'odham examples cited so far involve the lexical category represented in (42), that is, the class of adjectives. Through derivation, these yield a class of intransitive verbs, which in turn enter into the so-called causative-inchoative alternation. In languages that recognize adjectives as a distinct morphosyntactic category, that category is a common source for verbs participating in the causative-inchoative alternation. However, many such verbs have no obvious adjectival origin; this is the case for the following O'odham verbs, based, so far as we know, on original purely verbal roots:

(47) *Intransitive*   *Transitive*
      huḍuñ   huḍuñid   'descend, lower'
      ceṣaj   ceṣajid   'ascend/rise, raise'
      hu:m   hu:mid   'empty'
      ṣu:ṣug   ṣu:ṣugid   'fill (iterative)'
      ha:g   ha:gid   'melt'
      mehĕ   mehid   'burn'
      heum   heumcud   'get cold (feeling)'
      gi'î   gi'icud   'fatten'

Within the class of alternating verbs under consideration here, the suffix
-*cud* appearing in *heumcud* and *gi'icud* is considered a co-alternant with
-*id*; -*cud* also occurs as a true causative.[4]

In the verbs of (47) and in the adjective-based alternating verbs, the
"causative" meaning of the transitive is unsurprising. However, this property is directly relevant to the larger issue that interests us, namely, the
constraints on possible argument structures. In order to pursue this question, it will be necessary to introduce some degree of tension into the
investigation by examining the behavior of other derivations, cases that
bring to light different properties.

In this light, let us consider the nouns and corresponding derived
denominal verbs illustrated in (48).

(48) ki: 'house'   ki:t   'build a house'
     juñ   'cactus candy'   junt   'make cactus candy'
     hoa   'basket'   hoat   'make a basket'
     ha'a   'pot, olla'   ha'at   'make a pot, olla'
     si:l   'saddle'   si:lt   'make a saddle'

The process involved here is very productive in O'odham, and it has close
parallels in other Uto-Aztecan languages as well (cf. Hopi, section 4.5).
The derivation involves a suffix -*t* (underlying /-ta/) attached directly to a
nominal root or stem. In essence, the derived verbs are verbs of "creation"
or "production" in which a nominal corresponding to the entity or material produced is "incorporated" into the verb; this is a notion we will
develop more concretely as we proceed (cf. Baker 1988). The verb that is
derived is normally used as an "intransitive"; that is, it generally appears
without an overt object argument in the canonical complement position.
However, it can occur with a preverbal quantifier, external to the verb
word itself but construed with the incorporated nominal, as in (49), where
the preverbal cardinality expression *hema* 'one' is construed with the
nominal *ki:* 'house' internal to the derived verb.

(49) 'A:ñ 'ant   o   hema ki:-t.
     I   AUX.T.1 FUT one house-make
     'I will build a house.'

The incorporated nominal can also mark plural number and the derived
verb can bear object agreement inflection (by prefix), in agreement with
the plural nominal. In addition, a quantifying preverb may appear.

(50) 'A:ñ 'ant   o   ha'i ha-ki:kĭ-t.
    I   AUX.T.1 FUT some 3p-house.PL-make
    'I will build some houses.'

In this respect, derived verbs of creation and production exhibit the
properties of essentially transitive predicates, clearly inviting an analysis
according to which the nominal appearing in them is, literally, incorporated from object position.[5]

Whether these derived verbs are fundamentally transitive or intransitive, they can themselves be transitivized, by means of the suffix *-cud*,
which (on the surface at least) displaces the suffix *-t*, as in (51).

(51) ki:cud   'make house for *x* (e.g., a person)'
    juñcud   'make cactus candy for *x*'
    hoacud   'make a basket for *x*'
    ha'acud   'make a pot for *x*'
    si:lcud   'make a saddle for *x*'

The glosses given in (51) are intended to reflect the fact that the transitives
derived from verbs of creation are "applicatives" (cf. Saxton 1982, where
the gloss *APPLIC* is employed). That is, they are "benefactives," and
accordingly the argument that is, so to speak, introduced in conjunction
with the transitivizing morphology is a *beneficiary*, as exemplified in (52)
(with truncated *-c* (< *-cud*), as usual in the perfective).

(52) Nt   o   hema ha-si:l-c   g   ñ-'a'aldag.
    AUX.T.1 FUT one   3p-saddle-APPLIC ART 1-children
    'I am going to make a saddle for my kids.'

The beneficiary argument (in this instance, *ñ-'a'aldag* 'my children (man
speaking)') controls agreement, while the "incorporated" nominal remains
construed with the preverbal quantifier.

The point of interest here is that while the derived transitives of (45) are
causatives, the derived transitives of (51) are applicatives, not causatives
in the usual sense. Why don't the verbs of (51) mean something like 'have
x build a house', 'have *x* make cactus candy', and so on? We know that
-cud is sometimes associated with the causative meaning; why is it *not* a
causative in (51)? This question extends to other transitives as well. While
the transitive members of the verb pairs in (47) are causative in the commonly understood sense, the transitive members of the following pairs are
applicatives, not causatives (note that both *-id* and *-cud* are implicated
here):

(53) *Intransitive*   *Transitive*

ñe'ĕ	'sing'	ñe'icud	'sing for *x*'
na:d	'make fire'	na:jid	'make fire for *x*'
cikpan	'work'	cikpañid	'work for *x*'
gikuj	'whistle'	gikujid	'whistle for *x*'
ku'ag	'get wood'	ku'agid	'get wood for *x*'

Why doesn't *ñe'icud* mean 'have *x* sing' or 'make *x* sing', instead of 'sing for *x*'? And similarly for the others. In general, why are some derived transitives causative while others are applicative? Is this simply random? Or is there some principled basis for it?

We believe that the observations made here reflect general principles that govern the limits on lexical argument structures. The contrast noted here is the same, in essence, as a contrast that is virtually universal among the languages of the world. Languages differ in detail, but the basic elements and principles are the same.

While both deadjectival and denominal verbs participate in processes of transitivization, denominal transitives are regularly applicative, not causative. This follows straightforwardly if simple creation verbs of the type exemplified in (48) are simple monadic structures of the form [$_V$ V N], as seems likely. These have no specifier, and hence no position for the surface subject. It is therefore clear why *ki:cud* cannot mean 'make *x* build a house, have *x* build a house'. In short, as (54) shows, there is no position for an argument (DP) corresponding to the grammatical object in the hypothetical causative.

(54)

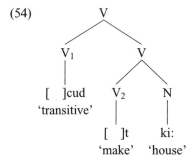

Assuming that verbs of production like *ki:t* 'build a house' are fundamentally monadic verb-complement structures, as in (54), there is no specifier internal to the V$_2$ projection. Therefore, there is no position for the DP argument that is necessary in the derived transitive. In and of itself, (54) is impossible, so far as we know. The principles of O'odham morphology will derive *ki:cud* automatically, by standard successive incorporation; the grammar of the language (or perhaps any language) will fail to permit a verb so derived to be related to the structure (54).

O'odham does have the verb *ki:cud* 'build house for *x*', and an indefinite number of like verbs. These have applicative, rather than causative, function. How do these arise? The secret, of course, is to find the structure that has the correct property, namely, an internal specifier that will function as the object of the derived verb. This suggests that it is mistaken to assume that the suffix *-cud* is a "causative," despite its use in that function in some verbs. The invariant fact about this element is that it forms transitive verbs. Suppose it is semantically empty, basically. And the "meaning" of a construction headed by *-cud* is to some degree a matter of the structure in which it appears; in particular, such "meanings" as causative, applicative, and inchoative derive from the structures themselves. The inner structure associated with the applicative relation is the dyadic type: [ᵥ DP [ᵥ V N]]. This birelational structure is what is implicated in expressing the "applicative" semantics, the semantics of having, giving, and producing something for someone. It is reasonable to propose that O'odham denominal applicatives like *ki:cud* consist of the dyadic structure embedded in the simple monadic structure, as shown in (55).

(55)

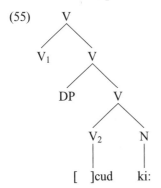

The semantics associated with this structure involves a relation between the specifier (DP) and the nominal complement (N). The individual denoted by DP "has" or "is with" the entity denoted by the complement nominal N. The upper verb V_1 and its complement are in the configuration standardly associated with the causative meaning, so that the whole means something like 'cause DP to have N'; this is the "bare bones," to be sure, but it is the essence of the semantics associated with the applicative of verbs of production. Crucially, for the syntax, this structure has the necessary feature—to wit, an internal specifier, accounting for the object of the derived verb. As usual, the surface morphophonological form is derived by incorporation, or conflation, of N into V_1 and then (the now complex) V_1 into V_2.

If these ideas are correct, then we might expect to find "direct" cross-linguistic evidence, in the form of actual linguistic expressions that *openly* reflect the abstract structures posited here. This expectation is fulfilled, in relation to the proposed structure of the nonalternating verbs, by Basque, where they are realized phrasally by a verb (*egin* 'do') accompanied by a nominal complement, as exemplified in the discussion of Navajo in section 4.2. While English, Navajo, and Miskitu use a *synthetic* form for these expressions, Basque uses an *analytic* form, reflecting directly the structure we assume is basic for all of the languages. O'odham verbs of production (in (48)), as well as the verbs of (54), can be assumed to be synthetic members of this type as well.

Analytic forms also exist in the case of verbs that we take to be adjective-based. In Miskitu, for example, some adjectives (primarily borrowings from Northern Sumu) form synthetic verbs, alternating between transitive and intransitive in the expected way.

(56) | *Intransitive* | *Transitive* | *Adjective* | |
|---|---|---|---|
| pih-w- | pih-k- | pih-ni | 'white' |
| pau-w- | pau-k- | pau-ni | 'red' |
| sang-w- | (sang-k-) | sang-ni | 'clear, green' |
| nuh-w- | nuh-k- | nuha-n | 'fat' |

But most Miskitu adjective-based verbal expressions are analytic, conforming to the pattern in (57).

(57) | *Intransitive* | | *Transitive* | |
|---|---|---|---|
| târa tak- | 'become large' | târa dauk- | 'make large' |
| yari tak- | 'become long' | yari dauk- | 'make long' |
| pihni tak- | 'become white' | pihni dauk- | 'make white' |
| yamni tak- | 'become better' | yamni dauk- | 'make better' |

Such analytic expressions exist in English, too, as noted earlier. And if the adjective is in the comparative degree, for example, the analytic form *must* be used (hence *make larger*, **enlarger*), predictably, since deadjectival verbs are formed from lexical heads, not from extended projections.

In this connection, it is relevant to consider the argument structures of O'odham verbs of the type represented by (47) and (54). These verbs, like most of the alternating and nonalternating verbs of English cited in the course of this discussion, give no direct evidence of an adjectival or nominal source. Nonetheless, the verbs of (47) behave like the overtly deadjectival verbs of (43) and (45), and the verbs of (54) behave like the denominals of (48) in lacking a causative derivative.

It is the behavior of a verb, not its form, that gives evidence of its argument structure. Since the verbs of (47) and (54) behave as they do, their argument structure type is defined straightforwardly. For example, the verb *gikuj* 'whistle' must represent the monadic argument structure. Certain details must be left underdetermined, such as the morphosyntactic category of the overt element, but this is not strictly speaking relevant to the argument structure (and corresponding syntactic) behavior of the derived verb. Thus, using R (root of indeterminate category) for the lexical base of the complement, the argument structure of *gikuj* 'whistle', by hypothesis, is (58).

(58)

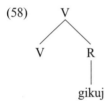

The complement, R, incorporates into the empty V, of course, to eliminate the empty matrix, thereby producing the required phonological form. Verbs of this type are the so-called unergatives of current linguistic literature. Their properties contrast with those of the so-called unaccusatives, whose argument structures belong to the dyadic type represented in O'odham by (43) and the intransitives of (47).

Since (58) is a monadic structure, it follows that it cannot be further transitivized as a causative. The transitive derivative that does exist, *gikujid* 'whistle for *x*', is an applicative or benefactive, not a causative. It is, therefore, a dyadic structure embedded in a monadic one, as shown in (59).

(59)

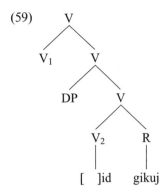

By successive incorporation, or conflation (of R into V_2 and V_1), this yields a configuration in which the overt verb *gikujid* appears in an S-Structure position (V_1) in which it governs a DP, as required of a transitive verb. The DP involved in this case, of course, is the specifier of V_2 and the object of the derived transitive verb.

The central theme of this discussion has been the idea that certain aspects of predicate argument structure are invariant. The claim is that the abstract monadic and dyadic structures involved in the derivations suggested here are basic to all languages. But a side theme has been the notion of diversity, the idea that the language-specific realizations of argument structures are far from invariant. Neither of these themes could be investigated without the linguistic diversity which exists in the world and which, sadly, is seriously imperiled in these times.

We would not be able to learn as much about these matters if, say, English were the only language. That the asymmetrical distribution of the causative-inchoative transitivity alternation is a systematic phenomenon, one to be explained within a theory of grammar, is perhaps dimly suggested by the English data themselves, but it is totally obvious in light of the simple comparison with Miskitu, Navajo, and O'odham (or any number of other languages). The point is amply supported by reflection on the history of related discoveries in linguistics—for example, the unaccusativity hypothesis (see Perlmutter 1978). Eventual understanding of unaccusativity in English did not have its origins primarily in research on that language; rather, it was due largely to foundational research done on Dutch and Italian, much enhanced by subsequent work on a variety of languages, and with important feedback from English (see Levin and Rappaport Hovav 1995).

Let us follow this theme a moment longer. If linguistic diversity is valuable in identifying problems (i.e., phenomena requiring explanation), it is an essential condition in the business of testing and supporting putative solutions and explanations. Thus, the idea that the nonalternating verbs are noun-based is suggested, somewhat, by the English data, but it is strongly supported by the existence of languages, like Basque, that use the hypothetical [$_V$ V N] overtly in the sentential syntax projected by lexical items corresponding to verbs of the type in question. And it is supported as well by the Tanoan languages, for example, where verbs corresponding to *work, speak, whistle, laugh, cry, sing,* and others, are likewise overtly noun-based, taking the form of N-V compounds.

The causative-inchoative transitivity alternation exemplifies the role of linguistic diversity in helping to suggest, support, and sometimes to "confirm" analyses. In the absence of diversity, there is little one can say about particular linguistic problems in many cases, perhaps in most cases; and, as noted earlier, the very existence of a linguistic problem is itself something that often goes completely undetected without the backdrop of diversity. This function of diversity is well known, and it is exploited with energy and enthusiasm by linguists in all frameworks. This is what might be called the *confirmatory* function of linguistic diversity. In the following section, these remarks will be further supported by material from Hopi, another member of the Uto-Aztecan family.

4.5   Uto-Aztecan: Hopi

Hopi possesses a productive transitivizing suffix *-na*, typically glossed 'causative' and customarily associated with the semantics of causation in the literature on the language. This element deviates from the straightforward causative meaning under certain conditions. The present discussion is a preliminary and highly tentative introduction to the study of Hopi transitivization from a comparative and theoretical perspective, with primary attention to *-na* and its interaction with other elements.

The following examples of *-na* are taken from Jeanne 1975. We use the Hopi morpheme itself to gloss the suffix, and we do the same for certain other suffixal morphology as well, in the interests of terminological neutrality at this point in our investigation.

(60) a. Pòokyaya munu.
       Pokyaya   fall
       'Pokyaya fell.'

b. Nu' Pòokyaya-t   múnu-k-na.
   I   Pokyaya-ACC fall-K-NA
   'I made Pokyaya fall.'

(61) a. Pòokyaya wa'ö.
        Pokyaya recline
        'Pokyaya lay down.'
     b. Nu' Pòokyaya-t   wá'ö-k-na.
        I   Pokyaya-ACC recline-K-NA
        'I made Pokyaya lie down.'

(62) a. Pòokyaya taatayi.
        Pokyaya wake.up
        'Pokyaya woke up.'
     b. Nu' Pòokyaya-t   taatay-na.
        I   Pokyaya-ACC wake.up-NA
        'I made Pokyaya wake up.'

(63) a. Pòokyaya pak-lawu.
        Pokyaya cry-LAWU.
        'Pokyaya cried.'
     b. Nu' Pòokyaya-t   pak-law-na.
        I   Pokyaya-ACC cry-LAWU-NA
        'I made Pokyaya cry.'

(64) a. Pòokyaya taya-ti.
        Pokyaya laugh-TOYI
        'Pokyaya laughed.'
     b. Nu' Pòokyaya-t   taya-toy-na.
        I   Pokyaya-ACC laugh-TOYI-NA
        'I made Pokyaya laugh.'

The examples in (60)–(64) illustrate transitivization by means of the suffix -na, deriving verb forms representing the semantics traditionally associated with causative or transitivized constructions. Accordingly, the verb pairs in these sentences exemplify the crosslinguistically well known causative-inchoative alternation, the na-form being the "causative," the intransitive base being the "inchoative."

Transitivization of this sort is extremely productive in Hopi. With a class of exceptions to be noted, virtually any monadic verb in Hopi can be transitivized in this manner.[6] The following brief lists give representative samples (taken from the Hopi Dictionary Project 1998). In each set, the intransitive is given first, followed by the transitive in -*na* and a brief gloss.

(65) k-*verbs*

eyo(k-)	eyokna	'ring (of metal, bell)'
homi(k-)	homikna	'shrink'
hoyo(k-)	hoyokna	'move'
kola(k-)	kolakna	'parch'
wari(k-)	warikna	'run (sg.)'

(66) yku-*verbs*

henanàyku	henanàykina	'start to trot'
horaràyku	horaràykina	'start to kick'
kwalalàyku	kwalalàykina	'start to boil'
tsölöl'öyku	tsölöl'öykina	'start to sprinkle (weather)'
yu'a'àyku	yu'a'àykina	'start to speak'

(67) va-*verbs*

hongva	hongvana	'stand up (pl.)'
kuyva	kuyvana	'sprout (of plant)'
tokva	tokvana	'fall asleep (pl.)'
yesva	yesvana	'sit down (pl.)'

(68) ti-*verbs*

alöngti	alöngtoyna	'change'
apiti	apitoyna	'be of use, do one's part'
hamànti	hamàntoyna	'become embarrassed'
kyaahakti	kyaahaktoyna	'get rich'

(69) ta-*verbs*

hotsitsita	hotsitsitoyna	'be zigzagging'
kwalalata	kwalalatoyna	'be boiling'
mururuta	mururutoyna	'be twisted together'
nàmtötöta	nàmtötötoyna	'be turning repeatedly'
làngta	làngtoyna	'be stretching out'

(70) i-*verbs*

kyaktayi	kyaktayna	'hurry'
laaki	lakna	'dry'
momori	momorna	'swim'
o'oki	o'okna	'stop crying'
qöövi	qöpna	'pout'
haani	hanna	'descend'

(71) *Ø-verbs*

hukya	hukyana	'cool off'
waaya	waayana	'escape (sg.)'
watqa	watqana	'escape (pl.)'
yooha	yoohana	'fracture, break'
peekye	peekyena	'decay'

There are two observations here that are relevant to our discussion.

First, verbs that transitivize in this way are morphologically complex, consisting in a root (R) of indeterminate (possibly verbal) category followed by a verbal suffix (represented as *V* in diagrams to follow). The latter element is the "verb" in the true sense, since it is the element that bears subsequent verbal inflection in finite clauses. Verbs in the final set, (71), are exceptions to this observation, since no detectable verbalizing suffix appears. We assume, for present purposes, that these verbs are not in fact exceptional but take a phonologically nonovert verbal suffix, symbolized -Ø.

Second, the transitivity alternation exemplified in (65)–(71) corresponds to the canonical, or standard, causative-inchoative alternation illustrated in the sentences of (60)–(64). Specifically, they have the property that the subject of the intransitive corresponds straightforwardly to the object of the transitive.

The issue we wish to address here is an extremely small and narrow one, but it has implications for a general study of argument structure relations in Hopi, in Uto-Aztecan languages, and in general.

Consider the following sentence pairs:

(72) a. Um yan-wat   kii-ta-ni.
        2sg thus-WAT house-TOYA-FUT
        'Build the house this way.'

    b. Itàa-ti   qa   na'önani-qa ita-mu-y   kii-toy-na.
        1pl-child NEG lazy-COMP 1pl-PL-ACC house-TOYA-NA
        'Because our child is not lazy, he built a house for us.'

(73) a. Itàa-taha inu-ngam tots-ta.
        1pl-uncle 1sg-for   shoe-TOYA
        'My uncle made shoes for me.'

    b. Pu-t   tiyòoya-t   katsin-na-'at   pu-t
        3sg-.ACC little.boy-ACC kachina-father-3sg 3sg-ACC
        tots-toy-na.
        shoe-TOYA-NA
        'The little boy's godfather provided him with shoes.'

(74) a. Pam piiki-t   nitkya-ta.
        3sg piki-ACC journey.food-TOYA
        'He prepared piki for the journey.'
    b. Pam koongya-y   piiki-t   nitkya-toy-na.
        3sg husband-3ACC piki-ACC journey.food-TOYA-NA
        'She prepared journey food for her husband.'

(75) a. Pam pas-ta.
        3sg field-TOYA
        'He prepared a field.'
    b. Nu' pu-t   a-ngqw   pas-toy-na.
        1sg 3sg-ACC 3sg-from field-TOYA-NA
        'I gave him a piece of (my) field.'

(76) a. Pam itàa-ki-y   paas   qeni-ta.
        3sg 1pl-house-ACC carefully place-TOYA
        'She cleaned/prepared our house carefully.'
    b. Pas   pu-ma nu-y   qa   qeni-toy-na-ya.
        PRTL 3-PL 1sg-ACC NEG place-TOYA-NA-PL
        'They don't make (any) room for me.'

The verb of the (b)-sentence in each of these pairs bears the familiar transitivizing suffix *-na*. These sentences involve a sequence of productive derivational suffixes, in fact. Preceding *-na* is the suffix *-toya*, which appears in its phonologically reduced form *-ta* in the (a)-sentences of (72)–(76). In these examples, *-toya* has a meaning that can be characterized roughly in terms of "creation" or "manufacture": thus, *kiita* 'make a house, build a house' (cf. *kii(hu)* 'house'). But the relation between the (a)- and (b)-sentences is *not* the one we are led to expect on the basis of the transitivity alternation exemplified by sentences (60)–(64)— that is to say, (72)–(76) do not represent the same simple causative-inchoative alternation represented by the verb pairs in (65)–(71).

Unlike in the standard causative-inchoative alternation, in the alternation seen here the object of the derived transitive is, so to speak, an introduced argument, in the sense that it does not correspond to the subject of the corresponding underived verb; in fact, it corresponds to no argument of the underived verb. Thus, the object of *kiitoyna* 'build house for *x*' is not a "causee" and does not correspond to the subject of *kiita*. The semantic role of the object of the derived verb is the role customarily termed "beneficiary," "recipient," or "goal" in current usage. In (77), we list the verbs of (72)–(76) with glosses reflecting approximately the semantic roles involved (with x corresponding to the referent of the object of the derived verb).

(77)

kiita	'build house'	kiitoyna	'build house for x'
totsta	'make shoe'	totstoyna	'make shoe for x'
nitkyata	'make journey food'	nitkyatoyna	'make journey food for x'
pasta	'prepare field'	pastoyna	'give field to x'
qenita	'prepare space'	qenitoyna	'make room for x'

Semantically, we have here the relation expressed by the dative in many languages—for example, Spanish, German, Warlpiri. This is the relation expressed by the prepositions *to* and *for* in English and, also in English and many other languages, by the "indirect object" in the so-called double object construction with verbs that permit that construction (cf. Tohono O'odham benefactive and applicative in section 4.4).

Let us use the term *benefactive* or *applicative* in referring to the derived *na*-suffixed verb of the Hopi alternation represented in (72)–(76). The first of these terms refers to the semantic role of the introduced argument. The problem we wish to address here can be stated in terms of this vague semantic label, as in (78).

(78) Why does the derived form of the verbs in (77) have the *benefactive* meaning, instead of the simple transitive, or causative, meaning associated with the derived verbs of (65)–(71)?

There are two issues here, in fact. First, why do the verbs of (77) have the benefactive meaning? And second, why *can't* the verbs of (77) have the causative meaning? For example, why must (79) have the benefactive meaning and *not* the causative meaning?

(79) Nu' i-ti-mu-y   kii-toy-na.
      I   1sg-child-PL-ACC house-TOYA-NA
      'I provided my children with a house.'
      ≠ 'I had my children build a house.'

The answer we wish to explore will require us to examine the internal structures of both kinds of *na*-derived transitive verbs and to determine the lexical argument structure configurations projected by the items of which both the transitive and intransitive verbs are composed. We are concerned in particular with the grammatical, or structural, aspects of the problem and, accordingly, we are especially interested in accounting for the syntactic observation embodied in (80).

(80) The object of the derived *na*-verbs of (77) is an internal argument
not present in the corresponding underived verb. In particular, the
object of the verbs of (77) does not correspond to the subject of the
underived verb. This is in contrast with the situation represented in
the canonical causative-inchoative of the verbs of (65)–(71).

The verbs exemplified in (77) share a property that is perhaps obvious
at this point. Like the standard causative-inchoative verbs, the verbs of
manufacture upon which the benefactive construction is based are complex, consisting of a root plus the verbalizing ending *-ta* (< *-toya*). This
ending also occurs in verbs of the standard causative-inchoative alternating sort (see (69)). But there is a systematic difference: the root element
in verbs of manufacture is consistently *nominal*, while the root element
of causative-inchoative alternating verbs is either verbal or categorially
underdetermined (hence our noncommittal use of *R* in glossing those elements). Thus, while *kwalalata* 'be boiling' is composed with a verbal root
(glossed *R*), *kiita* 'build a house' is composed with a nominal root
(glossed *N*).

(81) a. *R-based verbal theme*
        kwalala-ta (< kwalala-toya)
     b. *N-based verbal theme*
        kii-ta (< kii-toya)

We will assume that the verbs of (65)–(71) and all others like them are R-
based; by contrast, the verbs of (77), and their like, are N-based. This is
relevant to the problem at hand, we believe.

We make the further assumption that these verb words are composed
in the first instance through the process called Merge. Thus, for example,
the verb of (60a), repeated here as (82), has the lexical syntactic structure
depicted in (83).

(82) Pòokyaya munu.
     Pokyaya   fall:PERF
     'Pokyaya fell.'

(83)

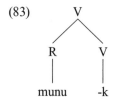

This is, of course, the *abstract* representation of the result of selecting the root *munu* 'fall (sg.)' and the verbal head *-k* from the lexicon and applying Merge, to form the syntactic configuration labeled *V*, in accordance with the principle that the head "projects" its category, labeling the construction formed by Merge. The actual word that receives phonological shape implicates another process, incorporation or conflation, which takes the root element and adjoins it to the head, producing a single word. We will abbreviate the result of this operation somewhat, simply placing the phonological matrix of the root element under the head V into which it conflates, as in (84).

(84)

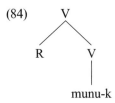

munu-k

The R-node left behind on the left branch is the trace of the incorporated element *munu*. As can be seen in (82), in the actual pronunciation of this particular form, and others like it, the *k*-suffix, being word-final and consonantal, is not pronounced; this is simply a fact of Hopi morphophonology. If the word is further suffixed, as in the transitive (60b), the *k*-suffix is pronounced. Similarly in (85), the future form of (82), in which the *k*-suffix is followed by the future ending *-ni*.

(85) Pòokyaya munu-k-ni.
      Pokyaya   fall-K-FUT
      'Pokyaya will fall.'

The verb *kiita* 'build a house' is likewise composed by Merge, giving the same bipartite syntactic configuration, with the verbal head *-toya* and the nominal complement *kii* 'house', as shown in (86).

(86)

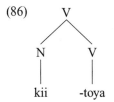

Here again, conflation (incorporation) applies, adjoining the nominal complement to the verbal head as shown in (87), forming a single phonological word.

(87)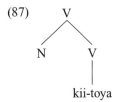

          kii-toya

Independent phonological processes reduce the verbal suffix to -*ta* in this case, giving *kiita*.

With this background, we can begin to consider answers to the question posed in (78) and, correspondingly, an explanation for the structural observation in (80). We emphasize that this is a mere beginning, since we are investigating only a small part of a large domain. We seek answers that are consonant with general principles of Universal Grammar.

In actuality, the answer that suggests itself is based on observations already familiar to us (recall the discussion of Navajo and Tohono O'odham in sections 4.2 and 4.4). The relevant observations are these:

(88) a. Denominal verbs resist simple transitivization; that is, they fail
to participate in the alternation represented by such Hopi
transitivity pairs as *munu/munukna* 'fall/make fall' and by such
English pairs as *clear/clear* 'become clear/make clear'.

     b. Verbs that do permit simple transitivization—verbs that
participate in the standard transitivity alternation exemplified by
the verbs cited in (a)—are typically composed with roots that
are not nominal, or at least give no evidence of being nominal.

These formulations are not exceptionless, but they point in a familiar direction, namely, that expressed in (89).

(89) The behavior of a given verb with respect to simple transitivization
is determined by the properties of the elements of which it is
composed.

That is to say, whether a verb undergoes simple transitivization depends upon its makeup. Verbs built upon nouns generally fail to undergo simple transitivization (i.e., transitivization with conventional causative semantics). Their failure to do so has something to do with the fact that they are denominal. Conversely, verbs whose composition involves, say, an adjective (in English) or a verbal root (in Hopi) readily transitivize, other things being equal.

If a verb's ability to undergo simple transitivization depends upon the properties of the lexical elements of which it is composed, then what are these properties? The Hopi verb *munu(-k)* 'fall' is composed of a verbal head V (-*k*) and a verbal root R (*munu*), as depicted in (90a), and the Hopi verb *kii-ta* 'build a house' is composed of a verbal head -*toya* and a noun *kii*, as depicted in (90b).

(90) a.   b.

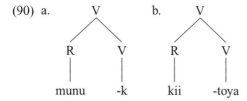

What is it about the combination in (90a) that permits simple transitivization, and what is it about the combination in (90b) that prevents it?

As noted in earlier chapters, the same questions and answers apply to the English alternating verb *clear* and the nonalternating denominal verb *laugh*, whose basic intransitive lexical structures are shown in (91), abstracting away from conflation.

(91) a.   b.

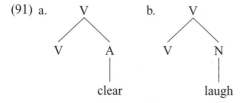

The order of elements in Hopi and English is represented as being different in these configurations, in recognition of the general head-final character of Hopi and head-initial character of English. From our point of view, this difference is of no consequence. We are interested not in linear order but in basic syntactic relations. Repeating observations made in earlier chapters, what we wish to express here is the head-complement relation, defining the complement relation as in (92).

(92) The complement is the immediate sister of the head.

It follows that the head and the complement are immediately dominated by the same node. The head is defined as in (93).

(93) The head is the constituent C that determines the label attached to the node immediately dominating C and its immediate sister.

Accordingly, we say that the head (H) "projects" its category to the node dominating it and its immediate sister. In this usage, the verbal head in (90) and (91) projects its category V to the node dominating the verbal head and its complement.

Let us now consider how transitivization takes place. In English, transitivization does not involve extra morphology: the verb appears without transitivizing morphology but within a configuration that permits it to take an object, the latter corresponding to the subject of the intransitive counterpart, as exemplified by the intransitive uses of *clear*. In Hopi, however, as in the other Native American languages discussed in this chapter, the transitive member of a given transitivity pair bears overt transitivizing morphology (the suffix *-na* in Hopi). We will assume for languages in general that transitivization involves a verbal head, null V in English, overt *-na* in Hopi. And we will assume that this transitive verbal head takes the intransitive construction as its complement. This is the basic notion of transitivization.

However, it will not do simply to insert, say, (90a) or (91a) into the complement position of the transitivizing verbal head, as in the hypothetical (94a), for Hopi, and (95a), for English.

(94) a.   b.

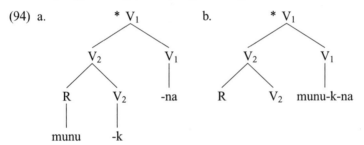

With conflation, applying cyclically to V_2 and V_1, we derive the correct form of the transitive verb *munu-k-na* 'make fall', as represented by (94b). But this structure is nonetheless ill formed. The derived verb has no object. There is no nominal argument (DP) within the structure to which the derived transitive verb can assign accusative Case. Hence, the structure fails. The same will be true of the English transitive *clear*, and other such deadjectival verbs, as in (95a) and its conflated counterpart (95b). Here again, the derived transitive has no object.

(95) a.

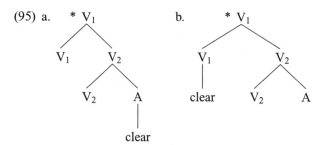

We will assume that the failure in (94) and (95) is fundamentally the same in all languages and, further, that it is to be traced to the fact that some property, or combination of properties, inherent in the component elements remains unsatisfied.

What *is* the essential property involved here? Notice that we *want* failure in the case of denominal verbs, since that would explain why they fail to participate in simple transitivization. Thus, assuming this line of thought to be correct, the ill-formedness of (96) and (97) is both expected and desirable.

(96) a.

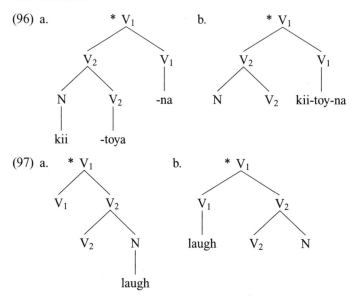

Hopi *kiitoyna* and English *laugh* exist as words in the two languages; they do not exist as simple transitives. Hence, it is expected that they would not take objects in the manner of the transitives of canonical alternating pairs like Hopi *munu/munukna* and English *clear/clear*. The ill-formedness of (96) and (97) is therefore expected.

What is it about alternating verbs that permits simple transitivization? How does the transitive member of an alternating pair acquire its object? And why does the object of the transitive correspond to the subject of the intransitive? If the answer to these questions has to do with the lexical properties of the elements involved, as we expect, then we must look at the lexical items themselves. In the clear cases, verbs composed with nouns behave differently from verbs composed with adjectives or verbal roots. What is the nature of this difference?

Let us suppose that, informally stated, the basic difference is as follows:

(98) a. English adjectives (A) and Hopi verbal roots (R) force the verbal head governing them (i.e., to which they bear the complement relation) to project a specifier position, normally occupied by a nominal argument (a DP).

b. Nouns do not force the projection of a specifier.

The specifier relation is defined informally as follows:

(99) The specifier is the immediate sister of the first nontrivial projection of a lexical head; the lexical head determines the label dominating the specifier and its sister.

If the Hopi verbal root *munu* forces the projection of a specifier, then the full lexical structure of the intransitive verb *munu(-k)* is as shown in (100).

(100)

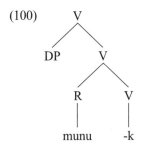

The DP (e.g., *Pòokyaya* in (60a)), represents the subject in the intransitive use of the verb. If we now transitivize this structure (i.e., embed it as the complement of the transitivizing verb *-na*), we straightforwardly derive the transitive counterpart in (101) (abstracting away from conflation, which produces the phonological word *munu-k-na*).

(101)

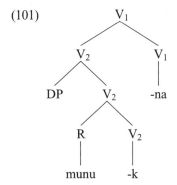

This gives a successful transitivization, since the derived transitive verb (ultimately assembled in V_1 through conflation) locally c-commands and governs DP, to which it assigns accusative Case, as required in sentential syntax, where DP is the object of the derived verb.

The derivation of English transitive *clear* is exactly parallel, as shown in (102), assuming that adjectives force the projection of a specifier in the lexical representation.

(102)

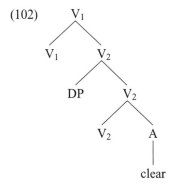

Like the derived transitive verb in the Hopi example just considered, the derived transitive *clear* in (102) (assembled at V_1 through conflation) is in the position required for assigning Case to the sentential syntactic object.

The appearance of the specifier, DP, as the sister to V_2 in these structures satisfies two requirements. It satisfies the lexical property of Hopi R (verbal roots) and English A (adjectives) that they must be appropriately situated in relation to a specifier, forcing the verbal head to project one. And it satisfies the sentential syntactic requirement of the transitivizing head that it have an object to which it assigns Case (in the normal course of events); this also "forces" the lexical head to project a specifier in the appropriate position.

By contrast, in the standard case, nouns do not force the projection of a specifier; and we assume that if a given noun does not force the projection of a specifier, it cannot do so. Such nouns, then, cannot appear in configurations comparable to (101) and (102), in which a DP appears in the inner specifier position. Again, this explains why there is no transitive *laugh* in English with the meaning 'make x laugh' (hence *The clown laughed the children*). And it explains why Hopi *kii-toy-na* is not the simple transitive of *kii-ta* 'build a house'; that is to say, *kii-toy-na* cannot mean 'make x build a house', 'have x build a house', or the like.

To this point, we have attempted to explain only half of the question posed in (78), namely, the part concerning the observation that Hopi denominal *ta*-verbs (like *kii-ta*) do not permit simple transitivization. We have not considered why derived transitive verbs of the form *kii-toy-na* exist and why this verb means 'build a house for x', 'build x a house', or 'provide x with a house'. That is to say, where does the benefactive meaning come from?

We will discuss this issue only briefly. There is a crosslinguistic observation to be made, incidentally. English verb phrases like *build John a house*, while grammatical, cannot mean 'have John build a house'; rather, they have the "benefactive" sense, like Hopi *kii-toy-na*, as illustrated in (79), repeated here as (103).

(103) Nu' i-ti-mu-y   kii-toy-na.
  I 1sg-child-PL-ACC house-TOYA-NA
  'I provided my children with a house.'

We propose that the structure involved in this use of the combination *-toy-na* is as shown in (104).

(104)

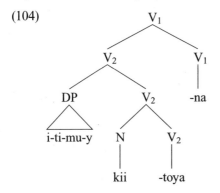

While the transitivizing function of -*na* is the same here as in all previous
examples, the nature of -*toya* is different. This is a homophonous but
distinct use of this element. In this function, -*toya* projects a specifier,
permitting successful transitivization by -*na*; and instead of its usual semantics of creation or manufacture, it expresses a "possessional" relation
between the entity denoted by its complement (*kii* 'house', in (104), the
possessum) and the entity denoted by the specifier (*itimuy* 'my children',
the possessor or beneficiary). The higher verb (V_1) represents its usual
"causative" function, so that the combination represented by (104) can be
paraphrased approximately as 'bring it about that my children have a
house'.

If this is the correct analysis, it might be expected that the inner verbal
projection (V_2) could appear without the upper verb, revealing the basic
possessive verbal construction. We believe this is true, although the actual
form of the verb in this use is different, as illustrated in (105).

(105) Um haqam ki-'y-ta?
       you where house-'Y-TA
       'Where do you live?' (Lit. 'Where do you have a house?')[7]

Here the verbal head is -'*y*- 'have'. -*toya* replaces it in (103) and (104) by
means of suppletive substitution, found regularly where the possessive
verb is transitivized by means of -*na*. The relevant structural features of
(105) are shown in (106).

(106)

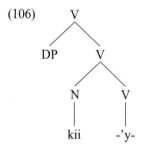

The key ingredient here is the verbal head, -'*y*-; this item projects a specifier. The verbal head -*toya* normally does not project a specifier. However, when it appears as the suppletive replacement of -'*y*-, it naturally
inherits this characteristic and necessarily projects a specifier, as shown in
(104). In this respect, the Hopi possessive verb -'*y*- (and its suppletive
proxy -*toya*) has the syntactic character of a postposition. Hopi postpositions, like adpositions crosslinguistically, have the fundamental lex-

ical and syntactic property that they take a complement and project a specifier, like -'y-. The following sentences further illustrate -'y- and its suppletive substitute:

(107) a. Itàa-tumtsoki qa   panaptsa-'y-ta.
       1ns-piki.house NEG window-'Y-TA
       'Our piki house doesn't have a window.'
    b. Ita-m tumtsoki-t   panaptsa-toy-na-ya.
       1ns-PL piki.house-ACC window-TOYA-NA-PL
       'We made a window for the piki house.'

In English, as in Hopi, there is a denominal verb *window*, which means 'provide with a window or windows' (see the entry for *window* in Webster's *New World Dictionary*). This is a member of the large class of English locatum verbs (Clark and Clark 1979), which includes *saddle, bridle, hobble, harness, clothe, salt*, and so on.

We think it is reasonable to propose that the benefactive, or transitive possession, verbs of Hopi are locatum verbs; that is to say, they are the structural equivalents of English locatum verbs. In English, of course, the internal head and upper heads are empty and are licensed at PF by conflation. Thus, *window the piki house* (for those English speakers who can say this) would have the basic structure depicted in (108).

(108)

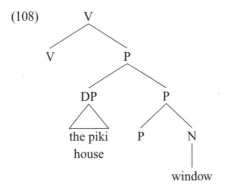

The bare noun *window* conflates with P, and the compound element [P N P] thus derived conflates with V, giving the surface form in which the phonological matrix of the noun is present in the verb only.[8] The English structure (108) differs from the Hopi structure corresponding to *panaptsa-toy-na* 'make a window for *x*, provide *x* with a window' in (107b) in the minor matter of the internal head. In Hopi, the internal head (-'*yi*~-*toya*) is verbal and hence has an intransitive use, as in (107a). In English, the

nonovert internal head is assumed to be nonverbal (perhaps prepositional, P), and hence there is no intransitive use.[9]

The notion that the behavior of the verbs under consideration here
stems from properties of their component elements raises the question of
the "deep" source of these supposed properties. Is there something more
that can be said about the property of nouns that they do not force the
projection of a specifier by the governing verb? And what of the other
categories—adjectives, for instance, or the Hopi verbal roots? At this
point, we can only mention a vaguely semantic correlate, hinted at in
earlier chapters and sections.

Nouns typically denote entities and normally correspond to arguments,
not predicates, in syntactic configurations. On the other hand, adjectives
must be attributed of entities; they are predicates or modifiers, demanding
an associated entity expression to satisfy this property. It is not surprising,
therefore, that adjectives should appear in lexical argument structure
configurations in which a DP also appears, in an appropriate position,
defining a sort of subject-predicate relation. Nouns, on the other hand,
might be expected to eschew precisely such configurations. The position
of verbs is somewhat variable. Evidently, Hopi verbal roots like *munu*
'fall' regularly force the projection of a specifier. In English, the situation
is not clear. While English and Hopi agree on the question in relation to
nouns, there is reason to believe that in English, verbs in and of themselves rarely force projection of a specifier. A verb not otherwise impelled
to project a specifier must take an external subject in sentential syntax;
this is standard for fully transitive verbs in English, and in Hopi as well.
The languages agree on the behavior of the verbal heads of simple
denominal verbs of creation. These do not force the projection of a specifier. Thus, Hopi *kii-ta* 'build a house' and English *laugh* cannot, in virtue
of the verbal head itself, acquire a specifier (an "internal subject"). Instead, the sentential syntactic subject of these verbs, like that of fully
transitive verbs, is the standard *external subject* (Williams 1980). If
this were not so, Hopi *kii-toy-na* could mean 'have x build a house' and
English *laugh* could mean 'make x laugh', contrary to fact.

Chapter 5

On the Double Object Construction

5.1 Introduction

The conception of argument structure developed in Hale and Keyser 1993, 1997b, sets a limit on the range of syntactic configurations that can be posited for the double object construction headed by verbs of the type represented in (1).

(1) a. She gave her daughter a book.
    b. He sent her a telegram.
    c. I feed my horse cottonseed cake.
    d. I wrote my love a letter.

However, while the range of syntactic structures that might be assigned to these sentences is limited, it is by no means obvious what the correct structure is, or even if there is in fact just one. Be this as it may, we will assume here that the double object construction is subject to the same constraints as lexical argument structures in general. Using x to symbolize a lexical head, y a complement, and z a specifier (required to complete a "lexical predication"), the structures projected by basic lexical elements (heads) are defined in terms of just two relations: head-complement and specifier-head. These define the elementary configuration types set out in (2), to which lexical argument structures are, by hypothesis, limited. Fundamentally, a head x is classified according to whether it takes a complement, a specifier, both, or neither.

(2)

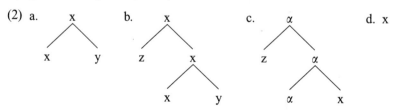

Concretely, of course, these lexical configuration types are realized variously in the morphosyntactic systems (parts of speech) of actual languages: in English, the (a)- and (d)-types are predominantly V and N, respectively, while both the (b)- and the (c)-types typically have more than one realization, with P and A, respectively, predominating (for some discussion, see Hale 1995 and Hale and Keyser 1997b).[1] In what follows, we will often refer to projection type (a) as *monadic*, and to types (b) and (c) as *dyadic*.

In proposing a structure for the double object construction, there are two temptations, at least. One is to assign a structure that "hugs the empirical ground," representing in rather direct fashion the order and hierarchical structure present in the S-Structure representation (cf. the thematic hierarchy in Grimshaw 1990). This view of the double object construction assumes that it consists of a (b)-type structure in the complement position of the (a)-type, as depicted in (3), with categorial realizations as indicated.

(3)

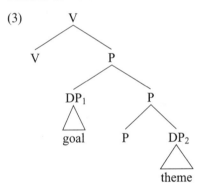

The DP variables correspond to the nominal phrases representing the goal or recipient (DP$_1$) and the theme (DP$_2$). The verb (V) corresponds to the class of elements that can head the double object construction (e.g., *give, send*). And the lower head, symbolized *P*, is assumed to be an empty category of the morphosyntactic category P, specifically, a preposition of "central coincidence" (see Hale and Keyser 1993), corresponding to the overt counterpart *with*, as in (4), the structure plausibly implicated in *I fitted him with new shoes, I supplied the rebels with arms, I provided them with books*, and the like.

(4)

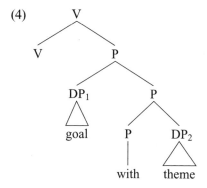

The configuration proposed in (4) is structurally isomorphic with that assumed for the *to*-datives in (5), customarily cited as near paraphrases of the sentences in (1).

(5) a. She gave a book to her daughter.
   b. He sent a telegram to her.
   c. I feed cottonseed cake to my horse.
   d. I wrote a letter to my love.

The structural configuration that suggests itself for the *to*-dative involves, again, the (b)-type structure as complement of the (a)-type, as shown in (6).

(6)

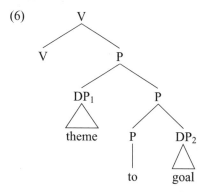

The difference is that the head of the inner projection is the P of "terminal coincidence," regularly overt in English, realized as *to* in (5) and so represented in (6). The argument variables are accordingly "switched," with DP$_1$ corresponding to the theme and DP$_2$ corresponding to the goal or recipient.

Within the framework assumed in this book, there is one aspect of (3) that is incorrect. An empty head must always fuse with the head of its complement. Thus, while (3) is the right structure for locatum verbs like *saddle*, *harness*, and *blindfold*, in which the complement "incorporates" into the empty P, it is not the right structure for the double object construction of (1), where the lower complement (DP$_2$) does not incorporate. At the very least, we must assume that the lower head is not P, but V; and it is not empty, but an overt verbal head *give*, *send*, and so on. The structural configuration might remain the same, with just the morphosyntactic category of the head changed, as in (7).

(7)

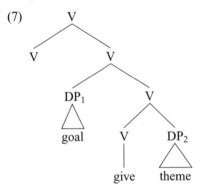

The thematic roles attributed to DP$_1$ and DP$_2$ are as in (3). The surface form is achieved by verb raising, as required for elimination of the empty head, that is, the upper V.

Let us assume, for the moment at least, that (6) is correct for the *to*-dative construction, with the theme argument (DP$_1$) higher than (i.e., asymmetrically c-commanding) the goal argument (DP$_2$). This is the reverse of the relations holding in (7), where the goal or recipient is higher than the theme. We will turn our attention to whether the latter structure is correct for the double object construction.

While (7) embodies the hierarchical arrangement we have assumed for the internal arguments of the double object construction (see Hale and Keyser 1993), and in fact the arrangement assumed for both the double object construction and the *to*-dative in some proposals (e.g., Takano 1996), it is theoretically possible, of course, that the hierarchical arrangement of arguments in (7) is wrong, for the double argument construction, at least. It is possible instead that the asymmetrical command relation shown there is not original but derived, from a more basic configuration in which the arguments are arranged as in the *to*-dative depicted in (6), with the theme higher than the goal. Bowers (1993) and Romero (1995) point out that secondary depictive predicates of the type represented in

(8) and (9) are construed consistently with the theme argument, not with the goal. This is consistent with a structural hypothesis according to which the initial syntactic configurations of the *to*-dative and the double object construction agree in the relative positioning of the goal and theme arguments.

(8) a. I gave the bottle to the baby full.
    b. I handed the baby to its mother crying.
    c. *I gave the bottle to the baby crying.

(9) a. I gave the baby its bottle full.
    b. I handed the mother her baby crying.
    c. *I gave the baby its bottle crying.

If this is the general pattern, secondary predication is regularly of the theme, not the recipient, in both the *to*-dative and the double object construction (see Jackendoff 1990, 203; Rothstein 1983). If we take the *to*-dative construction to be correctly represented by (6), then the secondary predication at issue here is of the higher of the two arguments.

If the same is true in the double object construction exemplified in (9), and this is what we take to be implied by the work of Romero (1995), then (7) is not the correct configuration for that construction. Instead, a structure more closely akin to that proposed by Larson (1988) must be assumed—to wit, a configuration in which the theme is higher than the goal, just as in the *to*-dative. In our terms, the structure would consist of a recursive (b)-type structure embedded in an (a)-type structure, as in (10).

(10)

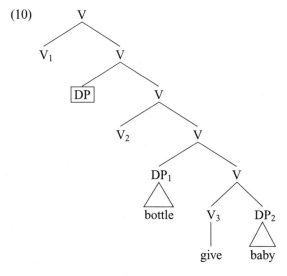

The lower V-projection presents the same relative arrangement of arguments as that assumed for the *to*-dative construction in (6)—with the theme higher than the goal. The surface configuration is derived by head movement, as required by the empty terminal nodes, raising the overt verb (e.g., *give*, as in (10)) first to V_2 and then to V_1, the position assumed by the overt verb in the sentential syntactic representation exemplified in (9a). The goal raises to the position indicated by the boxed DP—that is, the specifier of the V_2-projection, where it appears as the S-Structure object.

The elements of the structural configuration presented in (10) are justified in the following manner. The verb *give* is intransitive; that is, it does not assign Case to its complement. This is the essential feature of the double object construction. As a consequence, DP_2 (*baby*) must raise to the position corresponding to the boxed DP, namely, the specifier of V_2. That verb must be present to permit this and appears there for this reason alone. The upper verb, V_1, is the standard transitive verb, projecting no specifier. The verb *give* raises to this position, thereby acquiring the ability to assign accusative Case to the raised DP_2 *baby*.

In the following section, we will explore the implications of this conception of the double object construction, and the *to*-dative construction as well.[2]

5.2   The Attachment of Depictive Secondary Predicates

Our decision concerning the structural location of depictive predicates will be made under certain assumptions we hold, naturally enough, including the general assumptions inherent in our conception of argument structure configurations. Depictive predicates are not arguments, and hence are not registered in the lexical argument structure of predicators. However, it seems reasonable to attribute to them a structural position and a structural relation. Let us suppose that the structural relation of a depictive predicate is that of adjunct and that it is "licensed" by virtue of standing in a structural relation with another phrase, an argument, which we can call its "associate" or "subject." Two questions follow immediately: (i) what is the nature of the adjunction relation, and (ii) what is the structural position of an adjoined depictive secondary predicate relative to its subject?

In partial answer to the first question, we simply extend to adjoined secondary predication an essential property of the argument structure types in (2), namely, the property of relational uniqueness, according to which a given node has one and only one sister (differing in this regard from Koizumi 1994, for example). We may or may not be correct in this assumption, but it nevertheless limits the range of possibilities, ruling out ternary branching by adjunction. An additional aspect of the first question has to do with the identification of possible sisters of an adjoined phrase. Specifically, we must ask now whether a depictive predicate can freely adjoin either to heads (X^0) or to projections of heads (X', XP), that is, phrases. We assume that a restrictive definition of the adjunction host is correct, and we appeal to a residue of X-bar theory to ensure this. Heads adjoin to heads, phrases adjoin to phrases. That is roughly the principle involved. Accordingly, a phrase—say, a depictive predicate— can adjoin to a head only if the head is also a phrase (as would be the case for a head that does not project; see Chomsky 1995). This imposes a certain restriction on the structural positioning of secondary predicates. Since secondary predicates are phrases (whether or not they are also heads), they cannot adjoin to any of the terminal verb nodes in (10), for example.

In answer to the second question, we appeal to the work of Williams (1980), who argues for a structural requirement to the effect that a predicate must be c-commanded by its subject and, further, that a predicate must be c-subjacent to its subject (see also Bowers 1993, 641, in relation to secondary predicates of the type under consideration here). This imposes an additional limit on the possible attachment sites available to a secondary predicate: the predicate must be within the c-command domain of its subject, and it must not be "too far below" its subject, structurally speaking. In fact, Williams suggests, mutual command is the "tightest," and presumably preferred, construction (Williams 1980, 204). However, immediate containment in a primary predicate, itself satisfying the mutual command requirement (as in *John$_i$ [became rich$_i$]$_i$*), is clearly possible. Hence, we must, with Williams, assume the "looser," but empirically justified, c-subjacency provision, which allows the predicate to be separated from its subject by one branching node.

With these observations in mind, we can narrow down the attachment possibilities for the secondary predicate *full* in (9a), whose corresponding structural configuration is (10), by hypothesis. The c-command requirement eliminates adjunction of *full* to any projection above DP$_1$, its subject. Three possibilities remain: (i) the V-node dominating V$_3$ (*give*), (ii) the subject DP$_1$ (*bottle*), or (iii) the goal DP$_2$ (*baby*). Any of these would satisfy the c-command requirement.

We know that only one of these can be correct. We might eliminate adjunction to DP_2 immediately. Apart from giving the wrong S-Structure order (*I gave the baby full its bottle), adjunction to that phrase can be construed as a violation of the c-subjacency requirement, depending on the precise definition of the c-subjacency relation. But this will not be enough in any event, because we must also contend with the possibility of adjoining to DP_1. This would not involve any ordering problem, but it makes available a plethora of unwanted adjunction possibilities. In general, we need to exclude adjunction of secondary predicates to their subject DPs (consider, for example, the to-dative (8c): *I gave the bottle to the baby_i crying_i). While DP-adjunction might be correct for modifiers (e.g., a page yellow with age), it is evidently not correct for secondary predicates. It seems necessary, therefore, to impose an additional limitation on the structural position of a secondary predicate: namely, the subject must exclude its predicate. This is not only a constraint on secondary predication. It also holds for the predication relation embodied in so-called small clauses (see Bittner 1994 for much relevant discussion), where the predicate does not exclude its subject. It does not hold for modification, however.

This leaves just one possible adjunction site: namely, the V-projection immediately dominating V_3, as shown in (11).

(11)

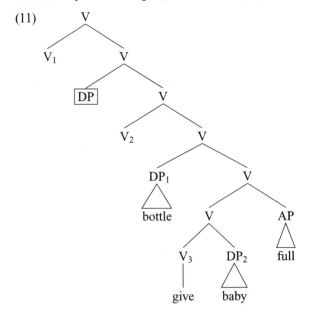

Here, DP₁ (*bottle*), and only that DP, satisfies the command requirements defined for secondary predication by AP (*full*).

Now consider the *to*-dative (8a), whose argument structure configuration is given in (6). The principles relevant to secondary predication of *bottle* by the adjective *full* limit adjunction to the P-projection dominating *to*, as shown in (12).

(12)

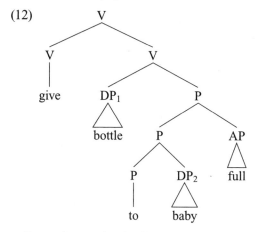

Returning to the double object construction—represented abstractly in (11), corresponding to (9a)—we suppose that its derived S-Structure form must be as in (13), by virtue of established principles of the framework assumed here.

(13)

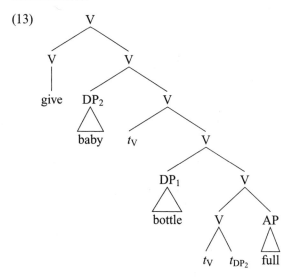

The verb (*give*) must undergo head movement and fuse with the empty V that governs it, successive cyclically in this instance, satisfying (among other things) the morphophonological requirement that an empty head incorporate its complement. The goal, DP_2 (*baby*), raises to assume the position of the boxed DP of (11), forming a chain whose foot is in the position corresponding to the complement of *give* in its original V_3 position. The reasons for this operation seem to be two. First, in this recursive (b)-type structure, V_2 must project a specifier; the raised DP_2 satisfies this requirement. Second, we must assume that DP_2 must raise to a position where it can be assigned structural Case, by the overt transitive verb *give*. The theme argument, DP_1 (*bottle*), receives inherent Case from *give*, in its base position, naturally.[3]

In (13), although DP_2 (*baby*) is now the higher of the two arguments, it cannot serve as the subject of the adjunct. For one thing, the adjunct AP (*full*) is not c-subjacent to DP_2. This may not be enough, however, to thoroughly preclude secondary predication of the raised DP_2 by some adjunct. Suppose an adjunct—say, *crying*—were adjoined to the V-node sister to the raised DP_2, giving (9c). All requirements identified so far would be met. But (9c) is impossible—in our speech, at least. This suggests to us that the original position of the raised DP is relevant to the predication possibilities in the double object construction. Secondary predication of *baby* by *crying* is impossible, because the former does not c-command the latter at D-Structure. We will assume, in light of this, that the c-command requirement is formulated in terms of argument chains. If DP_{CH} is the chain, trivial or nontrivial, that an argument DP consists of, then the c-command provision for secondary predication requires that the subject be an appropriate DP_{CH}: the predicate must be c-commanded by its subject, a DP_{CH}. The ill-formed (9c) fails the c-command requirement, regardless of which of the two possible adjunction sites is employed.

In summary, an adjoined depictive secondary predicate must conform to the following principles of attachment:

(14) a. The subject (DP_{CH}) must c-command and exclude the predicate.

   b. The predicate must be c-subjacent to its subject.

For secondary predication within a double object or *to*-dative construction, (14) correctly limits the attachment of the adjunct to a position from which it is predicated of the higher VP-internal argument, namely, the theme—assuming the structures (10) and (6), and rejecting (7). We now consider additional implications of the structures proposed here.

5.3 Derivational Morphology and Empty Heads

The verb *grow*, as in (15), has both intransitive and transitive uses.

(15) a. Corn grows (fast, well).
     b. We grow corn.

There is also a related derived nominal, *growth*, which involves only the intransitive variant (see Chomsky 1972).

(16) a. the growth of corn (is fun to measure)
     b. corn's growth (is fun to measure)
     c. *our growth of corn (started in 1955)

Under our assumptions, *grow* is a (c)-type element, appearing in the structure shown in (17).

(17)
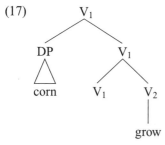

Thus, while *grow* is morphosyntactically a member of the category V, its argument structure is that of a (c)-type head, typically represented by an adjective in English. Be that as it may, *grow* takes a verbal host (specifically, an (a)-type host), and it forces its host to project a specifier, in order to satisfy its fundamental lexical property, that of taking a "subject" (e.g., *corn*). As usual, the empty host V incorporates its complement, giving the simple verb *grow*.

The structure assumed in (17) is crucial to understanding the derivational asymmetry embodied in (16). At least, it is crucial in the framework we assume. The derivational suffix *-th* selects a limited set of lexical items—generally adjectives, such as *long, wide, high*, and *strong*, but also the verb *grow*. That is to say, *-th* strongly selects lexical items, which we interpret to mean that it takes them in complement position, in a (b)-type configuration like (18) that it heads (see Marantz 1995 for a conceptually similar view within the Distributed Morphology framework).

(18)

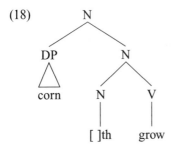

It follows from this fact of selection that *-th* cannot nominalize the transitive variant of *grow*. The transitive structure is as in (19).

(19)

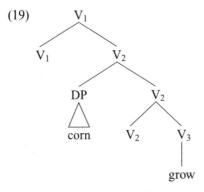

The derivational suffix *-th* selects just the members of a small set of phonologically overt predicators, as noted above. It cannot, therefore, select the transitive structure (19), as that would involve selecting an empty head, V_1, impossible by hypothesis, and in contrast to "productive" derivational morphemes, like *-able*, which are restricted only by category, not by list (see Pesetsky 1995, chap. 3, for much relevant discussion within a distinct framework).

   We believe that this line of reasoning is also appropriate in attempting to explain the derivational asymmetry observed in relation to *gift*, the putative nominalization of the double object verb *give*, as in (20).

(20) a.   our gift of a book to the children, our gift to the children of a
          book
     b.   *our gift of the children (of) a book
     c.   the children's gift of a book (**the children* as goal)

We assume that the derivational morphology involved here has the property of strong lexical selection: it selects the members (overt members) of a restricted list.

Since strong lexical selection involves selection of a complement (i.e., a sister, or more accurately, the head of a sister), it follows that the derivational morphology of *gift* can combine with the *to*-dative structure—for example, that represented by (6), where the head V is an actual lexical verb—but not with the double object structure represented by (10); hence the ill-formedness of (20b) and the lack of ambiguity in (20c). Selection of the double object configuration represented by (10) would violate the strong selectional requirements of the derivational morphology involved in *gift* (also *rental, payment, allotment, presentation,* and others, from Pesetsky 1995, 127–128, citing Kayne 1984). This is because the double object structure is headed by an empty V, not by a lexical verb; the *to*-dative, by contrast, is indeed headed by a lexical verb.

This account of *growth* and *gift* is an attempt within the present framework to express the principle inherent in the restriction on derivations that has come to be known as Myers's Generalization.

(21) Zero-derived words do not permit the affixation of further derivational morphemes. (Myers 1984)

Although our claim is that certain derivational morphemes select members of a particular set of stems, and therefore do not select empty heads (which have no morpholexical properties at all), the effect is closely similar to the idea expressed in (21). However, we believe with Fabb (1988) and Pesetsky (1995) that (21) is properly contained in a larger generalization about derivational morphology.

The generalization has to do specifically with the selectional properties of derivational morphemes. Some derivational morphology is "productive"; some is not. The morphemes at issue here are generally nonproductive, being restricted to particular stems, and are therefore incapable of selecting an entire morphosyntactic category (say, verb), including both overt and nonovert members. Thus, because of the local nature of selection, it is in the lexical representation itself that a "zero head" is prohibited from intervening between derivational morphology (of the type involved in *growth* and *gift*) and a stem element (*grow, give*). For this particular type of derivational morphology, symbolized here as Y, there can be no lexical configuration of the following type, where X is a stem and V is an empty head of category V:

(22) $[_Y [_V [X] V] Y]$

Although Y might indeed select X, it cannot appear in this structure, because it cannot select V, by the very nature of both V and Y. This is the sense in which Y-type morphology cannot be separated from X by an empty (i.e., zero) element. Since it is a fact of selection, the prohibition is in force in lexical argument structure representation. Furthermore, since it is a fact of *selection*, it is not really a fact about empty, or zero, morphemes, an observation we owe to Fabb (1988), who argues in detail for the view that selection is what is at work in constraining affixation in English (and see Pesetsky 1995 for development of an explicit theory of the multiple consequences of this idea within a different view of the relevant derivational morphology).

It follows, then, that V of (22) could in fact be overt, just not selected by Y. Under our assumptions, however, where V in (22) happens to be empty, it is necessarily eliminated by incorporation of X; that is to say, its empty phonological matrix is "filled" through fusion with the overt phonological matrix of its complement, this being a fundamental feature of this conception of derivational morphology.[4]

Returning to the basic argument structure syntax involved in the double object construction, we would like now to make a brief comment about the English possessive verb *have*.

5.4 *Have*

It has often been suggested that double object *give* is a "causative" of *have*: to "give the baby its bottle" is to "cause the baby to have its bottle." We have proposed here that the double object construction is a recursive (b)-type configuration embedded as the complement of a configuration of the (a)-type. If the "cause to have" paraphrase of *give* is correct, then *have* could be just the recursive (b)-type structure, bereft of the (a)-type host (differing, therefore, from Hale and Keyser 1997a and Harley 1995, which propose a different analysis).

Accordingly, the possessive sentence (23) might correspond to the lexical argument structure configuration (24). Here again, we will use the informal terminology of thematic relations, referring to the higher argument as the possessum (or "theme"), the lower as the possessor (or "goal").

(23) The baby has its bottle.

(24)

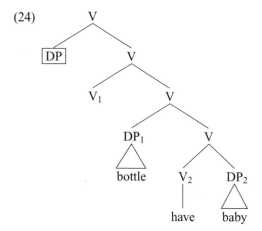

The difference here, of course, is that the overt verb (V_2, *have*) undergoes head movement just once (i.e., just to V_1) in deriving the sentential syntactic form of the verb itself. But, just as in the double object construction, here also the lower (possessor) DP raises to the specifier of V_1, the position indicated by the boxed DP, to satisfy the projection requirements of V_1—that is, to satisfy its need for a specifier. The resulting structure is shown in (25).

(25)

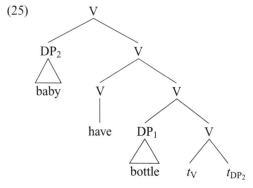

The possessor DP_2 will, of course, not be Case-marked in its raised position. It will therefore raise in sentential syntax to the specifier of IP to satisfy, among other things, its Case requirements, as exemplified in the surface form (23).[5]

We must now face the obvious question of how depictive secondary predication works in relation to the possessive constructions headed lexically by *have*. In truth, it is not easy to decide the matter. The verb *have* is involved in a variety of constructions (see Ritter and Rosen 1991; Déchaine, Hoekstra, and Rooryck 1995), and it is sometimes difficult to be sure what construction (or constructions) a particular example illustrates. But consider, for example, the following:

(26) She had a copy of *On Raising* [hot off the press].

It seems relatively clear to us that the phrase *hot off the press* is a secondary predicate and that it is predicated of *a copy of On Raising* (i.e., of the possessum, or "theme"), as predicted on the expectation that depictive secondary predication is of the higher of the two arguments in the basic form. If the depictive is replaced here with one that is appropriate to the subject *she*, such as *excited beyond words*, it does not seem to us to be acceptable, as expected, since *she*—that is, the chain headed by the subject—does not c-command the secondary predicate on the attachment assumptions we have made.

In the next section, we briefly shift our focus to the uppermost component of the structure attributed to the double object configuration.

5.5 Cause

A great many English predicators participate freely in the causative-inchoative alternation—for instance, *break*, *clear*, *lower*, *sink*, and many others (see Levin 1993); indeed, this is a popular alternation crosslinguistically. In the present framework, the intransitive (or inchoative) member of the alternation is a (c)-type configuration, as in (27).

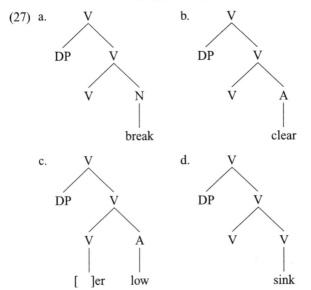

In these particular instances, the verbal head of the (c)-type structure is empty (or partially so, in the case of *lower*) and, accordingly, must incorporate its complement; it is the latter that supplies the overt ingredient, and it is this ingredient that forces the appearance of a specifier (DP). This is a common source of surface monomorphemic inchoative verbs in English, although the (c)-type also occurs with overt V, yielding an overt verb-complement phrase (as in *turn green, get drunk*, and the like; see chapter 1).

The DP constituent shown in (27) will, in the normal course of events, raise to an appropriate specifier position in sentential syntax, as in the intransitive sentences of (28).

(28) a. Hundreds of windows broke (in the storm).
     b. The (computer) screen cleared.
     c. Prices (eventually) lower.
     d. Ships (often) sink.

To say that a verb of this sort participates freely in the causative-inchoative alternation is to say that it can freely appear as the complement in an (a)-type structure, as in (29).[6]

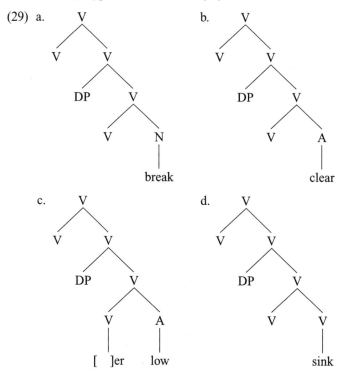

(29) a.
b.
c.
d.

The head of the (a)-type structure has the syntactic property that it does not, in and of itself, force the projection of a specifier. The argument structures of (29), therefore, find their subjects (assuming they enter into verbal sentential syntax) externally, eventually in the specifier position of an appropriate functional projection (e.g., the conventional specifier of IP). The DP pictured in (29) is, of course, the very same argument as the one that assumes the surface subject function in the intransitive variant. Here, however, it is an internal argument, assuming the surface object function and receiving Case from the higher V, realized as a phonologically overt verb (*break, clear, lower, sink*) through successive-cyclic incorporation and fusion, as required.

Our interest here is in the nature of the upper V, head of the (a)-type argument structure configuration. In verbs of the type represented in (29), the upper V is utterly empty, except for its morphosyntactic category (part of speech) V. It has no "meaning." It is not, for example, a "causative verb," like English *make, cause,* or *have.* And it does not define a predicate that requires, suggests, or implicates agency or volition on the part of its subject. On the other hand, it is obvious that a sentence using one of the transitive verbs in (29) involves the phenomenon of "cause." The entity denoted by the subject is in a clear sense "the cause" of the eventuality described in the predicate; where the eventuality is actual, it is so "because of" the entity denoted by the subject. In (30a), for example, the windows broke because of the storm, and analogously for (30b–d).

(30) a. The storm broke hundreds of windows.
     b. My fumbling at the keyboard cleared the screen.
     c. Competition lowers prices.
     d. Loose lips sink ships.

There is no sense of agency here, only of "cause" (although, in figurative speech, of course, agency might be "imputed" to the subject; we are assuming normal, nonfigurative usage, however).[7] We assume that this "cause" interpretation is simply the normal interpretation of the configuration $[V_1 \ [V_2]]$, where V_1 heads the (a)-type configuration and is the unmarked empty verb, and where V_2 is a verbal construction of one sort or another appearing as the complement of V_1. That is to say, "cause" is an interpretation assigned to certain structures and, hence, is unlike the "agent" or "instrumental" component of verbs like *cut, stab, smear,* and so on. Verbs of the *break* class can, of course, take agentive subjects or instrumentals, but they differ from the *cut* class in that "agent" and "instrument" are not inherent components in their lexical entries. The element responsible for the transitive use of the *break* class (i.e., the (a)-type host) contributes only the upper head-complement structure and the verbal category. The "cause" interpretation is attributed to the structure alone, as suggested.

Let us assume for present purposes that the foregoing is correct, and that the kind of "pure cause" interpretation is due to the presence of an (a)-type host itself devoid of such semantic components as "agency," "volition," and "instrumentality." On this assumption, we can extend this observation to the double object construction and the *to*-dative, which differ, among other things, in the presence versus absence of an (a)-type head-complement host superstructure.

In his important study of these constructions, Oehrle (1976) observes that double object sentences like (31) are ambiguous and, of particular relevance here, that one of the readings is what he terms "causative."

(31) Nixon gave Mailer a book.

Oehrle's "causative" reading is the one we have referred to here as "(pure) cause," and it corresponds to the situation in which Mailer got a book because of Nixon or, in Oehrle's paraphrase, 'Mailer wrote a book which he wouldn't have been able to write if it hadn't been for Nixon'. Nixon is not an agent here, but a cause (or Causer; see Pesetsky 1995 for much relevant discussion). There is, of course, an "agentive" reading of (31), corresponding to the situation in which Nixon performed the action of transferring possession or ownership of a book to Mailer. The latter reading is the only one available for the corresponding *to*-dative.

(32) Nixon gave a book to Mailer.

It is to be expected from this that the two constructions will differ in acceptability according to the nature of the subject appearing with them (Pesetsky 1995, 193–194). Cause subjects go well in the double object construction (e.g., *The interview gave Mailer a book*), but, for many speakers, they do not go so well in the *to*-dative construction, which requires an agent subject (*The interview gave a book to Mailer*).

The interpretations of these two constructions follow, we suggest, from the difference in their basic argument structure configurations. The double object construction contains, as its uppermost component, the (a)-type structure, with empty V. This is precisely the element that, we have argued, contributes the cause interpretation to the verbs that allow it. By contrast, the *to*-dative does not allow this interpretation. To be sure, it is not always easy to separate the cause interpretation from an interpretation that might be called "figurative"; for example, *The interview finally gave answers to Mailer* might possibly have a figurative agentive reading. Problem cases aside, however, the *to*-dative favors an agentive subject, while the double object construction imposes virtually no constraint, permitting the cause interpretation freely, as well as agentive interpretations where appropriate. This is to be expected given the structures assumed here, we believe.

5.6 Backward Binding

Before concluding our discussion of the double object construction, we wish to take up the issue of problematic (anti-c-command) "backward binding." Two cases have been discussed in the literature, and we will attempt here to determine whether they fall into a single family of problems and consequently imply a single explanation.

Several scholars argue that it is the goal, not the theme, that is the higher argument in the sense relevant to secondary predication (see Takano 1996 and references cited there; and see Koizumi 1994 for a corresponding theory of secondary predicate attachment). In the English case, at least, evidence for this comes, in part, from the "connectivity effect" seen in sentences like (33).

(33) I showed each other's pictures to the boys.

If standard c-command is involved in interpreting the reciprocal here, this example suggests that the *to*-dative (i.e., goal) phrase is higher than the theme at the relevant point in the derivation (and that *the boys* c-commands the anaphor in the relevant structure). However, examples like (34) seem to us, and to others as well, to be almost equally acceptable.

(34) I put each other's crowns under the thrones of the king of France and the queen of Holland.

In fact, we see nothing particularly wrong with backward binding in all cases of the same general type.

(35) a. I set each other's drinks down beside Max and Harriet.
      b. I strapped each other's spurs on Leecil and Wayne.
      c. We led each other's colts up to Monica and Chiquita.

At worst, these may merit a question mark, but in all honesty, we do not think they are degraded even to that degree. Thus, except for our hesitancy to judge these as marginal, we essentially agree with Takano (1996) and others who have made this point.[8]

This kind of backward binding is not limited to the *to*-dative but smacks of something more general and common. Even so, we are not absolved of the need to explain these cases of problematic backward binding. On the face of it, at least, they violate Condition A of binding theory. Before we address this problem, however, let us introduce the other case.

So-called object-experiencer verbs have been cited to illustrate the second case of problematic backward binding (Belletti and Rizzi 1988).

(36) a. Each other's outbursts frightened Marx and Hegel.
　　 b. The stories about himself bothered Clinton.
　　 c. Each other's foibles angered Bernice and Vinnie.

By contrast, so-called subject-experiencer verbs fail to display the backward binding effect.

(37) a. *Each other's mothers love Bill and Hank.
　　 b. *Each other's students respect Noam and Morris.
　　 c. *Each other's relatives hate Biff and Chauncey.

We would like to explore briefly the idea that the distinction is to be understood in terms of feature binding in the sense of Hale and Keyser 1999, rather than in terms of a movement operation.

Consider first the backward binding relation illustrated in (36). Using (36c) to represent the type, we assign it the structural representation shown in (38), augmented by relevant feature indices.

(38)

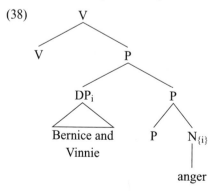

The plain index *i*, assigned to the specifier *Bernice and Vinnie*, is the familiar referential index of binding theory. The bracketed index $\{i\}$ is a different kind of element. It represents not only the standard referential index but also the relevant semantic features of the nominal complement of the preposition P. In this case, and in the case of the other examples of (36), this nominal is proximate. That is to say, the semantic features of the nominal are locally bound, by the specifier, a circumstance that corresponds to the observed interpretation of (36c), where the emotion of anger is attributed to Bernice and Vinnie.

Compare now the case of subject-experiencer verbs, using (37a) as an example. In configurational structure, the verbal projections of (37a–c) are parallel to those of (36a–c).

(39)

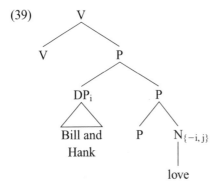

However, the parallelism does not extend to the binding relations. Here, the bracketed index is obviative (i.e., disjoint from the internal argument) and bound instead by the subject, an external argument.

One reflex of this distinction is the behavior of these verbs in relation to the middle construction. Proximate verbs participate in the middle construction, while obviative verbs do not (see chapter 2 for discussion).

(40) a. Bernice angers easily.
      b. *Bill loves easily.

These verbs' behavior in relation to the middle follows straightforwardly from their special indexing. Since the proximate verbs are internally bound, the formation of the middle is possible because the bracketed index is "activated" within the verbal projection, and the elimination of the external argument has no effect on that requirement. But since obviative verbs are externally bound, elimination of the external argument prevents the bracketed index from fulfilling the requirement that it be activated.

With this background, we turn to the problem of backward binding. We propose that whether or not a verb projects a structure permitting backward binding depends upon the activation of the bracketed index. And this, we assume, takes place at the node that most locally dominates both the antecedent and the nominal bearing the bracketed index. In the case of the proximate verb of (38), this is the node P dominating the constituents of the prepositional projection. An activated bracketed index is a pronominal, by hypothesis. Backward binding occurs as a result of projecting the activated bracketed index to the first node that c-commands the subject, as shown in (41).

(41)

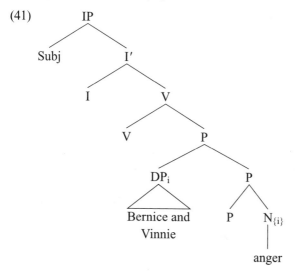

At I′, the bracketed index c-commands the subject and can therefore bind an anaphor within it.

By contrast, in the obviative case, depicted in (42), the bracketed index is not activated within the relevant projection—that is, not earlier than IP—and, consequently, cannot bind an anaphor within the subject.

(42)

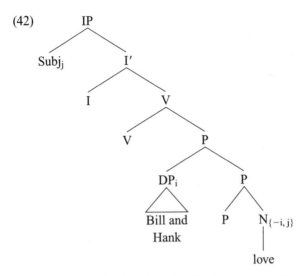

At I′, the obviative bracketed index is not yet activated.

A bracketed index counts as a pronominal, as it consists of an indexed nominal feature together with semantic features representing relevant aspects of the content of the nominal root appearing as the complement of P (and conflated with V at PF). And a bracketed index may project to dominating nodes provided the process is limited to the extended projection of the most immediately dominating verb, in accordance with the principles of extended projection outlined in Grimshaw 1991.

Complex verbal constructions vary according to whether a bracketed index may project from an embedded predicate into the domain of a dominating matrix verb. Compare the following constructions:

(43) a.   Each other's quirks make John and Mary angry.
       b.   *Each other's relatives consider John and Mary angry.

Evidently, the bracketed index projects without hindrance into the extended projection of the causative verb *make* in (43a) and is able there to bind into the subject of that verb, as shown in (44).

(44)

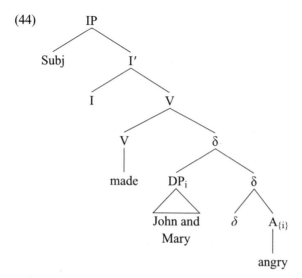

This is evidently not possible in the case of the verb *consider*. Thus, while the bracketed index may project to the node I′ in (44), it is prevented from doing so in (45), the structure assumed for the verb phrase of the ill-formed sentence (43b).

(45)

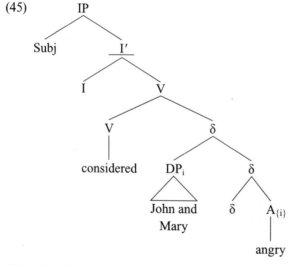

This disparity parallels that observed in the following pair, in which the bare infinitive is allowed only where the matrix verb imposes a tense dependency on the embedded verb:

(46) a.   We made her speak Spanish well.

     b.   *We considered her speak Spanish well.

The ability of the causative verb *make* to "impose a tense dependency" on the embedded predicate, whether verbal or a small clause, results from the structural relation according to which *make* directly selects the embedded predicator and is, therefore, not separated from the embedded predicate by any node belonging to a functional category, such as I or C. In (46), *make* satisfies this relation, since no functional category intervenes between that verb and the embedded predicate. By contrast, the verb *consider*—like most other verbs, in fact—fails in this regard, since it does not directly select the predicate of its complement.

    We ask at this point whether a similar account can be given for the *to*-dative construction, as exemplified by (33), repeated here as (47).

(47) I showed each other's pictures to the boys.

Assuming that the structure of this type of *to*-dative construction is the same as that posited for *to*-datives generally, the constituents are arranged as in (48).

(48)

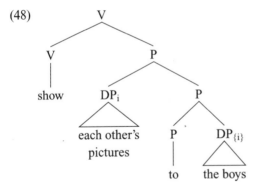

In our judgment, all such structures permit backward binding, regardless of the preposition. Our account implicates the bracketed index on the prepositional object. This is activated by the upper projection of P, and it can therefore bind into the specifier *each other's pictures* at the first projection of P, where it c-commands the specifier.

    Obviously, matters cannot stand as they have been formulated up to this point. Abstractly, the structural relations depicted in (48) parallel exactly those seen in the upper portion of (42). However, our account permits backward binding in the case of (48), but not in the case of (42). The difference, we suggest, depends on locality. In (48), the domain of activation and the domain of binding are local, in the sense that they are within a structure defined by a single category, the relevant arguments being dependents of the same P-projection. In this case, we maintain, activation and binding coincide, permitting backward binding. The situation represented in (42) is different. There, activation and binding must be taken separately. Local activation is impossible, given the obviative character of *love*. Backward binding, while theoretically possible, fails at the critical point, because the bracketed index is not activated and therefore not pronominal.

5.7 Concluding Remarks

The grammar of depictive secondary predication, insofar as we understand it, has persuaded us to consider assigning to the double object construction a lexical syntactic structure (i.e., argument structure) that is simultaneously (i) more "complex" than would seem to be warranted, on initial observational grounds, and (ii) in evident conflict with the surface hierarchical arrangement of the internal arguments, implying the further complication of a movement operation.

On the other hand, the lexical configuration required for the double object construction has characteristics that can be invoked to explain not only the behavior of depictives but also limitations on certain derivational morphology and the availability of the (nonagentive) causative interpretation.

Naturally, the analysis proposed here for the English double object construction raises questions for other constructions in the language. For the purposes of this concluding section, we will content ourselves with discussing the *with*-construction, to which we assigned the structure shown in (4), repeated here as (49).

(49)

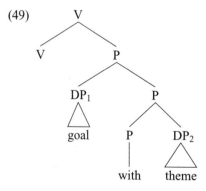

The correctness of this structure (like that of (3) and (7), now discarded for the double object construction) comes into question when we consider depictive predication.

(50) a. We supplied the soldiers with rations (*drunk).
        (cf. We brought the soldiers to the armory drunk.)
     b. We fit the mule with a harness (*unbroken, *green).
        (cf. We brought the two-year-old to the home place unbroken.)

Since the first DP cannot take a depictive secondary predicate, we must assume that its advanced structural position is derived, as in the double object construction, and that it heads a chain that fails to c-command the predicate. That is to say, the basic argument structure configuration that must be attributed to the *with*-construction is essentially identical to that of the double object construction (i.e., the structure embodied in (10)). There is a difference, however. In the *with*-construction, the argument assigned to the specifier position is not a "bare DP" but an overt Case preposition (symbolized *K*, heading a "Case Phrase," KP), as shown in (51).

(51)

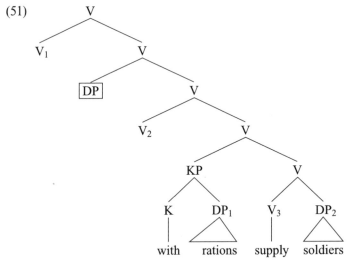

Thus, as in the double object construction, in the *with*-construction the verb assigns inherent case to its specifier. Here, however, the case is realized overtly as *with*, in accordance with the lexical property of verbs like *supply*, *provide*, and *furnish*. This overt element, like a "true" preposition, prevents DP_1 from c-commanding any depictive predicate. Accordingly, neither of the two internal arguments in the *with*-construction can function as the subject of a secondary predicate.

As expected, given the structure assigned, the *with*-construction occurs easily with a pure "cause" subject, as in (52).

(52) a. The hurricane furnished us with a lot of free lumber.
b. Nixon supplied us with plenty of good copy.

And while *provision* is a well-formed derived noun, it cannot be a nominalization of the *with*-construction, as expected.

(53) *Our provision of the soldiers with rations was fortunate.
(cf. Our provisioning the soldiers with rations was inappropriate.)

This follows if, as we suspect, *-ion*, though relatively "productive" in terms of sheer numbers, nonetheless selects a particular class of lexical items, however large this may be. In any event, unlike *-able*, for example, it does not select items freely and cannot select the empty V heading the double object and *with*-constructions.

The examples of depictive predication we have used here have all involved predicates with two internal arguments, the depictive being construed with the higher of the two (in the basic argument structure configuration). This raises the natural question of well-known examples like *eat the meat raw* and *drink the whiskey neat*, in which only one surface internal argument appears. We must admit, at this point, that we do not know how examples of this type work, since we do not have an argument structure analysis of verbs like *eat* and *drink*. There is one class of verbs, however, that conform to our predictions. These are the locatum verbs, like *saddle*, which have a single internal argument on the surface but which we assume to have the more complex underlying argument structure shown in (3), repeated here as (54), with the "theme" (*saddle*) in the lower position, complement of an empty P (of "central coincidence"), and the "goal" (*horse*) in the specifier position projected by P.

(54)

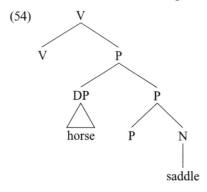

We rejected this structure for the double object construction, for the reasons given. But it is probably correct for the locatum verbs, derived by successive-cyclic head movement of N, first to P and then to V, satisfying the phonological requirements of these empty heads (see chapter 3 for discussion of the conflation alternative to head movement). Although there is some resistance to it, which we do not understand, we believe that it is possible here to adjoin a depictive predicate in the allowed manner— that is, to the P-projection immediately dominating N (*saddle*)—where it can be predicated of the DP, as in (55).

(55) I saddled my horse drunk (after it got into the fermented apples).

This is ambiguous, of course, but we can easily get the reading according to which the secondary predicate is of the surface internal argument *my horse*. If so, then this can be taken as a further example of the general rule that secondary predication is of the higher internal argument in the lexical argument structure configuration.[9]

Chapter 6

There-Insertion
Unaccusatives

There exists a class of English verbs whose members are customarily held up as paradigm examples of the unaccusative class. Unlike the much larger class of unaccusatives of the *break* type, which enter freely into the standard transitivity alternation, verbs of the *arrive* type at issue here do not transitivize; but—to some degree, at least, though often with a tinge of reduced acceptability—they participate in the *there*-insertion construction, as exemplified in (1b).

(1) a. Many guests arrived (at the party).
    b. There arrived many guests (at the party).
    c. *Arrived many guests (at the party).
    d. *John arrived many guests (at the party).

Following Moro (1997), we maintain that the surface subject of (1a), and the postverbal subject in (1b), originate in the specifier position of a "small clause" complement to the verb *arrive*. In terms of the theory of argument structure being employed here, this verb heads the monadic, (a)-type lexical configuration and takes as its complement the basic dyadic, (b)-type configuration (see (24) in chapter 1), resulting in the structure shown in (2).[1]

(2)

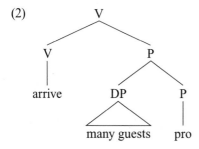

The inner dyadic component in this construction can, of course, be a fully overt prepositional projection, as in *arrive (many guests) at the party*, but it is a particular lexical feature of the verbs of interest here that they can take a special pronominal element, *there*, construed either with an overt P-projection or with a nonovert locative pronominal, as depicted in (2).

English, as is well known, satisfies the Extended Projection Principle (EPP) with *overt* nominal subjects. Consequently, one of two things must happen in order to derive a well-formed English sentence on the basis of (2), avoiding the pro-drop variant (1c). The specifier DP may raise to sentential subject position, arriving ultimately in an appropriate specifier position in the functional matrix, giving (1a). Alternatively, the expletive *there* may be inserted in subject position instead, satisfying the English EPP in that manner. This overt element, we can assume, is inserted only where it is needed—hence, only to satisfy the EPP (see Chomsky 1991), and not in the base position dominated by P, where pro is evidently possible, perhaps by virtue of incorporation into V (as in Moro 1997), a detail we will not consider further.

Either of the two processes just outlined will prevent the ungrammatical (1c). But what prevents (1d)? Transitivization of *there*-insertion unaccusatives is, so far as we can tell, generally impossible.

(3) a. i.   There arose a problem (in the research design).
      ii. A problem arose (in the research design).
      iii. *We arose a problem (in the research design).
    b. i.   There appeared a blemish (on the surface of the vase).
      ii. A blemish appeared (on the surface of the vase).
      iii. *We appeared a blemish (on the surface of the vase).
    c. i.   There occurred a riot (on the streets of Laredo).
      ii. A riot occurred (on the streets of Laredo).
      iii. *They occurred a riot (on the streets of Laredo).

The acceptability of the *there*-insertion sentences (the (i)-sentences) is, to say the least, variable among speakers, but there seems to be no variation in judgments of the transitive sentences (the (ii)-sentences), among adult English speakers, at least. They are uniformly judged ungrammatical.

These are not "ordinary" unaccusatives—unlike the familiar *break*-type unaccusative, they do not transitivize "automatically." This, at least, would follow straightforwardly from the structure assigned to them in (2). Automatic transitivization is freely possible by virtue of the head-complement relation. It is accomplished by inserting a dyadic structure into the complement position of the monadic, (a)-type lexical configuration, and it is successful precisely because the inserted structure is dyadic, that is, projects a specifier that functions as the surface object of the derived transitive verb. However, (2) is not dyadic in the relevant sense. It *contains* a dyadic structure, but it is not itself dyadic and, therefore, projects no specifier; hence the impossibility of (4) as a transitive of *arrive*.

(4)

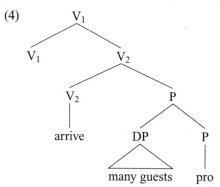

If this were all that needed to be said about the matter, we would have an explanation for the ungrammatical transitives of (1) and (3). But we must go further. What is to prevent the structure in (2) from simply appearing with an *external* subject in sentential syntax? Couldn't *John* in (1d) simply be an external subject, of which (2) is predicated in sentential syntax? This is precisely what happens with other verbs built directly on the monadic argument structure: canonical unergative verbs, for example, have external subjects (e.g., analytic *make trouble, build houses, have a puppy,* and synthetic *laugh, sneeze, pup*). And canonical location and locatum verbs—having a structure putatively very like (2)—are consistently transitive (e.g., *put the books on the shelf, fit the mare with racing shoes, shelve the books, shoe the mare*). So why can't (2) take an external subject, giving (1d)?

Before we answer, let us summarize. We can set aside the question of automatic transitivization of *arrive*-type unaccusative verbs. It is impossible, to be sure, given the argument structure proposed for them, but we are left with another possible source of transitivity: simple predication of an external argument. However, while ergative and transitive verbs may function as predicates in sentential syntax, taking external subjects, *arrive*-type verbs cannot. This is as yet unexplained.

There is a natural temptation to appeal to Case theory in explaining this asymmetry. If *arrive*-type verbs are simply unable to assign Case to a nominal they govern, then sentences of the type represented by (1d) would be impossible on those grounds. The *there*-insertion variant is, in any event, possible by virtue of a Case transmission mechanism assigning nominative to the postverbal subject (see Safir 1982, 172 et passim). And the alternant with subject raised from the specifier of P is derived in the usual manner associated with raising predicators lacking the capacity to assign accusative Case, like English *seem*, *be*, and the passive participle. However, while it is certainly true that *arrive*, and its like, do not assign accusative Case and are therefore "raising" verbs in the standard sense, this is probably a symptom, rather than the root cause, of the overall lexical and syntactic behavior they exhibit. The verbs are simply "not transitive," and their key property is that they do not take an external subject. If they were closet transitives, they might be expected to appear in the passive, circumventing the Case problem, contrary to fact (hence, **Many guests were arrived at the party*).

Seen in this light, a somewhat more apt comparison is between the *there*-insertion unaccusatives and the "pure" unaccusatives—that is, the inchoative alternants of the *break*-type unaccusatives. Intransitive *clear*, for example, appears in the composite dyadic lexical projection depicted in (5).

(5)

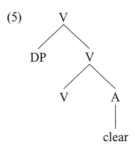

This shares with (2) the property that it cannot appear directly in sentential syntax with an external subject. Again, the reason could be Case, DP being unable to "get Case" if prevented from raising to the specifier of the appropriate functional projection (I(nfl), or T). This is an idea worth exploring, but it is not actually clear that Case theory, in and of itself, could rule out the use of (5) with an external subject. Suppose, for example, this structure were in fact to enter into construction with an external subject, as in (6).

(6)

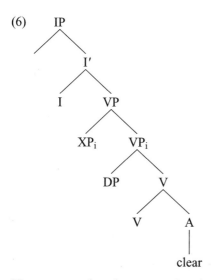

Here, we employ the conventional symbol *VP* to represent the maximal projection of V, an inconsequential notational deviation from the practice used in (5). The external subject (XP_i) is a "distinguished adjunct" to VP—it is the argument of which VP is predicated in sentential syntax, a relation indicated by coindexing (see Bittner 1994, following Williams 1980). The subject is external to VP, since it is not dominated by VP (i.e., it is not dominated by all segments of VP). But its structural position does conform in basic outline to what is generally termed the "VP-internal subject hypothesis" (as formulated, e.g., in Koopman and Sportiche 1991), since XP_i is dominated by a segment of VP. In (6), we have also supplied VP with a relevant portion of its extended projection, which we symbolize as I projecting to IP.

The structure dominated by VP is the lexical structure defined by the heads V and A, the latter the complement of the former. It corresponds to (5). Thus, (6) is the structure that results if (5) is supplied with an external argument together with an appropriate extension by functional category. This structure cannot succeed, however. There is no well-formed issue from it. First, it cannot result in a transitive sentence like the well-formed *John cleared the screen*. In that clause, the verb c-commands the object (DP); in (6), it does not. Any other theoretically possible output is simply ungrammatical. But why?

As suggested above, it is not clear that the business can be laid entirely at the doorstep of Case theory. Not entirely. An uninteresting reason for this is that Case theory is simply too much in flux at the moment; there are too many ways to "block Case assignment" to one or another argument position. A more interesting reason is that (6) fails *in spite of* Case theory. There are a number of theories of Case in which Case licensing is accomplished fully and naturally in configurations of the type represented by (6). These are theories according to which ergative-accusative typology is defined, in part, in terms of the ability of V to assign accusative Case (e.g., Bok-Bennema and Groos 1984; Bittner 1994; Bittner and Hale 1996a).

Framing the matter in accordance with the principles of Bittner's (1994) Case-binding theory, an argument A satisfies its Case-licensing requirements by one or the other of these two means:

(7) *Case licensing*
   a. A is Case-licensed if it is Case-bound.
   b. A is Case-licensed if it is governed by a Caselike head (i.e., by K, a Case particle or affix, or C(omplementizer)).

Simplifying somewhat, Case-binding is a relation between a head H and an argument A standing in a structural relation characterized jointly by the following criteria:

(8) *Criteria for Case-binding*
   a. H delimits a small clause.
   b. H locally c-commands A.
   c. H governs a (bare DP) Case competitor for A.

Looking now at (6), the candidate Case binders are the two heads I and V. The first delimits a small clause (i.e., a predicate with a distinguished adjunct, in this instance [$_{VP}$ XP$_i$ VP$_i$]). It does so by virtue of governing it; this is one of two ways in which a head can delimit a small clause. And V delimits the same small clause by virtue of projecting it. Hence, both I and V satisfy (8a). However, V fails in relation to the other two criteria; although it locally m-commands DP, a potential bindee, it does not c-command it; there is in fact no A such that V locally c-commands it. And V fails (8b) as well, since, while both XP$_i$ and DP are potential competitors (structurally), V governs only DP, since XP$_i$ is beyond V's governing domain. But I fares better. As noted, it delimits a small clause. Furthermore, it locally c-commands XP$_i$. Now, in relation to (8c), if VP is a barrier, then I does not govern DP, a potential Case competitor. But if DP raises to the specifier of IP, then I *does* govern DP and, therefore, satisfies all of (8a–c). In fact, DP must get into the governing domain of a Caselike head; this is accomplished by raising to the specifier of IP, within the governing domain of C. Thus, according to the provisions of the Case-binding theory, both arguments in (6) are Case-licensed. The external subject is Case-bound, and the specifier DP is licensed by raising to the governing domain of C, a Caselike element.

The scenario just presented is precisely what happens in a so-called raising ergative language, according to the Case-binding theory. Raising ergative languages, like West Greenlandic Inuit and Dyirbal of North Queensland, are those in which the object achieves a prominent structural position, not unlike that of a subject; this prominent position is, by hypothesis, effected by raising from a position internal to VP (i.e., specifier or complement) into a specifier position in the matrix functional configuration (i.e., the specifier of IP in this case). So why can't (6) be realized as an ergative construction? An uninteresting answer is that English simply does not have an ergative case. But what prevents a sentence like (9), in which the Case-bound subject, XP, realizes its ergative case as a preposition—say, *by*?

(9) *The screen cleared by John.

Here, the DP *the screen* functions as "surface subject," being moved to sentential syntactic subject position from the specifier of VP. And *by John*, the ergative, is postposed, as is usual for prepositional phrases in English.

Curiously, (9) is "almost good" in English. However, we assume that it should in fact be taken as ungrammatical, on a straightforward ergative reading; the interpretation it weakly receives is, for us at least, one in which *by* is short for something like *by virtue of* or *by the good graces of*. In any event, (9) is not the grammatical equivalent of the standard transitive *John cleared the screen*, as it would be if it were a true ergative construction.

We will assume (though it is not quite true) that we have eliminated Case as the factor responsible for the inability of (5) to take an external subject. We are left, then, with the original problem. Why is this so? Why can't a simple dyadic argument structure appear with an external argument, as in (6)?

There is an intuitively clear reason for this, it seems to us. The fact is, (5) is "complete," or "saturated." All arguments that are required in order for (5) to enter directly into sentential syntax are present in the lexical projection itself. There is no "open position" in (5). Consequently, an external subject is entirely supernumerary and is precluded by virtue of the principle of Full Interpretation (Chomsky 1986, 98 et passim). This is the explanation we favor for well-formed (5) and ill-formed (6).

Now let us reconsider (2), which we take to be representative of intransitive structures headed by verbs of the *arrive* type. Let us redraw the structure of (2) to include the full P-projection, instead of the pro element depicted in (2). This gives a configuration of the type shown in (10).

(10)

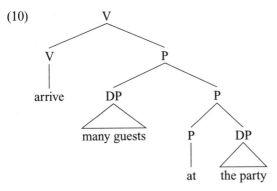

Automatic transitivization is excluded, given this structure, for the reasons already given. But we are still left with the question of why (10) cannot simply take an external subject in sentential syntax. As suggested above, Case theory might be invoked to account for this; the idea is worth reconsidering in this instance, because Case might play a role here, in fact, though we will argue that it is not the sole determining factor. The Case-theoretic account would be that *arrive* and its fellow *there*-insertion unaccusatives are inherently intransitive, unable to assign accusative Case. The specifier DP in (10) is unable to get Case in its base position and therefore raises to the specifier of IP (stopping first in the distinguished adjunct position, i.e., the "true subject position"). The established existence of a class of raising predicators (like *seem, be likely,* etc.) serves as a precedent for this, it could be argued.

Assuming the Case-theoretic explanation for the present, (10) fails to take an external subject because that subject would occupy the very position into which the "internal" subject (the DP in the specifier of the P-projection) must move to satisfy its Case requirements. Of course, this smacks of the explanation given for (6), that is, for the inability of (5) to take an external argument. That is to say, there are too many potential subjects around. This would follow if (10) were complete, or saturated, in essentially the way (5) is complete.

We think this is part of the answer; more exactly, the effect at issue is due to an interaction of Case theory and argument theory (the θ-Criterion, if you will). However, there is more that must be done, because the configuration represented in (10) is, in its essential structural details, precisely the configuration associated with the completely productive and fully well formed transitives derived "automatically" on the basis of dyadic structures like *clear*, as in (5); see (11a). And (10) is likewise identical in purely configurational respects to the structure assigned to location and locatum verbs like *shelve* and *saddle*; see (11b).

(11) a.

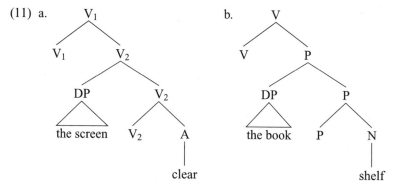

These structures take external subjects, of course. They are not complete, and they *must* take an external subject in sentential syntax. Why aren't these structures complete, the way (10) appears to be? In general, a verbal argument structure is complete (in relation to sentential syntax) if its apical V-node immediately dominates a specifier. While the dyadic subparts of (11a,b) are complete in this respect, the whole structures are not: the highest V does not immediately dominate a specifier.

So what is the fundamental difference between (11a,b) and (10)? Configurationally, at least, they share the property that the apical V-node does not immediately dominate a specifier. Yet the first, being incomplete, accepts an external subject, while the second behaves as if it were complete, rejecting an external subject. In this respect, verbs putatively assigned the structure in (10) exhibit canonical "unaccusative" behavior, like the simple unaccusatives having the structure depicted in (5). The essential observational generalization about these "*there*-insertion unaccusatives" is that their sentential syntactic surface subject is linked to an internal position, either the specifier of the P-projection or the P-projection itself; in the latter case, the surface requirement is fulfilled by the "proxy" expletive element *there*. The same generalization holds of simple unaccusatives like *clear* and *break*, of course, but with the difference that here, the specifier is the sole internal source of the required sentential syntactic subject.

As suggested above, Case theory has a role to play here; at least, it is implicated in the context of the theory of Case briefly outlined above. But in order to show this, it is necessary to say something about how accusative Case is assigned, under the assumptions of the Case-binding theory.

Consider again the structures in (11), in which the dominant V locally c-commands the DP in the inner specifier position. This arrangement is one of the primary ones in which a verb is properly poised to assign Case to a DP, or to Case-bind it, in our terms. The verb in question delimits a small clause (by projecting it), and it locally c-commands the potential bindee (i.e., the specifier DP), since there is no closer head that also c-commands that argument. Hence, the dominant V in (11a,b) meets two of the requirements set out in (8). But if the verb is to Case-bind DP there, it must have within its governing domain a Case competitor, completing the essential set of requirements.

Most theories of Case attribute to certain nuclear categories (e.g., V, P) the ability to "assign Case." Moreover, assignment of structural Case is generally held to be a capacity that may be present or absent in a given head. In the Case-binding theory, the ability of a head to Case-bind an argument depends in part on the presence of an appropriately situated Case competitor. In an accusative language, like English, the verb is said to "assign" accusative Case—by Case-binding an argument that it locally c-commands. The Case-binding theory claims that the ability of a verb to Case-bind an argument is due to the presence, within the verb itself, of a nominal element that serves the function of Case competitor. Being a part of the abstract morphology of the verb, this element is often nonovert, as in English, where its presence is discernible only by virtue of its syntactic effect. But it is often overt, where it is realized in "object agreement" on the verb (see Bittner and Hale 1996b). In the typical accusative language, this V-borne Case competitor is categorially a determiner (D), hence pronominal in nature; and it is adjoined to the verbal head, as shown in (12), a modified version of (11a).

(12)

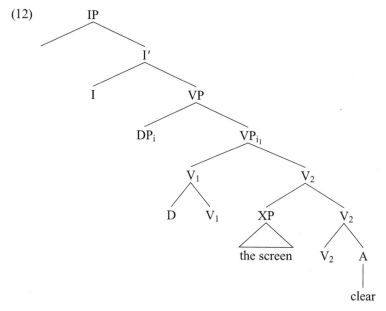

The relation of interest here is the one that holds between V_1 and XP. That verb projects, and therefore delimits, a small clause. It locally c-commands XP, a potential bindee, and it governs a Case competitor. The subject, DP_i, cannot be the Case competitor here, obviously, since that argument is beyond the governing domain of the verb. By assumption, it is the V-adjoined D that fulfills this role; that is the only other possibility. The upper verb, V_1, therefore Case-binds XP, the specifier projected by the inner verb in accordance with the basic lexical property of its complement, the adjective *clear*. It is the so-called accusative Case that is realized (overtly or covertly) on an argument in the structural position of XP in (12), in which the Case binder is a verb. In contrast, as mentioned earlier, the ergative Case is associated with an argument Case-bound by I.

We can return now to a consideration of the structure assigned to *there*-insertion unaccusatives like *arrive*. Let us begin with the structures assumed for them, as represented in (2) and (10). In those structures, there is a verb appropriately positioned to Case-bind an argument occupying an internal specifier position, exactly as in the case of (11a), the transitive configuration based on the simple unaccusative. But the *there*-insertion unaccusatives cannot transitivize, as shown earlier, because their sentential syntactic subjects must come from an internal position. This result is obtained if we simply assume that V in (13), modified from (12), lacks the

adjoined D that would otherwise function as a Case competitor and force
the verb to Case-bind the DP in the specifier position that it locally c-
commands.

(13)

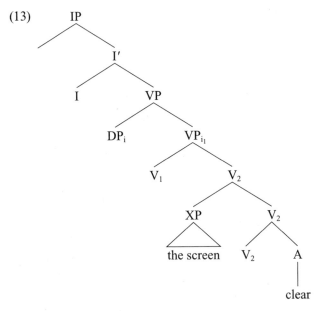

Since that DP is not Case-bound, it must "satisfy the Case Filter" by
moving to a position in which it is governed by a Caselike head, namely,
C. It accomplishes this by moving first to the external subject (distinguished adjunct) position, as shown (leaving a copy in its base position),
and then to the specifier of IP (not shown), where it is governed by C.

This "works," but it is unsatisfactory, since it fails to relate the apparent intransitivity of *there*-insertion unaccusatives to *there*-insertion itself.
We will attempt to make a connection. However, what we will suggest is
provisional and, at present, somewhat clumsy.

As noted, the V-adjoined D of (12) is sometimes overtly realized as
object agreement. Many languages have "locative" or "areal" agreement
in addition to conventional person and number agreement. Navajo is
such a language.

(14) a. Béégashii yish'į́.
       cow   3o.YPERF.1s.see.PERF
       'I see the cow.'

    b. Bikooh-góyaa   hweesh'į.
        arroyo-down.along AREALo.YPERF.1s.see.PERF
        'I see down along the arroyo.'

English is not normally thought of as having this type of agreement, but we would like to suggest that this is exactly what is involved in constructions based on the *there*-insertion unaccusatives. In place of the V-adjoined D, *there*-insertion unaccusatives have an adjoined locative determiner (L), as depicted in (15).

(15)

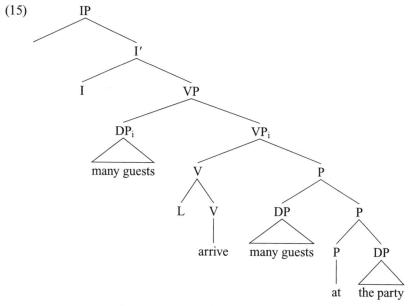

The adjoined L is not, strictly speaking, nominal, belonging to the category normally associated with the extended projection of P, rather than of N. If this is true, then V in (15) cannot Case-bind the DP it locally c-commands. This circumstance permits—and, other things being equal, forces—that DP to raise in order to satisfy its Case requirements, giving (1a).

    As noted, however, another alternative is available—namely, the *there*-insertion structure itself, as in (1b). We take the V-adjoined L to be construed with the complement of the verb, that is, with the P-projection. This is consistent with the notion that it is locative, or areal, agreement. *There*-insertion, however it is actually achieved, is quite possibly a mechanism whereby the P-projection can be "represented" in subject position.

Let us assume that *there*-insertion involves insertion of *there* in subject position and coindexation of *there* with the V-adjoined L. The latter is, of course, coindexed with P by virtue of agreement. Accordingly, the proposed structure for (1b) is as shown in (16).

(16)

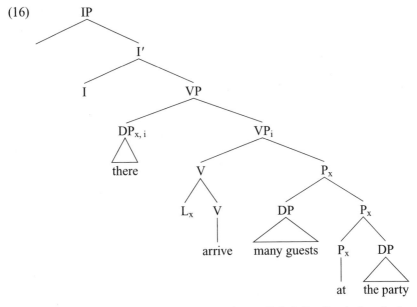

The subject, *there*, is an expletive heading a "chain" of coindexed elements whose foot is P. Ultimately, it raises to the specifier of IP, where its Case requirements are presumably met through its proximity to C.

But how is the DP in the specifier of P licensed? We think it is licensed by the same governing head, namely, C. The Case-binding theory recognizes two types of languages within each of the two large classes belonging to the typology of Case. Both ergative and accusative languages can be classified as either transparent or raising. Transparent ergative languages, for example, are those in which the object (the absolutive, or nominative argument) is licensed in situ, unraised. These are the "morphologically" ergative languages, so called because the object does not give evidence of being in a prominent or high structural position. They are in the majority among ergative languages, evidently. In contrast, raising ergative languages are those in which the object must raise to satisfy the requirement that it be governed by a Caselike head. The difference depends on transparency to government: if IP and VP are barriers to government from C, then raising is necessary, as in Inuit and Dyirbal. If these categories are transparent (i.e., do not function as barriers), then raising is not necessary (and precluded, presumably), as in Warlpiri, Mayan, and ergative Polynesian. The same division among languages is found in accusative languages: if IP is a barrier, raising of the nominative subject is required, as in English; if IP is transparent, the nominative subject is licensed in situ. One way in which transparency can be induced is by verb raising (V to I and then to C), creating, in effect, a composite head. This establishes a head-to-head dependency that effectively removes the barrierhood of the maximal projection of each head. Another circumstance that gives rise to transparency is the presence of an a priori dependency across maximal projections (see Bittner and Hale 1996b).

We suggest that the DP in the specifier of P in (16), and generally in structures of this type, is licensed in situ. It is governed by C by virtue of transparency. The transparency relation is established by *there*-insertion, which creates a chain extending from the specifier of IP to P. We assume that this removes the barrierhood of both IP and VP, at least for the purposes of licensing the argument in question—namely, DP in the specifier of P. This argument is, so to speak, parasitic on *there* for its Case requirements. Transparency also accounts for the agreement relation between I and DP.[2]

Chapter 7
Aspect and the Syntax of Argument Structure

7.1 Events and States

In this chapter, we deal briefly with questions of stativity. Our discussion is much more speculative here than elsewhere, because this is an area in which we feel somewhat insecure. We begin with a discussion of the category Adjective.

Adjectives pose an immediate problem for the framework assumed in Hale and Keyser 1993. This is the case, in particular, for adjectival nuclei that take just one argument—specifically, an argument that stands in the relation of specifier, not complement. The problem resides in the fact that the appropriate cooccurrence of the adjective and the specifier it requires cannot be effected by Merge. The creation of a syntactic constituent by merging DP and A(djective) results in the complementation configuration, putting the DP in the wrong relation to the adjectival nucleus. What is required is a configuration in which the DP occupies a position in which the adjective will be attributed, or predicated, of the DP—a relation that can be expressed notationally by coindexing DP and an appropriate projection of A. This is the essential adjectival requirement, and it can be satisfied in a configuration in which the DP is suitably close to the A-projection but is not a sister to the A-head. By *suitably close*, we mean that the specifier DP locally c-commands the relevant (whether maximum or intermediate) projection of the adjective and the latter is c-subjacent to the former (see Williams 1980).

The problem is resolved in the argument structure configurations of deadjectival verbs like *clear, narrow, redden, darken*. These are assumed here to have a structure like (1) in which a verbal head serves not only to project the verbal category (i.e., to "verbalize" the adjective) but also to host the specifier required by A (here a maximal projection, trivially).

(1)

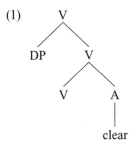

As usual, this diagram represents the properties of the heads involved. It is the "virtual" structure, not the actual "output": Merge applied to V and A results immediately in conflation, giving the verb *clear*, as in *The sky cleared*.

But what of the adjective when it appears to lack a host for the specifier it requires? Consider, for example, the structure of an adjectival small clause, of the type illustrated in (2).

(2) a. We found [the sky clear].
     b. We consider [our students brilliant].
     c. With [the sky clear], we can fly today.
     d. With [my clothes wet], Mom wouldn't let me in the house.

If *the sky* in (2a) is in a specifier position, what head projects that position? We have assumed that A itself does not merge directly with the phrase that satisfies its specifier requirement, since the resulting relation would be indistinguishable from that holding between a head and its complement, not the required relation here. And in (2) there is no other obvious candidate to host the specifier—a problem, on the face of it. The solution can be seen by considering the difference between conflation constructions like (1) and freestanding adjectival predicates like those in (2).

In the conflation construction, the adjectival component is an unprojected head—that is to say, a bare adjective. In the small clause construction, however, we assume that the freestanding adjective is the lexical head of an extended projection. In (2), it happens that no part of the extended projection is overt, since the adjective is in the absolute degree. In the examples in (3), however, elements of the extended projection are overt.

(3) a. We found [the sky so clear that it hurt our eyes].
     b. With [the sky clearer than glass], we can fly.
     c. We found [the sky as clear as glass].

It is the functional category defining the extended projection of A, we suggest, that projects the specifier position required to complete the licensing of the adjective. This is depicted abstractly in (4).

(4)

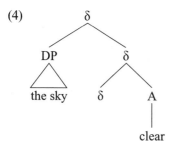

Among the elements that occur in the head position δ are Ø, the nonovert head of the absolute degree, exemplified in (2a), and -er, the affixal head of the comparative degree, exemplified in (3b); these both implicate conflation, eliminating the empty phonological matrices. Other members of the category δ presumably include *so, as, too, very.* The δ-projection exemplified in (4) appears as the complement of a verb in (2a,b) and as the complement of a preposition in (2c,d). In (5), it appears as the complement of raising predicates, including the copula.

(5) a. The sky seems [*t* clear].
    b. The sky is [*t* as clear (as glass)].
    c. The sky is [*t* clearer (than glass)].

The adjective conflates with the phonologically empty head in (5a) and in (5c), the empty matrix being associated with the comparative degree suffix *-er*.

The structures (1) and (4) share the property that they are dyadic; in both cases, the head projects two "argument positions," corresponding to the relations termed "complement" and "specifier."[1] There is an important difference between the two structures, a difference that resides in the nature of the head. While V and δ both select adjectival complements and DP specifiers of the same general sort (appropriate to the adjective), they differ consistently in stativity. The V-based structure is active (nonstative) and the δ-based structure is stative.

In this discussion, we will be concerned in large part with the question of stativity, and with its "source" and proper representation in the grammar. We will take a number of detours, however, in order to discuss structural matters that come up. We begin by considering the possibility that stativity correlates with lexical category or part of speech.

7.2 Stativity and Category

It is not unreasonable to ask whether it is a general principle that verbs project structures associated with an active (nonstative) interpretation while other categories project structures associated with a stative interpretation. In some languages, such as Warlpiri, this is true without exception. But it is of course well known that, in a great many other languages, including English, there are verbs that are stative according to standard tests (the progressive, imperative, telicity, etc.). Subject-experiencer psych verbs are generally classed as stative (examples taken from Tenny 1994, 65).

(6) a. John feared the truth.
    b. John knew the truth.
    c. John admired the truth.
    d. John liked the truth.
    e. John respected the truth.

What accounts for the stativity of these verbs? One possibility is that they involve the dyadic structure projected by the category P—specifically, the covert P of central coincidence—like that found in locatum verbs such as *saddle, hobble, clothe.* Accordingly, these verbs would have paraphrases involving *give,* as in *John gave the truth his respect,* or, more accurately, *John got the truth (to be) with his respect,* where *with* corresponds to the overt possessive preposition, a prototypical preposition of central coincidence, also illustrated in secondary predicates like *with gifts,* as in *They came with gifts.* Of course, the preposition putatively implicated in (6) is empty and nonovert, and it necessarily conflates with its complement. Under these assumptions, the dyadic structure underlying the verb phrases of (6) is as shown in (7) (using *respect the truth* to illustrate).

(7)

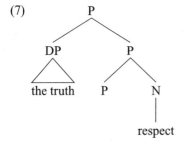

As usual, the structure depicted in (7) abstracts away from conflation, according to which the phonological matrix of the noun *respect* is spelled out in P.

If (7) is projected by a central coincidence P, we can assume it is inherently stative, like any small clause based on central coincidence P, as in *We found [him with money]* (i.e., *in possession of money*), *We found the [horse saddled]*.[2] The stative uses of subject-experiencer verbs correspond structurally to certain expressions based on the structural head realized by the verb *have*, which is also stative.[3]

(8) a. Mary has my respect.
       (cf. I respect Mary.)
    b. She has the boss's esteem.
       (cf. The boss esteems her.)
    c. He has his children's love.
       (cf. His children love him.)
    d. Cowboys have my envy.
       (cf. I envy cowboys.)
    e. Leecil has our admiration.
       (cf. We admire Leecil.)

The structural correlation is this, taking (8a) as the model and comparing it with (7). The subject of the *have*-construction (here, *Mary*) corresponds to DP in (7), and the object of *have*, (here, *my respect*) corresponds to N, the complement of P; *have* itself corresponds to P. In essence, then, the predicates in (8) are structurally identical to (7). The differences between them are matters of realization and selection: (7) is headed by an empty P, whose complement is a bare N, while the predicates of (8) are headed by an overt, morphologically verbal element *have*, whose complement is a full DP, specifically a possessive construction linked to the external subject.

We will resume this structural comparison at a later point. For the present, let us return to the issue of stativity. We ask whether the suggested categorial affiliation of the head of (7) could be the source of the stativity of the verb phrases of (6). This would be in line with the proposal that nonverbs head stative projections.

The usual fate of a P-headed structure like (7) is to enter into construction with another category, as when it appears as the complement of the lexically monadic V-head, as shown in (9).

(9)

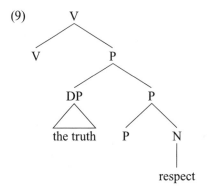

respect

This is a verbal construction, of course, and by hypothesis should be nonstative. And we think this is true, in fact. That is to say, subject-experiencer psych verbs like *respect, love, like,* and *hate* are "ambiguous": they can occur in the imperative and the progressive, and in contexts akin to those commonly used in typing nonstative verbs.

(10) a. Respect your parents.
     b. He is liking his new job.
     c. The troops respected their new commander in minutes.

Often, to be sure, some invention must be employed to show these verbs in canonical nonstative environments, perhaps because their characteristic, unmarked use is as statives. But we maintain that the usage exemplified in (10) is real and must be accounted for, as it is under the assumption that these verbs can in fact enter into the construction presented in (9), essentially the structure of locatum verbs.

If the stative predicates of the *have*-constructions of (8) are structural paraphrases of (7), then the *give*-construction predicates seen in the slightly stilted (11a–c) are structural paraphrases of (9).

(11) a. I give my respect to Mary.
     b. The boss gives her his esteem.
     c. His children give him their love.

Here again, the difference is one of realization and selection: the head is overt in (11), nonovert in (9), and the complement in (11) is a possessive DP linked to the external argument.

However, if (9) accounts for the nonstative use of subject-experiencer psych verbs, what accounts for their allegedly more fundamental stative use, as in (6)? On the view that the stative counterparts are lexically nonverbal, a rather natural suggestion can be made. The head of (7), as given, is nonverbal; it is P, by hypothesis. By contrast, the head of (9) is verbal. Of course, the two are homophonous, taking the form *respect*. But this follows from the fact that both result from "conflation" of the same bare nominal *respect*. This gives overt phonological form to P, yielding the P-based predicator *respect*. The same nominal root gives phonological form to V in (9), deriving the verbal variant of *respect* exemplified by (10a).

If the distinction between stative and nonstative subject-experiencer predicators like *respect, love,* and *fear* can be attributed to lexical category (V, P, etc.), then the suggestion we are entertaining now could in principle resolve the problem of stativity: statives are P-based, nonstatives are V-based. There is another part of the problem, however. The stative is just as much a "verb," in the traditional sense, as the nonstative is. That is to say, contrary to what is expressed in (7), the stative variant of *respect* assumes the same commanding position that its V-based active homophone does. And like the latter, the stative variant enters into the same inflectional relations (e.g., tense inflections) as the nonstative, unquestionably verbal variant does.

One possibility is that the P of (7), while not itself verbal, must inflect with verbal morphology—in violation, to be sure, of the principles that generally hold in extended projections. If this morphological eccentricity were in fact a property of P in (7), then its satisfaction would require P (with conflated N) to be raised to a position from which it c-commands its original position and those of its arguments. For the present, let us suppose that P raises and merges with its own maximal projection, as shown informally in (12).

(12)

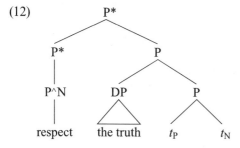

Assuming that this is a legitimate structure, it has the desired characteristics.[4] It not only brings P (P*) into its observed S-Structure position, but also places it in a position where it can assign Case to the specifier DP, as required. The alternative of having P raise straightforwardly to the functional head T is not tenable, we think, since alleged P raises in the absence of T in causative constructions of the type represented by (13a,b) and to the proximity of a functional head, without adjoining to it, as in the infinitive illustrated by (13c,d).[5]

(13) a. That made John respect the truth.
　　b. We had John learn Spanish.
　　c. That'll teach John to always respect the truth.
　　d. We forced John to learn Spanish.

Thus, the motivation for the putative P-raising in (12) is not straightforward. It is not simply the case that P in the stative constructions at issue "needs" verbal inflection. Rather, we think, the putative P here has the verblike property that it must head a predication to which a "t-value" is assigned. This requires that this P, like a verb, be situated in a certain structural position. Specifically, it must head a predicate, and it must itself be c-subjacent to a head that sets the t-value of the predicate: for example, T itself, assigning a "tense" in the traditional sense; the infinitive *to*, involved in assigning a dependent or relative tense; or a causative predicator, like *make*, which likewise assigns a dependent tense to its complement (by contrast to verbs of the type represented by *expect*, which assigns no t-value, as is evident from such examples as *We expect John learn Spanish*).

This analysis purports to account for the stative readings of certain subject-experiencer verbs by attributing their stativity to the lexical category of their heads. By implication, it is imagined that the whole business of stativity might be explained in terms of category: to put it simply, verbs are active, nonverbs are stative. Before taking up this issue in more detail, we need to consider certain problems and consequences related to the basic structural relations involved in this proposal.

First, the subject of subject-experiencer verbs is evidently an external argument. Thus, verbs of the type *respect* and *envy* cannot "freely" transitivize (or rather, further transitivize), in the manner of verbs like *break* and *clear*.

(14) a. *That respects John the truth.
　　　　(... makes John respect the truth.)
　　b. *That envies me his talent.
　　　　(... makes me envy his talent.)

This follows straightforwardly in the V-headed structure, (9), assigned to alleged active variants of these verbs, assuming that the verbal head is of the unmarked type for that category (i.e., the type that projects no specifier). We must assume that the same is true of the P-head in (12). But the category P is prototypically dyadic, necessarily projecting a specifier. Hence, transitivization—for example, insertion of (12) into the complement of the canonical verbal configuration—should be freely possible, leaving (14) unexplained. Persisting for the present with the idea that the head of (12) is categorially P, we appeal to the fact that the raised P (P*) is the head of a chain and hence the member of a single lexical item whose properties are satisfied in the projection initiated at the tail of the chain, that is, at the point of first Merge. On this assumption, (12) presents no upper specifier and, hence, cannot automatically transitivize. As in the putative active variant, in the stative variant the subject-experiencer is an external argument.[6]

While this account is not really a satisfactory solution to the problem of transitivization, it is workable and appeals to an established principle— the uniqueness principle inherent in the theory of argument structure relations, restricting a given lexical head to at most one complement and one specifier—and it therefore accounts for the fact that (12) must lack an upper specifier.[7] But by assigning to stative subject-experiencer psych verbs the representation in (12), we have forced the issue, claiming that their stativity is a matter of category, with V nonstative and P stative. But this is an artifice, a trick designed to make category and stativity coincide. Moreover, we have not investigated the consequences of the kind of head movement invented here to derive the structural configuration in (12), and we have probably violated the principles underlying the relations involved in the extended projections that define sentential syntactic constructions, principles strongly suggested by our intuition that the very definition of the category V is the morphological one according to which a verb takes tense and aspectual morphology.[8] See chapter 2 for discussion of the structural and semantic properties of psych predicates, and of predicates isomorphic with them. There, we consider these predicates' variable behavior with respect to the English middle construction and show that it is not to be related to stativity directly but to another factor: specifically, an opposition having to do with *obviation* in the anaphoric binding relations involving semantic manner and means features inherent to specific lexical root elements.

7.3   True Stative Verbs

To say that subject-experiencer verbs of the kind exemplified in (6) (*feared, knew, admired, liked, respected*) are stative is probably inaccurate. This is suggested both by the fact that they are open to nonstative interpretations in appropriate contexts and by the findings documented in a rich body of literature on aspect that demonstrates copiously that stativity, telicity, and the aspectual classes (activities, accomplishments, achievements) pertain not to verbs but to the predicates they head (see Dowty 1979; Tenny 1987, 1994). It would be reasonable to entertain the possibility that these notions, and stativity in particular, are never features of individual lexical items—for example, of verbs, nouns, adjectives, adpositions, . . .—but features of whole predicates.

But this does not seem altogether satisfactory either, for some heads are entirely consistent in their behavior in relation to so-called stativity. For example, the functional head (covert or overt) defining the extended projection of the category A is consistently stative. Thus, while the verb phrase *turn greener* is nonstative, this is a property of the verb phrase headed by *turn*; the adjectival extended projection headed by *-er* (putative category δ) is itself "stative" (as it is in (3b) and (5c)), a property evidently attributable to the functional head.

The category V is not entirely left out here, since some verbs head predicates that are "classically stative."

(15) a. That house costs fifty thousand dollars.
     b. This bull weighs one ton.
     c. Two and two equals/makes four.
     d. Three books comprise the entire collection.

These are stative in much the same way copular sentences with *be* are stative.

(16) a. That house is fifty thousand dollars, if you are interested.
     b. This bull is one ton in weight.
     c. Two and two is four.
     d. These three books are the entire collection.

Furthermore, if we take the position that the verbs of (15) are in reality copulas, sharing certain essential properties with the copula *be*, then their most renowned property can be explained—namely, their failure to participate in the passive construction.[9]

(17) a. *Fifty thousand dollars is/are cost by that house.
   b. *One ton is weighed by this bull.
   c. *Four is equaled/made by two and two.
   d. *The entire collection is comprised by three books.

Suppose that the verbs of (15) are copulas, in fact, differing from *be* by virtue of their lexical (as opposed to functional) status and correspondingly richer semantic content, sometimes paraphrasable by means of a prepositional modifier, as in (18a,b).

(18) a. That house is fifty thousand dollars in cost.
   b. That bull is one ton in weight.

Under this interpretation, the verbs of (15) do not select an object complement; instead, they select a predicate, as pointed out often in the literature on these topics. Thus, while the expression *fifty thousand dollars* is a standard (plural) object DP in the passivizable (19a), it is a predicate in the unpassivizable (19c) (cf. (15a) and (17a)).

(19) a. The counterfeiter printed fifty thousand dollars.
   b. Fifty thousand dollars were printed by the counterfeiter.
   c. That house costs fifty thousand dollars.

If this suggestion is correct, then the unpassivizability of the verbs of (15) follows. The measure phrases appearing in those sentences are predicates there, albeit nominal in category; and if they are assigned Case at all, it is not the accusative Case ordinarily assigned by a verb but some other Case, perhaps the nominative, assigned "across the copula." Thus, the sentences of (15) simply do not have the properties of sentences that participate in the standard active-passive voice alternation. This is consistent, incidentally, with the well-known fact that the measure phrase in (20) does not require *of*-insertion.

(20) That house is worth (*of) fifty thousand dollars.

The lexical head that projects the clause in this case—*worth*—is nominal in category, requiring support by the auxiliary *be*, as expected. But it is syntactically a copula, and its structural complement, the measure phrase, is a predicate and not the sort of complement that is expected to be Case-marked by the head that selects it. Hence, *of*-insertion (which is otherwise required, as in *the worth of her suggestion*) is not applicable.

Although the details are far from clear, it is possible that a similar analysis is appropriate to another class of verbs that fail to passivize (see Perlmutter and Postal 1984, 92).

(21) a. This trailer sleeps (up to) three (gorillas).

b. This couch seats (up to) four (people).

Here again, the complement is a measure phrase of sorts, a capacity phrase. It is possible that the proper conception of this construction is one according to which *(up to) three (gorillas)* and *(up to) four (people)* are measure predicates, as suggested for the measure phrases in the putative copular constructions of (15); if so, the passive is expected to be inapplicable. Verbs like *hold (three gallons)* and *contain (five books)* share the property of nonpassivizability with the verbs of (21), possibly for the same reason. A copular paraphrase in these cases, while generally awkward and difficult to contrive, is sometimes weakly possible, as in *This can is three gallons (in capacity)*.

Let us return to the matter of stativity, which has again drifted away as something that seems essentially beside the point. It appears to be true, however, that the verbs in (15), in the "copular" use we have alleged for them, are genuinely stative. The question is, then, to what is this to be attributed? It is probably true that virtually any verb can be used to denote an eventuality that is a state. But in (15), something else is going on. The verbs of (15) are stative because they are copulas, and copulas are essentially stative. Why are copulas stative, if that is so? And why is *be* in (22a) inherently stative and a legitimate copula, while *turn* in (22b) is not a copula and only derivatively stative (if at all), given that the two evidently select identical complements (here, *yellow*)?

(22) a. The leaves are yellow.

b. The leaves are turning/have turned yellow.

7.4   Stativity as a Feature Relation

If the copula is inherently stative, then it is reasonable to ask whether other syntactic heads have this property as well. The hypothetical category δ is also stative, in the generally accepted sense. So the answer is affirmative: different syntactic heads can share the property of consistently projecting a stative predicate. But is this an autonomous property? Or, as we asked in the beginning, is this a matter of category—true verbs are variable in stativity, while other categories are steadfastly stative, copulas falling outside the class of "true verbs," despite their fully verbal extended projection?

The idea that stativity is a matter of category, pure and simple, is belied by the copula. To say that the copula, where that is understood to include verbs like *cost* and *weigh*, is not a verb flies in the face of conventional understanding of the parts of speech of English. Thus, if stativity is a property at all, it is evidently autonomous. Now, consider the behavior of the category P, in the small clause construction.

(23) a. With Annan in Baghdad, we can relax.
  b. With Kirsten at Lincoln Center, ballet remains supreme.

(24) a. *With Annan to Baghdad, we can relax.
  b. *With Kirsten from Lincoln Center, New York will boycott the ballet.
  c. *With Annan go to Baghdad, we can relax.

The prepositions in (23), like the putative δ in (12), project a predication that is evidently stative. At least, it is stative in the same sense that small clauses appearing in this construction generally seem to be. Verbal small clauses are clearly impossible here, as shown in (24c), though this is not in and of itself relevant, since *all* verbs are precluded, regardless of their relation to stativity—that is, *bare* verbs are precluded; not gerunds, which are stative and therefore allowed. It is trivially true, therefore, that eventive predicates projected by bare verbs are precluded in the *with*-construction.

The category P, however, is not uniform in relation to this construction. The instances of P in (23) project small clauses that are perfectly possible there, while those in (24a,b) do not. Some prepositions, such as *in* and *on*, are permitted on one reading, but not on another.

(25) a. With Father Jim in the room, we have to watch our language.
   (≠With Father Jim entering the room,...)
  b. With Clint on his horse, all's right with the world.
   (≠With Clint getting on his horse,...)

The plain prepositions *in* and *on* can express a relation in which the argument in specifier position (i.e., derived S-Structure subject) corresponds to an entity that moves or is arrayed along a path ending at the place denoted by the complement, like the related prepositions *into* and *onto*.

(26) a. Frankie walked in(to) the room.
  b. Clint got on(to) his horse.

But this is not the reading that comes through in the *with*-construction exemplified in (25). Instead, in those examples, the understanding is that the location of the entity denoted by the specifier in the P-projection coincides in a certain sense with the place denoted by the complement.

The opposition that emerges in (23) and (24) appears to be rather pervasive in the lexical and functional systems of the grammars of natural languages. It is probably to be identified with the well-known telicity opposition, and with the *central* and *terminal coincidence* opposition to which we have referred on occasion (see Hale 1986). The prepositions of (23) project the dyadic structure in (27) characteristic of the lexical category P.

(27)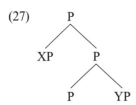

The prepositions that project dyadic structures compatible with the *with*-construction of (23) share the property of expressing the relation of central coincidence, holding between the figure (specifier) and the place (complement). Those that cannot appear in that construction express the relation we have labeled "terminal coincidence." The various manifestations of this fundamental opposition are well known by a variety of names, including *stasis* and *change*. We employ the terminology of "coincidence" here to reflect the dyadic nature of the relations. In any event, we suspect that this opposition is a true reflection of inherent properties— relevant to the notion traditionally referred to as "stativity"—in certain lexical and functional heads that project dyadic structures in syntax. Central coincidence consistently corresponds to stativity. Terminal coincidence, on the other hand, corresponds to change and therefore to the various active, dynamic, and otherwise nonstative event types.

If participation in the coincidence opposition is indeed a fundamental property of certain syntactic heads, and if stativity is identified with central coincidence, then it is very probable that this identification is the *only* way in which stativity is attributable to a *head*, as opposed to a *construction* (as in structures projected by the subject-experiencer verbs; see chapter 2).

Let us assume that this is correct. Then which categories participate in the opposition? In particular, which heads are associated with central coincidence, and to that extent, with stativity?

We have suggested three nuclear types that are inherently stative in this sense: (i) the head that defines the extended projection of A (i.e., the category δ, as in (2) and (3)); (ii) a subclass of the category P (e.g., *in*, *at*, as in (23a,b)); (iii) the copula, morphologically a subclass of V (e.g., *cost*, *weigh*, as in (15)).

The first of these can be illustrated by means of the small clause in (2a), repeated here as (28), with the structural representation in (29).

(28) We found [the sky clear].

(29)

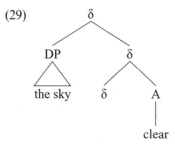

This is claimed to involve central coincidence because its specifier, *the sky*, corresponds to an entity that possesses the attribute denoted by the complement, namely, the adjective *clear*. That is to say, the relation between the specifier and the complement is not one of change. The entity denoted by the specifier possesses the attribute. It does not come to have the attribute, or come to lack the attribute; rather, the entity and the attribute coincide to define a set whose members are at once *the sky* and *clear*. Contrast (29) with (31), corresponding to the inchoative—terminal coincidence, hence nonstative—sentence in (30).

(30) The sky cleared.

(31)

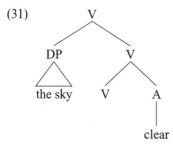

The dyadic head V, like the majority of verbs, has the property of projecting a structure expressing the terminal coincidence relation. The entity denoted by the specifier undergoes a change whose end point is possession of the attribute denoted by the complement.

Central coincidence prepositions, like *in* in (23a), repeated here as (32), project a wide variety of structures showing a correspondingly wide range of interpretations. In this case, the preposition is used to express its customary locational sense and function.

(32) With [Annan in Baghdad], we can relax.

(33)

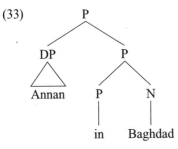

The entity denoted by the specifier, *Annan*, coincides with the location denoted by the complement, *Baghdad*. Here again, no change is expressed in the small clause (33). Rather, the preposition identifies the location of the entity denoted by the specifier with the place denoted by the complement: the two locations coincide centrally, not terminally, insofar as that is physically possible. By contrast, in *They led Annan into Baghdad*, the preposition expresses terminal coincidence (the place, Baghdad, being the *terminus ad quem*).

Turning now to the stative copula, we believe that central coincidence is what defines that category of verbs. In a predication of the type represented by (34), employing the prototypical copula *be*, the property denoted by the syntactic complement, the predicate nominal *a calf roper*, is attributed to the entity denoted by the subject.

(34) Leecil is a calf roper.

This is central coincidence: the property (*a calf roper*) coincides temporally and spatially with the entity (*Leecil*). In this respect, the copula *be* contrasts minimally with the nonstative, terminal coincidence verb *become*, which likewise relates a subject and a predicate and, to that extent, is a copula.

(35) Leecil became a calf roper.

In this case, the predicate nominal denotes a property that corresponds to the end point of a change undergone by the entity denoted by the subject—a relation comparable to that in (30), and unlike that in (32), which is to be compared rather with (34). The verbs *be* and *become*, in (34) and (35), constitute a minimal pair, so to speak, for the central versus terminal coincidence opposition.

We conclude that stativity is not itself a feature of heads. Rather, it is a property of constructions and arises in the semantic composition of meaningful elements. However, among the elements that contribute to a stative semantics is one that is attributable to syntactic heads. This is the semantic opposition just discussed, coincidence. Some heads must be identified with central coincidence. Among these are certain verbs. The stative copulas (e.g., *be, cost, weigh, equal*) are clearly members of this class. We leave open the question of how widely central coincidence is distributed among the rest of the verbal lexicon.

7.5   Stativity as a Structural Relation

We have suggested that there is a property of syntactic heads—specifically, the central value in the coincidence dimension—that is responsible for the stative interpretation of certain predicates. That is to say, central coincidence is the origin of stativity, in some cases at least. Let us assume that this is so, for the sake of argument. The question then becomes, what is the nature of this element? Is it a feature—say, [central], with values plus and minus—or is something else going on? It is hard to imagine this as a feature opposition, in the traditional sense, that is, as the presence or absence of some property. Suppose the feature is [central]; absence of a property "central" does not really make sense. Suppose the feature is [terminal]; "minus terminal" makes some sense (i.e., absence of movement to or from an end point), but only in relation to some other element, that is, a place (path or ground). The latter is fundamental. Thus, the simplest "events" involve a place. If a terminal relation is involved, it is in addition to the place. Thus, what we have called "terminal coincidence" is more complex than "central coincidence." If this relative complexity were expressed in structure, then central coincidence would involve a simple dyadic structure, like that defined by the projection of the preposition *in*, as in the bracketed small clause of (36), with structure (37).

(36) With [the baby in bed] we can relax.

(37)

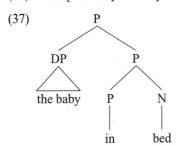

By contrast, as illustrated in (39), the terminal coincidence preposition *into* implicates a complex structure (as suggested, in this case, by the form of the preposition itself; see Jackendoff 1983).

(38) Getting [the baby into bed] is hard.

(39)

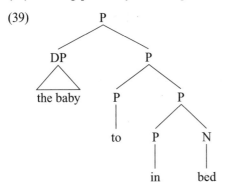

Some lexical items are characterized by containing P-projections belonging to one or the other of these two types. The pair in (40) exemplify intransitive verbs belonging to the central coincidence and terminal coincidence categories, respectively, with the structural representations shown in (41).

(40) a. Leecil stayed in Tucson.
     b. Leecil went to Tucson.

(41) a.

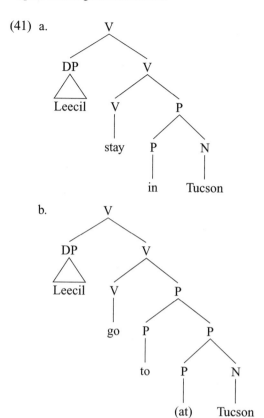

The verbs *stay* and *go* select the P-projections indicated. They do not themselves have the property of central or terminal coincidence. That property derives from the P-projections. Accordingly, the verbs are not necessarily stative. Any stativity that might adhere to these sentences is due to the P-projections, and it correlates with the central and terminal coincidence distinction inherent in the configurations. The simple P-projection (as in (41a)) corresponds to central coincidence, and the more complex structure (P within P, as in (41b)) corresponds to terminal coincidence.

Transitive counterparts to (40a,b) are (42a,b), with the structures shown in (43).

(42) a. We keep the calves in the corral.
 b. We put the calves in the corral.

(43) a.

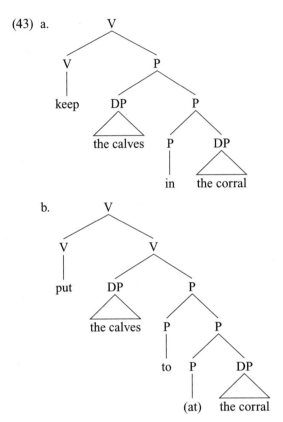

With these examples, we claim that a genuine opposition exists between two kinds of verbs, depending on the type of P-projection that appears in their lexical structures. A central coincidence verb is built upon a simple P-projection. By contrast, a terminal coincidence verb is built upon a complex P-projection, consisting of a P that takes a second P as its complement.

7.6   Concluding Remarks and Observations

What is the relationship between aspect and argument structure? The question makes sense, of course, if the terms are defined. We define argument structure as the system of structural relations holding between lexical heads (nuclei) and their arguments within the syntactic structures projected by nuclear items.

In general, we conclude that aspect is orthogonal to argument structure. Whenever we deal with questions of interface and interaction in this domain, we observe that argument structure is for the most part autonomous. Its properties and characteristics are strictly local, being defined in terms of the structural relations of complement and specifier. To be sure, any argument structure configuration associated with an actual predicate in sentential syntax will be interpreted in terms of one or another aspectual type (achievement, accomplishment, etc.) and its arguments will be associated with one or another aspectual role (measure, path, terminus, etc.; Tenny 1994). But argument structure is a distinct and separate component of grammar.

Chapter 8

On the Time of Merge

8.1 Introduction

In theory, apart from any empirical considerations, a prepositional projection like *on the wall* ([P [DP]]) could take its required specifier DP, for instance *mud*, immediately, as it appears to do in *The kids splashed mud on the wall*, or it could take it later, following the introduction of a verb, as in *We heard mud splash on the wall*. In both of these configurations ([*splash* [*mud* [*on the wall*]]] and [*mud* [*splash* [*on the wall*]]]), the specifier requirement of P is met, assuming that local c-command is the structural relation that must hold between the specifier and the P-projection. The relevant structural relation is between phrases, exemplified in this instance by *mud* and *on the wall*. The c-command relation is local here because no other phrase intervenes; it does not matter that a head (V) intervenes in the case of *mud splash on the wall*. Any number of heads can "intervene" in this sense, as will become clear momentarily.

The question that concerns us here is the point at which Merge operates in the composition of the relevant syntactic structures. In the first configuration mentioned above, Merge can be said to be effecting "immediate gratification" in relation to the specifier requirement of P; for the second configuration, the appropriate metaphor is "delayed gratification." So far as we can see, nothing precludes these alternatives in principle. Pretheoretically, on the other hand, they represent an embarrassment of riches, overgenerating far beyond the empirical base. They must be appropriately constrained and motivated. This is the purpose of the present chapter, in which two case studies are discussed: the grammar of particles and the grammar of the *spray/load* alternation.

8.2 Particles

In earlier work on the syntax of argument structure (e.g, Hale and Keyser 1993, 1999, 2000), we postponed discussion of one of the most interesting and characteristic grammatical phenomena of English, namely, verb and particle constructions of the type exemplified in (1).

(1) a. She put her saddle up on the fence.
    b. He put his tackle down on the ground.
    c. She put her saddle up.
    d. He set his tackle down.

Fortunately, there exists a study of particles, by Den Dikken (1995), which has many of the characteristics we take to be fundamental in a syntactic theory of argument structure. Here, we will consider some of the data and problems Den Dikken has discovered, with a view to determining how they bear on the issue of the operation of Merge in relation to the specifier requirement of lexical and functional heads.

We agree with Den Dikken and many others that particles of the type we are concerned with here are nuclear elements, heads, projecting structures of some sort. Consequently, we are compelled to ask what properties these heads have that determine the structures they project. To this end, let us consider first the particles in the shorter sentences (1c,d), the natural question being whether or not they are in some sense elliptical or possessed of a nonovert complement (e.g., a dropped or nonovert PP like those found in the longer sentences (1a,b)).

We conclude that the answer is at least in part negative, based on evidence suggesting that an empty category of an understood sort (e.g., the type associated with movement, i.e., a trace) cannot appear in the position corresponding to that of the complement of the particle. For example, the PP in (1a) is not an appropriate answer to (2).

(2) a. Where did she put her saddle up?
    b. On the fence.

The dialogue in (2) makes sense—for us, at least—only if *on the fence* is taken to refer to the location of the event as a whole, as in the more likely scenario in (3).

(3) a. Where did she put her saddle up?
    b. In the tack room.

The PP in (2b) cannot be taken to represent the "nonovert sister" of the particle in (2a). The same holds for the following dialogue:

(4) a. On which rack did she put her saddle up?
    b. On the farthest rack.

Again, there is an interpretation for (4a), but it is not one according to which the phrase *on which rack* heads a chain in which the trace occupies the position of the PPs in (1a,b). The question and the answer alike would only make sense if the agent were herself *on the farthest rack*, there *putting her saddle up*, on a peg, or the like. We assume, therefore, that the trace that appears in the acceptable readings of the (a)-sentences in (2)–(4) is not a complement of the particle. Thus, the structure in (5), where the hypothetical trace is indeed in the complement relation to the particle, is not possible.

(5) $[_\pi \; \pi \; t]$, π a particle

It follows then that the (a)-sentences in (2)–(4) are unambiguous, corresponding roughly to the paraphrase 'Where was she when . . .', and not to the sense in which the end point of the saddle is questioned—and therefore not to the sense in which the trace is, by hypothesis, in the structural position shown in (5). This issue is taken up by Den Dikken (1995), who proposes that π is not a fully lexical category and, unlike a true preposition, cannot license a trace. We will assume that this is the correct analysis, with one minor proviso. In the case of $\bar{\text{A}}$-movement traces, while true particles cannot be "stranded" through extraction, some occurrences of *up* and *down* are not true particles but full prepositions (P), hence "lexical" in Den Dikken's sense. These can strand in the familiar manner.

(6) a. Which road did Leecil run down?
    b. Which rope did the ants crawl up?

Though the category π is possibly a type of preposition, as suggested by Den Dikken, it is not lexical in the sense of a nuclear element capable of licensing a trace, and members of the category are not to be confused with homophonous fully lexical prepositions that exist in some cases.

It is tempting to assume further that this analysis extends to the bare particles of (1c,d); that is to say, there is no "hidden" PP complement following the particle, since such an empty category cannot be supported by π. However, a highly plausible alternative analysis is developed by Svenonius (1996), according to which a "bare" particle is in fact underlyingly "transitive," on the analogy of unergative denominal verbs. Its complement is "incorporated," or "conflated" with the particle, and is therefore nonovert. This implies that bare π actually *is* followed by an empty category, licensed through antecedent government in virtue of incorporation. The status of incorporation, or conflation, is somewhat questionable as a resource to account for denominal verbs, but a selection-based account of such verbs (see Hale and Keyser 2000), extended to bare π, would also posit an empty category in complement position. We will assume Svenonius's proposal for bare particles.

We agree with Den Dikken's thesis that particle constructions of the type represented in (1) are small clauses. For us, this means a particular thing, since "small clauses" are not an autonomous structural entity in our conception of syntactic configurations projected from the lexicon. A small clause, in our view, is defined in terms of the relations complement and specifier. This commits us to a certain structure for the particle constructions in (1).

Let us begin by considering the bare particle type exemplified in (1d), repeated here as (7a).

(7) a. He set his tackle down.
    b. He set his tackle right down.

The small clause of (7a) consists of the string *his tackle down*. Given Svenonius's proposal that bare particles have incorporated complements, abstractly, the "short" particle constructions of (7) and (1c,d) are syntactically homomorphic to the "long" versions in (1a,b). Both versions are head-complement constructions. The particle category π, like its prepositional cousin P, forces the projection of a specifier—directly, as in (8a), or by delayed gratification, as in (8b), where Den Dikken's modifier category is presented as an intervening head arbitrarily labeled μ.[1]

(8) a.

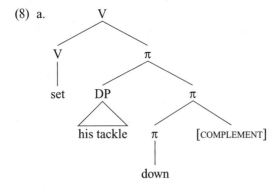

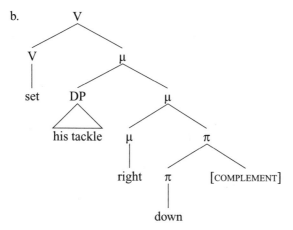

Returning to the longer sentences of (1), it is evident that the particles there (*up* and *down*) select a prepositional complement; this is what we must assume, given our view of syntactic configurations. The question we are concerned with is how the specifier is introduced into the structure. That is to say, which of the projections is the specifier combined with at Merge? It is clear from the surface form that the specifier combines with the π-projection, at least, as shown in the structure corresponding to the verb phrase of (1a), *put her saddle up on the fence.*

(9)

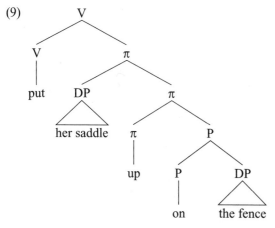

Here, the particle (π) selects the prepositional projection (P) as its complement. The construction as a whole requires a specifier (DP). If we maintain that (9) reflects the actual "history" of the applications of Merge in the derivation of the full π-construction, then we are adopting what we have termed the "delayed gratification" account of the satisfaction of P's requirement of a specifier; in short, we are saying that it is possible to wait until the π-projection to introduce the specifier required by P.

But there is another alternative, one similar in nature to the analysis proposed by Den Dikken. This is the "instant gratification" scenario shown in (10), according to which the specifier is introduced by Merge at the P-projection and then again, via Move, at the π-projection.

(10)

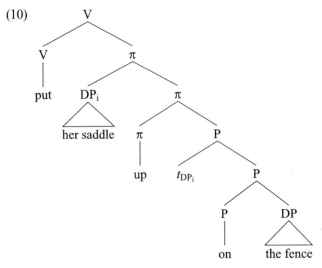

We maintain that the delayed gratification account in (9) is correct, and that the alternative in (10) is impossible. This conclusion would be inevitable if, for example, (9) were more economical than (10) and therefore preempted it. This is in fact what we assume.

There may be some empirical support for delayed gratification. Consider the following pairs:

(11) a. She put her saddle up on the fence.
     b. *She put up her saddle on the fence.

(12) a. He threw the cat down into the well.
     b. *He threw down the cat into the well.

The ungrammaticality of the (b)-sentences here would follow from the delayed gratification account, where the structure underlying these sentences is not possible. Whether this is truly relevant depends on a more general understanding of particles, however. If particles themselves require specifiers, then that requirement would also account for the (b)-sentences. So far as we can see, particles do not *in and of themselves* require specifiers. They are "defective," not only in the sense identified by Den Dikken, accounting for their inability to support an empty category in complement position, but also in the sense that they function only synergetically with their overt complements in the projection of specifiers.

The following data presented by Den Dikken (1995, 45, 54) are relevant:

(13) a. They made John out a liar.
      b. They made John out to be a liar.
      c. They made (*it) out that John is a liar.
      d. They find *(it) painful that John is a liar.

A predicate nominal, likewise an infinitival predicate, requires that a specifier be projected, as in (13a,b), where the particle projects the specifier. But a fully saturated structure, like the embedded CP of (13c), does not require—in fact, does not permit—that a specifier be projected. In this case, the particle *out* projects no specifier, rejecting even a proxy (*it*) construed with the embedded CP. This is in contrast to the situation represented by (13d), where proxy *it* is required in specifier position, for well-understood reasons: the adjective *painful* requires that a specifier be projected.

The particle *out* evidently cannot project a specifier, except synergetically, or parasitically. It cannot project a specifier on its own. If this property holds of all or most particles, it is an additional reflection of the idea that the category is less securely lexical than its prepositional cousin, a proposal Den Dikken (1995, 56) expresses in terms of L-marking.

(14) Particles are nonlexical prepositions, hence do not L-mark their complements.

The principle of delayed gratification, ruling out (11b) and (12b), will also account for the following contrasts (Den Dikken 1995, 55–56):

(15) a. They painted the barn up red.
      b. *They painted up the barn red.

(16) a. They made John out a liar.
      b. *They made out John a liar.

(17) a. They made John out to be a liar.
      b. *They made out John to be a liar.

An adjective forces the projection of a specifier, this being an essential property of the category. Delayed gratification ensures that (15a), but not (15b), will be generated. The same can be said of predicate nominals; the same logic rules out (16b).

In relation to (17b), and the (b)-sentences of (11) and (12) as well, there is some dispute. Den Dikken assigns (17b) a parenthetic question mark only, and he judges (18b) (his (52b)) as fully grammatical.

(18) a. They put the books down on the shelf.
     b. *They put down the books on the shelf.

As indicated, however, we think that (18b) is no better than the (b)-sentences of (11) and (12). However, we concur with his judgment of (19b) (his (53b)).

(19) a. They sent a schedule out to the stockholders.
     b. They sent out a schedule to the stockholders.

We have a disagreement about the data. For the moment, let us assume Den Dikken's judgments, in order to see how he accounts for them.

Consider the following set:

(20) a. *They made out John a liar.
     b. *They painted up the barn red.
     c. (*)They made out John to be a liar.
     d. (*)They put down the books on the shelf.

Den Dikken appeals to (14) to account for the ungrammaticality of (20a,b). The particle is "insufficiently lexical" to L-mark the specifier of the P-projection. And assuming that the maximal projection of P is a barrier, the verb cannot assign Case to *John* and *the barn*. On the other hand, (20c,d) are permitted, on his account, by virtue of the particle's defective-P status, according to which the particle is attached to P in a manner indistinguishable from that of an adjunct, so that the node dominating it is a "segment" of P, not a maximal projection. The verb can therefore assign Case to the specifier of P, as usual in an exceptional Case-marking configuration. The infinitival predicate of (20c) is assimilated to this analysis on the view that *to* is categorially a preposition (Den Dikken 1995, 60).

This is an interesting idea, but we believe it will not hold up, because (20c,d) are—for us, at least—ungrammatical, as expected under the delayed gratification account. However, there is a problem for our account as well: (19b) is perfectly grammatical. This is rather puzzling, because the stringwise similar (11b) and (12b) are impossible, for us.

The problem, we believe, is that there is an interpretation of (19b) that belongs to another class of structures, exemplified in (21).

(21) a. He wrote out a poem for his class.
     b. They sent out a message for decoding.
     c. They laid out a trousseau for the bride.
     d. They put out a schedule for the stockholders.

We do not know exactly what the structure of these examples is, but we doubt that the particle here takes the PP as a complement, and we will assume that the latter is an adjunct, not a complement. The ordering of the particle and the following DP in (21) is to be understood, we believe, in terms of the well-known alternation shown in (22).

(22) a. i. He sent a message out.
        ii. He sent out a message.
     b. i. They laid the trousseau out.
        ii. They laid out the trousseau.
     c. i. They put a schedule out.
        ii. They put out a schedule.

We contend that these are not relevant to the issues we have been discussing. It is very possible that they represent a true linearization rule, subject to certain morphophonological constraints.[2] Interestingly, if the conditions are right, the particles of (11)–(12) can participate in this alternation.

(23) a. i. She put her rigging up.
        ii. She put up her rigging.
     b. i. He set his tackle down.
        ii. He set down his tackle.

In general, it appears, the particle-before-DP order is not possible if the particle has an overt true complement, suggesting that the PP constituents in (21) are not complements of the particles. And we would claim further that the PP constituent in the relevant structure of (19) is also not a complement of the particle. The following comparison is relevant:

(24) a. To which stockholders did they send out the schedule?
     b. *Into which well did he throw down the money?

(24b) is impossible for the reasons we have suggested. The DP *the money*, by delayed gratification, must appear in the specifier position projected by the particle, leaving no way to derive this sentence; and extraction of the complement PP is impossible, in any event, for the reason given earlier. (24a) is permitted (i) by virtue of the linearization alternation exemplified in (22)–(23), and (ii) by the extractability of adjoined PP, as in sentences like these:

(25) a. i. For whom did they lay out a trousseau?
     ii. For whom did they lay a trousseau out?
  b. i. With which recipe did he conjure up those demons?
     ii. With which recipe did he conjure those demons up?
  c. i. In which room did they put up decorations?
     ii. In which room did they put decorations up?

If the extracted prepositional phrases in (25) are adverbial adjuncts, and not complements, then the variable positioning of the particles is to be expected, on the assumption that the linearization alternation corresponds to a rule of "transportation" (see Keyser 1968) inverting the order specifier-particle under appropriate conditions, including the condition that the particle not have an overt complement. This process of particle transportation may also apply, of course, when the adverbial PP is not extracted.

(26) a. i. They laid out a trousseau for the bride.
     ii. They laid a trousseau out for the bride.
  b. i. He conjured up those demons with a new recipe.
     ii. He conjured those demons up with a new recipe.
  c. i. They put up decorations in the kids' room.
     ii. They put decorations up in the kids' room.

A formal account of transportation must take several things into account. First, as a number of our examples have already shown, a particle cannot front leaving an overt complement behind, as in (11b) and (12b), repeated here in (27) and (28).

(27) *She put up her saddle on the fence.

(28) *He threw down the cat into the well.

To be sure, these are partially accounted for by the principle that Merge takes place in conformity with delayed gratification (where possible). But they are not entirely accounted for by that principle; if there is an independent process of particle transportation, inverting the particle and the inner specifier (*her saddle, the cat*), what prevents it from taking place here? Setting this problem aside momentarily, and considering the cases in which particle transportation can indeed take place, we need to account for the following contrast noted by Svenonius (1996):

(29) a. The doorman threw the drunks out.
     b. The doorman threw out the drunks.

(30) a. The fans considered the runner out.
     b. *The fans considered out the runner.

Svenonius argues that a special selectional relation (Pesetsky's (1995) l-selection) holds between the verb and the particle in (29). He proposes further that l-selection is a condition on particle shift, and that it is not met in (30); hence the ungrammaticality of (30b). We adopt Svenonius's view in part, and we argue that the relevant selectional relation is not between the verb and the particle alone, but between the verb and the substructure composed by the particle and its complement. And it is this substructure, not the particle alone, that is attracted to the verb in particle transportation. There is in addition an independent and well-known "weight requirement" according to which a particle together with its complement may attract to the verb only if the combination comprises a single word. With these assumptions, together with Svenonius's proposal that bare particles involve abstract incorporation of their complements, it is possible to account for the ill-formedness of (27)–(28) and (30b). The former are ruled out by the requirement that the particle front with its complement, the latter by the fact that the verb *consider* does not l-select a particle in this, or possibly any other, construction.

Svenonius has developed an analysis in which it is unnecessary to appeal to any sort of weight condition on particle transportation. A particle that moves to the left is attracted there by a certain feature F that needs to be checked by a nominal element. This will succeed if the particle carries the required nominal element. This will in turn be the case if the particle has incorporated its complement, a nominal. From this, the rest follows. Stranding of an overt complement will be impossible, and the leftward movement will take place only if the particle carries with it a nominal element and is therefore able to check F.

We are not able to adopt this part of Svenonius's analysis since we do not posit a nuclear item bearing the attracting feature F. We think, however, that the l-selection requirement is sufficient to account for the observed phenomena. In a pair like (31a,b), it is clear why particle transportation fails.

(31) a. Leecil threw his bullrope down on the ground.
     b. *Leecil threw down his bullrope on the ground.

Particle transportation is not possible here because the verb *throw* does not l-select the particle and its complement. The complement here is entirely free. We are assuming, of course, that we are correct in requiring that the *complement* of the particle enter into the l-selection relation with the verb. It seems to us obvious that adpositions, for example, and even more so the category π, can be "transparent," permitting a verb to select their complements (see Hale and Keyser 2000). To repeat, there is no l-selection here, in the original sense of selection of a particular or "listed" lexical item. Consequently, (31b) is not possible. However, in (32), the particle, together with its abstract incorporated complement (as in Svenonius 1996), does count as a listed, hence l-selected, item: the abstract complement belongs to the prototypical l-selected category, since it is the single member of the set to which it belongs.

(32) a. Leecil threw his bullrope down.
     b. Leecil threw down his bullrope.

It is perhaps appropriate to mention that both l-selection and standard π-selection imply a certain relationship to the verb, affecting certain morphological possibilities. Consider the following sentences:

(33) a. They set the tortoises free.
     b. They set free the tortoises.
     c. *They reset the tortoises free.
     d. *They reset free the tortoises.

(34) a. They painted the barn red.
     b. They repainted the barn red.
     c. *They painted red the barn.

In (33), the verb *set* and the "(deadjectival) particle" *free* are in an l-selection relation with the verb; the verb l-selects the particle.[3] In (34), by contrast, the adjective is not l-selected by the verb. The difference is reflected not only by the transportation possibilities (*free* can shift, *red* cannot) but also in the use of the prefix *re-*. Following Keyser and Roeper (1992), we might suggest that attraction of a particle depends upon the availability of a "clitic position" into which the particle can "fit." In

(33c,d), this position is filled by *re-*; hence, particle transportation is not possible. This idea might be extended to account for the apparent optionality of particle transportation. The proposal would be that particle transportation is obligatory: in (33a), it applies at LF; and in (33b), it applies in syntax, its result being visible at Spell-Out. The ill-formedness of (34c) follows, of course, from the fact that the l-selection requirement is not met.

This effect is not limited to l-selected elements, as can be seen from the following case, in which, by hypothesis, the complement of the particle is not l-selected:

(35) a. *He rethrew his bullrope down on the ground.
     b. *They repainted the barn up red.

This observation might make sense if particles themselves were *always* l-selected by the verb and if that relation were implemented by LF particle transportation, filling the clitic position proposed by Keyser and Roeper. Syntactic particle transportation, on the other hand, necessarily involves a composite consisting of π and an l-selected complement.

Before concluding this section, we want to return to the question of delayed gratification and to consider certain exceptional cases. First, consider the following pair, illustrating the ideal situation:

(36) a. We got the kids up into the loft.
     b. The kids got up into the loft.

Both of these conform to the principle of delayed gratification, assuming that Merge introduces the specifier, *the kids*, at the π-projection (and not first at the P-projection followed by raising). But if this is so, then why are there two different sentences here? This is also perfectly consistent with delayed gratification, and it is the expected situation in verbal projections. Consider first the situation represented by (36a), the transitive. In that sentence, the specifier DP has combined with the π-projection by Merge, and at this point, of course, the resulting structure is the maximal projection achieved. There is no violation of delayed gratification, clearly. This π-projection (*the kids up into the loft*) subsequently combines with the verb *get*, giving the V-projection *get the kids up into the loft*. This is well formed, and again there is no violation of delayed gratification. In (36b), the intransitive variant, the specifier DP, *the kids*, is introduced by Merge at the V-projection (*get up into the loft*), in accordance with delayed gratification. A violation of that principle would be an alternative derivation in which DP is first introduced at the π-projection and is subsequently raised to the V-projection.

The derivations just sketched represent the unmarked case, given delayed gratification. Other things being equal, the expectation is that all verb-particle constructions will behave the same in this regard, projecting both transitive and intransitive structures.

However, not all things are equal. It is not always the case that verb-particle constructions enter into the transitivity alternation exemplified in (36). Consider the following cases:

(37) a.   He turned out rotten.
     b.   *We turned him out rotten.

(38) a.   He ended up a Democrat.
     b.   *His education ended him up a Democrat.

The verbs themselves are labile. Nothing prevents their participation in the transitivity alternation: *turn* appears in both *The cloth turned red* and *Turn the cloth red*, and *end* appears in both *The war ended* and *End the war*. But in (37) and (38), only the intransitive is possible. The specifier is introduced only at the V-projection; the alternative of being introduced at the π-projection is blocked, resulting in the ill-formed (37b) and (38b).

The circumstance exemplified in (37) and (38) correlates with another fact about these particular structures.

(39) a.   He turned out rotten.
     b.   *He turned right out rotten.
          (cf. get right up into the loft)

(40) a.   He ended up a Democrat.
     b.   *He ended right up a Democrat.

We assume that the mechanism involved here is enclisis. The particle combines with the verb in a manner that prevents both the appearance of a μ-projection (*right, straight*) and the establishment of a Case-binding relation between the verb and its object (see Bittner 1994; Bittner and Hale 1996a). If this is correct, then the ill-formedness of (37b) and (38b) is explained. The inner DP can be licensed only if it is introduced as a specifier at the V-projection.[4]

We turn now to the opposite situation, in which the transitive is permitted while the intransitive is not. Consider the following pairs:

(41) a.   They made Leecil out a liar.
     b.   *Leecil made out a liar.

(42) a. We brought our kids up honest.
    b. *Our kids brought up honest.

We believe that this is another situation that must be explained in terms of the lexicon. The verbs *turn* and *end* appearing in (37) and (38) have both transitive and intransitive uses when they occur independently, outside the verb-particle construction. By contrast, the verbs *make* and *bring* appearing in (41) and (42) never participate in the standard transitivity alternation, inside or outside the verb-particle construction. They are inherently transitive, and must Case-bind an argument, this being a basic lexical property pertaining to them. It follows that the (b)-sentences above are ill formed, since they contradict the Case-binding requirements of the verb (as described in Bittner 1994).

8.3 The *Spray/Load* Alternation

In this section, we will be concerned with the alternation exemplified in (43).

(43) a. They loaded hay onto the truck.
    b. They loaded the truck with hay.

In his important study of predicate forms, Basilico (1998) argues that (43b) involves an inner predicate in relation to which the DP *the truck* is the external argument. We do not use the term *external argument* for this relation. But let us take the term to mean that the DP *the truck* is external to the projection in which *hay* appears, that is, external to the PP. Under these assumptions, the structure of (43b) would be as in (44).

(44)

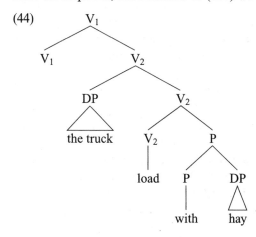

For us, the claim would be that delayed gratification is expected in (44) and achieves in addition the result that the specifier (*the truck*) is external to the P-projection. By contrast, in the structure of (43a), shown in (45), the specifier (*hay*, in this instance) would be internal to the P-projection, namely, by Merge with immediate gratification.

(45)

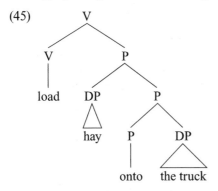

Before investigating why these structures must be the way we claim them to be, we will present one of the arguments Basilico has advanced to demonstrate that the asymmetry in fact exists.

Consider the following sentences, from Basilico 1998, 551.

(46) a. The farmer loaded a bale of hay onto every truck.
     b. The farmer loaded a truck with every bale of hay.

Basilico observes that these two structures differ in their scopal properties. The first sentence is ambiguous, while the second is unambiguous, allowing only the interpretation according to which *a truck* has scope over *every bale of hay*. This might follow if the specifier were located above and outside the lexical projection that contains the object of the preposition, an arrangement that obtains in (46b) but not in (46a). In (46b), the specifier is in the V-projection and thus outside the prepositional phrase, that is, outside the P-projection. The idea would be, then, that the specifier and the object of the preposition cannot interact in the relevant sense in (46b), which therefore lacks the scopal ambiguity. In (46a), by contrast, both arguments are within the P-projection and, presumably, can interact scopally: either argument can be in the scope of the other.[5]

Let us turn again to the structures we have assigned to these sentences, beginning with (45). This is the minimal configuration we must assume given the properties observed. The verb is transitive, hence must stand in a structural relation in which it can Case-bind the specifier in sentential syntax, a circumstance that obtains in (45), being achieved by immediate gratification at the P-projection. Coincidentally, immediate gratification is required here by virtue of the fact that the manner feature of the verb— namely, the semantic feature {load}—is obviative and hence bound by the external argument. The "adverbial" component of *load* in this construction refers to certain aspects of the actions of the agent in the prototypical "loading" event type; the farmer gets a bale of hay onto every truck in a manner consonant with the dictionary, or encyclopedia, definition of "loading."

We hasten to mention that this may be the wrong way to think about the linking of manner features in this case, and others like it. Instead, {load} may simply be unspecified for obviation, in which case the features of *load* are interpreted either in the way suggested, as a set of manner features linked externally, or else as a feature linked to the specifier (*a bale of hay*), or to the event itself. Since *The hay is loaded* is probably true if *They loaded the hay onto the wagon* is true, the more flexible view of the linking of manner features—permitting features to be unlinked—is perhaps more nearly correct. This would permit the observed ambiguity of *He loaded hay onto the truck until it (the hay, the truck) was completely loaded.*

As for (44), on the other hand, linking of the semantic features of *load* is crucial to the structure. In that structure, repeated as (47), the specifier DP, *the truck*, appears above the verb bearing the semantic features {load}. This is the result of Merge and delayed gratification. It is necessary, furthermore, to obtain proper binding of the relevant semantic features.

(47)

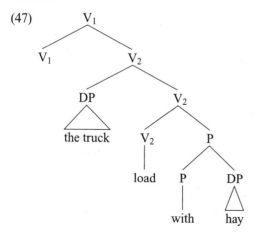

In this structure, {load} is bound by the specifier, as a constant feature of
the semantics of the verb. If *They loaded the truck with hay* is true, then
They loaded the truck is true. And *The truck is loaded* is true, by virtue of
the acquired property (*loaded*) of the entity denoted by the DP. This
reflects the so-called holistic character of this member of the *spray/load*
alternation (Levin 1993, 51), accounting for the oddity of the sentence
*He loaded the truck with hay until it was completely loaded, for example.
Our perception that the semantic features of the verb are *bound* by the
specifier is our reason for assuming that *the truck*, in accordance with
delayed gratification, appears in the position in which it c-commands the
verb. More must be said, however. The verb *load* is inherently transitive
and must be permitted to Case-bind a nominal argument. To make this
possible, head movement must apply, raising *load* to the higher V-position,
indicated in (47).

The principle of delayed gratification, partially responsible for the
structure depicted in (47), has another effect that is relevant to Basilico's
(1998) scope observations. Consider the following sentences:

(48) a. The farmer crammed a bale of hay frequently into a feeder.
      b. The farmer crammed a feeder frequently with a bale of hay.

The relevant observations are these. In (48a), the adverb has ambiguous
scope. According to one reading, the same bale of hay enters the feeder
repeatedly. According to the other reading, multiple bales of hay are
crammed into the feeder. By contrast, (48b) is unambiguous with respect
to the scope relations between the specifier DP *a feeder* and the adverb.
The latter is unambiguously within the scope of the specifier; the sentence
speaks of a single feeder, not multiple feeders. This follows from the
theory according to which the specifier DP is introduced by Merge at V_2,
and not by Merge at P with subsequent Move and Merge. Since the DP *a
feeder* is not the head of a chain and linked to a trace in the P-projection,
and therefore has no presence in the P-projection, it does not interact with
the adverb. Hence, (48b) lacks the ambiguity associated with (48a). This
difference between the prepositional alternant and the locatum alternant
(the *with*-construction alternant) holds regularly.

(49) a. They supplied a case of Grolsch frequently to a softball team.
      b. They supplied a softball team frequently with a case of Grolsch.

(50) a. She smeared a pat of butter frequently on a piece of toast.
      b. She smeared a piece of toast frequently with a pat of butter.

Basilico discusses a number of other constructions that we are setting aside for the present, either because we have so far not been able to propose a solution for them within the assumptions inherent to our framework, or because we are not convinced about the data. An especially interesting opposition he discusses is the inversion construction exemplified here:

(51) a.   On the farmer's truck was loaded a bale of hay.
     b.   ?*With a bale of hay was loaded the farmer's truck.

Basilico explains this distinction in terms of Case; (51b) violates the Case Filter. This explanation is not available to us for various reasons, the principal one being that Basilico's particular Case-theoretic account implicates categories and structures not available in the framework we are developing.

Linguistic data we are not sure about in our own minds include *there*-insertion constructions of the following type:

(52) a.   There was hay loaded onto the wagon.
     b.   There was a wagon loaded with hay.

Basilico claims that the first of these asserts the existence of an event, while the second asserts the existence of a wagon that is loaded with hay. We feel that both interpretations are possible in both sentences.

8.4   Final Remarks

This discussion has been concerned primarily with the manner in which the specifier relation is introduced into syntactic structures. Prototypically, specifiers are "required" in those syntactic structures in which they appear. They are "projected" by nuclear elements alone (as in the case of P) or by a nuclear element as a function of its complement (as in the case of V and an A complement).

The question is, what is the "timing" of the introduction of specifiers? Structurally, a specifier is the immediate sister of the first nontrivial projection of a head. But if a nuclear element requires a specifier, must that specifier be introduced (via Merge) exactly at the first nontrivial projection, as in (53a), or at a later point (i.e., after another head has been introduced into the structure), as in (53b)?

(53) a.

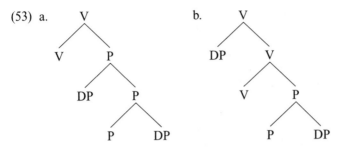

In (53a), the specifier required by P, as an inherent property of that category, is introduced within the P-projection itself. This is the circumstance we have referred to as "immediate gratification." In (53b), on the other hand, the specifier is introduced not in the P-projection, but in the immediately superordinate V-projection. This is "delayed gratification." Without argument, we have taken this to be a possible construction. We have assumed that the relation between the specifier DP and P is sufficiently local to establish the "predication-like" relation that holds between DP and [P DP] in both constructions (see below).

If it is correct to believe that both delayed and instant gratification are possible in the projection of syntactic configurations, what determines which of the two operates in a given instance?

The answer depends on the elements and structures involved. In a structure like (9), repeated here as (54), delayed gratification is required.

(54)

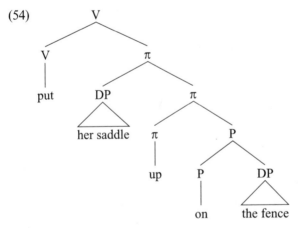

Immediate gratification of P's specifier requirement, by introduction of the specifier *her saddle* at P, would not be successful, since the specifier would not be licensed. The particle would intervene between the specifier, DP, and its licenser, V.

By contrast, in (45), repeated here as (55), immediate gratification is possible, by introduction of the specifier at P. Delayed gratification, introducing the specifier at V, would not succeed in this case, since *load* is transitive (and possibly externally linked), as required in order to license the DP *hay*.

(55)

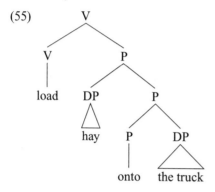

Labile verbs like *splash*, represented in (56), show an alternation between delayed and immediate gratification.

(56)

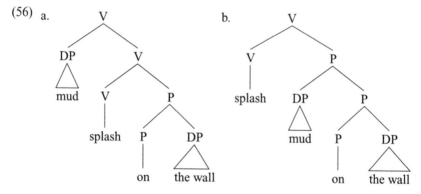

Both alternants—(56a) by delayed gratification, and (56b) by immediate gratification—satisfy the principle of derivational economy that, among other things, abjures the use of Move. The first is the unaccusative and gives rise to the sentential syntactic intransitive exemplified in (57a); the second is the transitive, implicating an external argument, the subject, as exemplified in (57b).

(57) a. Mud splashed on the wall.
    b. The horses splashed mud on the wall.

In essence, the principle that constrains delayed gratification is this: delayed gratification is possible if it gives a convergent derivation, and economy requires delayed gratification where its use avoids Move (i.e., immediate gratification and subsequent Move). This prevents a derivation of (57a) according to which DP (*mud*) is first introduced by Merge at P and subsequently raises to combine with V by Merge.

The configuration in (56a) does not violate "locality." DP is not excessively distant from the category (P) that requires it. This is because the intermediate V inherits the specifier requirement of its complement. In other words, V comes to require a specifier (by virtue of P), and V must project a specifier accordingly. This circumstance is familiar from the derivation of deadjectival verbs, in which A requires a specifier but cannot itself project it, relying on a host V to assume that function.

Notes

Chapter 1

1. The term *sentential syntax* is used here to refer to the syntactic structure assigned to a phrase or sentence involving the lexical item, its arguments, and its extended projection (Grimshaw 1991) and including, therefore, the full range of functional categories and projections implicated in the formation of a sentence interpretable at PF and LF. The internal structure of a lexical projection is also properly speaking a "syntax," but it is the structure included within the projection of the lexical head and is defined strictly in terms of heads and arguments.

2. The appearance of a sentential syntactic subject with predicates like those in (1) is forced by a general principle of grammar (see Chomsky 1982; Rothstein 1983) that, following an established tradition within generative grammar, we will refer to as the "Extended Projection Principle" (EPP). Following Bittner (1994; and see also Bittner and Hale 1996a), we will assume that the subject (whether external or raised from an internal position) enters into a "small clause" relation with the VP predicated of it (see Koopman and Sportiche 1991); it is structurally an adjunct to the VP and, moreover, a "distinguished adjunct" coindexed with the VP, a formal notation corresponding to predication (see Williams 1980). In this view of the matter, an external subject, being an adjunct to VP, is in a minimal sense "internal" to VP, as in the VP-internal subject hypothesis, but it is not internal to the lexical configuration projected by a lexical head, since it occupies neither a complement position nor a specifier position within that projection.

3. This is a claim, of course, and it could be false. The force of the claim will become more evident as the discussion proceeds. For now, we note that obvious apparent counterexamples, like the causative construction exemplified by *make John bake a cake*, are sentential syntactic constructions in which the object of the causative verb *make* is an extended projection of the verbal head, despite its traditional designation as a "bare infinitive"; compare the passive, in which the *to* of the infinitive surfaces, and the negative, as in *make John not bake a cake, not raise Cain, not whistle a tune*. Thus, while the causative verb *make* is a lexical entry (lp-monadic), the causative construction is not. The internal composition of the clausal complement of causal *make* is entirely free. It is not "listed" in the lexicon. Moreover, it is an extended projection, not a bare V-projection, and therefore includes functional categories, however reduced or impoverished.

4. The verb does not, in and of itself, motivate the appearance of a specifier. In fact, we suspect that this is quite generally true of verbs in English; that is, verbs typically project the monadic structure including just a complement. It is not surprising, therefore, that *turn* does not project a specifier (capable of appearing as a sentential syntactic object) in all instances, and particularly when its lexical complement is nominal, as in *turn the corner* (cf. **turn the car the corner*).

5. We borrow the term *conflation* from Talmy (1985), extending it to phenomena somewhat different from those he uses it for.

6. We indicate here only the purely morphophonological effects of conflation. We assume that the syntactic effect is head adjunction, inasmuch as conflation is a variant of head movement (though subject to the more restrictive constraint that it is limited in effect to incorporation from the complement position; see Travis 1984).

7. The head designated *Head* in (24c) may represent a simple head, without further projection, or it may represent a full phrase, since this is a complement and thus occupies an argument position within the larger structure headed by Head*.

8. Following a suggestion by Jim Higginbotham (personal communication), there is another exponent of this preposition, namely, the *-ed* in *The horse is saddled* (the horse is "with saddle").

9. This case is not as clear as that exemplified in (37), since ill-formed (38) might also be explained in terms of sentential syntax: a verb must be licensed there by functional categories (e.g., Tense); the internal verb, V_2, cannot be licensed since it is not raised to V_1.

Chapter 2

1. The phrase *has just the features of a verb* is not meant to imply that the lexical categories (V, N, etc.) are themselves basic features of grammar. The categories may well be identified with the configurations they project (see Romero 1997). The following correlations hold in general, with certain regular exceptions: in the maximal configuration [Head-Complement], the head corresponds to "V," reflecting the property that verbs generally take external subjects; in the maximal configuration [Specifier [Head-Complement]], the head corresponds to "P"; and in the configuration [Head], the head corresponds to "N." Adjectives are a secondary category, morphosyntactically diverse among languages of the world, with the special property that they must be attributed of some argument, attained parasitically and accounting for one class of exceptions to the otherwise general, specifierless configuration associated with verbs (the other being the class of exceptions under consideration here for P-complemented alternating verbs like *splash* and *drip*).

2. One of the complications alluded to above is the following. Suppose the configuration (15) were merged with a verbal head, becoming the complement of the V in a larger structure, a transitive structure in sentential syntax. The adverbial index would be bound and the structure would succeed (apparently, and perhaps actually). This is again the reflection of a redundancy in the system: there are two

derivations for *Leecil smeared saddle soap on my chaps.* We are setting this problem aside for present purposes, but see chapter 8 for a suggested analysis eliminating this redundancy.

3. For an important crosslinguistic analysis of the classical system of obviation, see Aissen 1997; and for a discussion of an extension of the term to other domains, attributed originally to a suggestion by Charles Hockett via Joseph Grimes, see Hale 1992 and references cited there. It is this extended use of the term that we adopt here.

4. It should be mentioned, perhaps, that judgments about the middle are not particularly stable. With a little thought, most middles can be made to sound acceptable, or at least imaginable. We assign stars to middles that require extra thought, recognizing that assessment is relative, in the sense, for example, that *This horse saddles easily* is more or less perfect, while *This wall kicks easily* is much less than perfect. Interestingly, (29bii) approaches perfect if the noun *punch* is taken to refer to a result or effect, rather than the action attributed to the external argument—that is, if *punch* refers to a "dent" or "depression" in the bag, an effect of "punching the bag" (cf. *This bag takes punches nicely*). In this interpretation, *punch* is more like verbs of the *cut* type (see text below).

Chapter 3

1. Tanya Reinhart (personal communication) points out that this use of the term *cognate argument* is too broad. Eventually, we will have to distinguish the true cognate object construction (e.g., *sleep the sleep of the just*) from hyponymous or metonymous argument constructions like those in (8). We will take this issue up in section 3.4.

2. (10a) has a meaning, of course, but not that corresponding to (11).

3. It should be borne in mind, we think, that it is possible, even very likely, that noun incorporation does not in fact exist as an operation in the computational part of a derivation. Rather, the so-called incorporate nominal is in situ, in its "thematic position." It is instead the unincorporated nominal that is moved in syntax—being raised or "shifted" out of the VP domain for purposes of Case licensing, or the EPP, or both (see Hale, in progress). An incorporate is licensed by virtue of its appearance within a verbal word (in the spirit of Baker 1996). In the Northern Athabaskan languages that have noun incorporation, this view of the matter is especially defensible (see, e.g., Tuttle 1996; Rice 2000). Be this as it may, while Baker (1988) and Baker and Hale (1990) imply that traditional incorporation, like conflation, cannot freely target a specifier, Den Dikken (1995) correctly points out that theories of argument structure such as the small clause theory developed in Hoekstra 1988, 1991, which share a crucial assumption with Hale and Keyser 1997c and subsequent work (specifically, that location and locatum verbs are built upon an internal substructure in which a specifier is projected), must necessarily permit incorporation of a specifier, as an empirical fact. To demonstrate this, he uses an example from Baker's own work (Den Dikken 1995, 13; Baker 1988, 90).

4. Again, it happens that (23a) has a meaning, but not the one of interest here, namely, the one associated with the structure shown in (24). That is to say, it does not mean 'Japanangka straightens spears', or the like.

5. We equivocate for good reason: there are very credible alternative views of these matters. There is an analysis of constructions like (25) that changes the nature of the problem entirely. This is the "nonincorporation" analysis proposed in Mithun 1986. There the issue becomes that of "cognate and hyponymous arguments," to be discussed later.

6. If N were designated the head, giving {N {N, V}}, the structure would fail, since the argument structure properties of V could not be expressed.

7. This notion of label must be reconciled with the virtually incontrovertible evidence for the Distributed Morphology principle of "late insertion" (Halle and Marantz 1993). In short, the concept "label" embodied in (33) cannot be taken to imply that the actual phonological representation of the head is given there, since that information is dependent on morphological relations effected in sentential syntax, hence unavailable in the structures projected from the lexicon.

8. It should be noted that some languages allow predications of precisely this form. To all intents and purposes, the Hopi sentence *Pam pas-mi* (he field-ALL) 'He went to the field' is of this form, adjusting for the head-final organization of phrase structure in Hopi. The sentence is headed by the allative postposition *-mi*.

9. It is possible that D itself might conflate with a head verb, of course. If this occurs in some languages (e.g., Irish, on some analyses of its agreement system), it is a language-specific possibility.

10. As mentioned in note 3, we agree with Den Dikken's (1995) reinterpretation of Baker's (1988) example (43c)—in particular, we agree that it illustrates incorporation into V from the specifier position of the complement of V. It should be pointed out, however, that under Baker's own analysis, the incorporation would proceed from the complement position itself, that is, from the position immediately sister to V. Baker assigns a structure different from the one that is necessarily assigned either in Hoekstra's (1988, 1991) small clause theory or in our own closely similar conception of the argument structures of location and locatum verbs, outlined in chapter 1 and assumed throughout.

11. We must assume that the government requirement of incorporation is met in (46); this would entail that a verb can govern into the extended projection of its complement, permitting extraction of N from DP in this instance. This is questionable, but it is implied in the claim that determiners can be stranded by incorporation. Baker discusses this phenomenon, citing it as *evidence* for incorporation (e.g., Baker 1988, 92–96), but he does so in the context of a categorial representation in which the lexical head N, not the functional head D, contributes its label to the nominal phrase as a whole. Thus, there is no extraction from DP in the representation Baker uses, so the government question, for possibly accidental notational reasons, does not arise, on the widely accepted view that a verb governs the head of its complement. The issue raises many questions, not the least

that of the true nature and linguistic status of standard syntactic incorporation. The outcome of this question, we assume, will leave intact the idea that conflation is a matter having to do with labels at Merge. It is not a movement operation.

12. Overt instantiations of the category PRED in Hopi include -va (interval) and -qa (extent), as in tsaa-va 'short' and tsaa-q 'narrow'. It is probable that the adjective of (47), wuupa, wuuwupa, contains the interval element -va (hardened to -pa). However, we will follow the HDP in not insisting on this here, leaving PRED nonovert in (47).

13. Incidentally, the verb hepma is itself the product of incorporation: specifically, of heeva, hep- 'seek' and the (suffixal) destinational purposive verb -ma 'go and'.

14. Nuclear D in possessive constructions is the morphological locus of the number category of the possessum, possessor agreement, and Case (of the DP as a whole). It is never overt on an incorporating lexical head N. The latter is a general fact, extending to other lexical categories as well; and it poses an interesting and nontrivial problem (see Li 1990, for relevant discussion), strongly suggestive of an alternative analysis of incorporation, uniting this process with conflation. According to this alternative, a head noun conflates (in our current sense) with its sister, an empty functional head; the projection of the latter in turn conflates with its sister (e.g., with the verb). For example, in (48), N conflates with empty D, and the maximal D phrase, bearing the p-signature of the noun, conflates with V (i.e., passes its p-signature on to V). This would be consonant with the fact that only "bare" lexical stems incorporate. But it would also require reconsideration of certain structures; for example, on the face of it, specifier incorporation would not reduce to conflation as we are now thinking of it.

15. Notice that the following is much better: *John laughed his last laugh and Bill laughed his too.* This is ellipsis (cf. *Bill laughed his last laugh too*), hence not a counterexample to the generalization exemplified by (52b).

16. The verb is also the structural sister to the node D, the extended projection of its complement. Any theory of the phenomenon we have given the name *conflation* must account somehow for the English fact that determiners do not conflate, just as prepositions do not conflate, except when substantiated by prior conflation (as in the case of location and locatum verbs). Whatever accounts for this selective nature of conflation will ensure in (59) that the p-signature of the noun, but not that of the determiner, will be copied into the label of the verb.

17. Suppose, however, that the functional category dominating a noun were itself phonologically nonovert. In this case, the noun would conflate (i.e., copy its p-signature) into the empty head of the functional category, and the functional head, thus substantiated, would conflate into the verb. In this situation, the source copy would not be spelled out, since no overt functional head would be left stranded.

18. It is natural to ask why K does not acquire a p-signature through conflation, of D, for example. The answer, we believe, is that this is a language-specific parameter. It is perhaps a matter still to be determined, but it seems reasonable to us

to propose that the often-observed fusion of D and Case is in fact conflation. In Pima of Ónavas (a Tepiman language of Sonora, Mexico), the determiners *id* 'proximate' and *üg* 'distal' fuse with accusative case to give *ik* and *ük*, respectively, as in *'Aan* [DP *ük ban*] *nüid* 'I see the coyote', with accusative case on the object, beside [DP *Üg ban*] *mür* 'The coyote is running', with nominative (unmarked) subject.

19. This putative property of English prepositions may not extend to adpositions generally (or to particles; see below). Moreover, it does not preclude the possibility that adpositions might incorporate in some languages (for discussions of P-incorporation, see Baker 1988; Craig and Hale 1988).

20. Case theory might be invoked to explain (62a); but it cannot be invoked for (62b–e). We are assuming that *on* and *in* in these cases are in fact prepositions. There is a class of particles, of course, and a few of these do have verbal uses in English, possibly by conflation—for example, *He downed a second glass of tequila*, *They upped the prices*. And verbs like *enter* and *mount* might in fact be analyzed as "morphologically rich prepositions" conflated into defective V, in which case they would presumably have p-signatures in syntax.

21. In some languages, conflation of nouns into adpositions is more common. Examples are the Navajo postpositions *-(ii)h* 'into' and *-(ii)'* 'in': *taah* 'into water', *taa'* 'in water', *leeh* 'into earth', *lee'* 'in earth'. Here, conflation is required where the postposition is defective—in this case, where it lacks the vocalic portion of its root.

22. We do not entertain the possibility that there simply is no complement N in *John danced*. This alternative is not well supported by a full consideration of English and, especially, by a crosslinguistic examination of unergatives of this type.

23. The verb *clear* can occur without an overt object, of course, as in *I'll clear (the dishes)*. But this is not the relevant *clear*, as is evident from **The dishes cleared*.

24. This might be true in general; that is, roots might always be categorially indeterminate, the notions N, V, and the like being "contextual" in the manner suggested. English and the Salish languages are particularly supportive of this, but languages like Warlpiri, of Central Australia, and most Uto-Aztecan languages, for example, show highly rigid class cleavage; here, the heads of verbal extended projections, and the heads of nominal projections likewise, are systematically distinct and category-faithful. In the case of Warlpiri, there is no crossover, so far as we are aware.

25. This cannot be the entire story, however. Not all presumed specifiers can incorporate, for reasons that are only partially understood. The grammatical object in the double object or dative construction steadfastly resists incorporation in languages that have fully productive incorporation processes (see Baker 1988 for discussion).

Chapter 4

1. Construct morphology (e.g., possessive -*ki* 1, -*ma* 2, -*ka* 3, and -*ka* plain CNSTR) is suffixed not to the word but to the first metric foot—hence *lih-ki-wan* 'my money', not **lihwan-ki*.

2. Tom Green (personal communication) suggests that the nonalternating verbs in -*ra* represent a class defined by an archaic thematic element. His evidence for this comes from the prosody of Ulwa verb roots, according to which each constitutes an iamb. If -*ra* were a part of the root in these cases, these verbs would be exceptions to this prevailing pattern.

3. The form *wegij* is the perfective (PERF) of *wegijid* 'redden, make red', formed by regular truncation (see Hale 1965). Other perfectives in (46) also involve truncation.

4. The distinction between simple "transitivizing" and "causative" emerges in combination with transitive and so-called unergative verbs; causative -*cud*, with "causative" force, may occasionally combine with such verbs, as in *ñu:kudacud* 'have *x* take care of *y*' (cf. *ñu:kud* 'take care of') and *cikpanacud* 'have *x* work'.

5. These derived verbs can appear with a "pseudo-object," a nominal expression referring to the material from which an entity (corresponding to the incorporated N) is made, as in *Hema 'at ki:-t g melhog* (one AUX.T.3 house-make ART ocotillo) 'He built a house of ocotillo' (from Mathiot 1974, 479). Pseudo-objects do not share the properties of true objects (e.g., they do not control object agreement, they cannot be construed with preverbal quantifiers, and they cannot be anaphors).

6. This fact renders questionable the use of the expression *causative-inchoative* in reference to the Hopi alternation exemplified here, since most intransitive verbs can be transitivized in this manner, including verbs that serve as the Hopi translations of English unergatives, a class generally excluded from the causative-inchoative alternation in the latter language (see below, where English *laugh* is briefly discussed). We employ the causative-inchoative terminology simply because it was familiar to the audience to whom this material was first presented. This may be a mistake, but we have no convincing evidence that it is in fact a mistake, since conventional translation relationships cannot be fully trusted in determining the "meanings" of verbs. Thus, translation does not reliably identify the unergative and unaccusative classes, for example. The only evidence we can truly count on is syntactic behavior—in this case, participation in the alternation at issue, as opposed to nonparticipation (to be exemplified presently).

7. The suffix -*ta* in (105) is aspectual, not to be confused with the reduced alternant of -*toya* seen in earlier sentences.

8. There are problems with the notion of conflation, not relevant here, which suggest strongly that it does not exist as such (see chapter 3). The Hopi counterpart of this process, however, is well established, belonging to the category of head movement operations known as incorporation.

9. James Higginbotham (personal communication) suggests, however, that the P-projections of locatum verbs do in fact occur outside the transitive construction,

as in *I found [the horse saddled]*, and for some speakers *When will we finally see [the cottage windowed]?*, and the like, *-ed* being the P head here.

Chapter 5

1. Although we maintain a distinction between the (b)- and (c)-types, Déchaine (1996) has pointed out that the two can be treated as variants of the same lexical structure. In our approach, the distinction resides in the location of the head *x* that forces the appearance of a specifier: in the (b)-type, this is the head of the maximal projection; in the (c)-type, it is the complement of α, a "host" that is forced by *x* to project a specifier. In both cases, *x* has the lexical property that it must appear in a relation we will refer to as a *(lexical) predication*; the specifier satisfies the "subject" required by this predication. The two structures can be unified, of course, since each involves the "formation" of a predicate from a structurally uniform head-complement subconstituent.

2. A number of works argue that the opposite view is correct—in other words, that the goal is higher than the theme (see Takano 1996 and references cited there; and see Koizumi 1994 for a corresponding theory of secondary predicate attachment). In the English case, at least, evidence for this comes, in part, from the "connectivity effect" seen in such sentences as ?*I showed each other's pictures to the boys*, which, if standard c-command is involved in interpreting the reciprocal here, suggests that the *to*-dative (i.e., goal) phrase is higher than the theme at the relevant point in the derivation. Since examples like ?*I put each other's crowns under the thrones of the king of France and the queen of Holland* are of roughly the same acceptability, we suspect that something special is involved with connectivity (see Minkoff 1994 for a theory that is probably relevant to this issue).

3. This may account for the marked character of the passive (??*The bottle was given the baby*), a construction that must evidently be specially learned and is, therefore, not uniformly distributed among English dialects (see Hudson 1992 for much discussion; and see below as well).

4. It is a fundamental (possibly erroneous) feature of our conception of derivational morphology that V in (22) cannot be a true zero affix. Consequently, the derived word will not contain a zero affix beneath an additional layer of derivational morphology. The illicit derivations are precluded by selection at the outset; and empty heads are eliminated by fusion in the course of incorporation. Thus, (21) is not actually operative, even in the generalized version that does not distinguish overt and nonovert affixes. Nonetheless, the spirit is the same, we believe, and we are much indebted to Myers (1984), Fabb (1988), and Pesetsky (1995) alike.

5. We leave undecided the question of the Case assigned to the possessum. There are two possibilities: (i) Structural case from *have*; (ii) inherent Case from the verb in its basic position. Our analysis of *have* likens it to an "intransitive" version of *give*. This may be right, in which case *have* assigns inherent Case to its "object" (i.e., to its specifier). This may be why the passive is marginal in the true posses-

sive sense: ??*The bottle is had by the baby* (note also ??*The bottle was given the baby*).

6. We acknowledge that something is lost in saying that causative-inchoative verbs "participate freely" in the alternation for which they are named. It does not seem to us that transitive *drop*, for example, permits the "pure cause" interpretation discussed below (see also Levin and Rappaport Hovav 1995, 86, for similar cases). We expect that the theory of supra-VP projections developed by Borer (1998) will, in many instances, make the proper distinctions between verbs that we classify together as projecting the transitive argument structure configurations in (29). We bear in mind the possibility that Borer's theory might succeed in making the VP-internal structures we posit unnecessary—a theoretical advance, if so.

7. We are not sure what relationship exists between "cause" of the type we are referring to here and the often discussed notion of "direct" versus "indirect" causation, as in *break the window* versus *cause the window to break* (see Jackendoff 1990, 150–151, and Pustejovsky 1995, chap. 9, for discussion). While the first is said to be "direct," it is nonetheless clear that it can be used in a situation involving mere "cause" in our sense, devoid of any agency.

8. See Minkoff 1994 for a theory relevant to this issue.

9. There is an alternative possibility that should not be lost sight of, namely, that secondary predicates "associate" with the highest internal argument. If there is only one, then of course that will be the highest. If this is the true generalization, then we cannot maintain the analysis suggested in this chapter. From our perspective, we take this as a challenge to show that all cases of observed secondary predication of a single internal DP argument implicate, in reality, a more complex basic argument structure in which the subject of the secondary predicate occupies a position from which it can at once exclude and c-command the predicate. Predication of a simple DP complement in an (a)-type structure is an obvious test case. But these are verbs of creation, and depictive (as opposed, say, to "resultative") secondary predication is, so far as we can tell, generally of a preexisting entity, or preexisting condition, making the test difficult to apply.

Chapter 6

1. The (a)-type argument structure is the configuration projected by a head that selects a complement but does not project a specifier; the (b)-type, typical of English prepositions, for example, is the configuration projected by a head that selects a complement and in addition projects a specifier. The (c)-type, like the (b)-type, has both a complement and a specifier; in the (c)-type, however, the appearance of a specifier is determined primarily by the complement, typically an adjective, in English (see chapter 1).

2. We must assume that the raising verb construction is also transparent, accounting for agreement in the (weakly) possible *There always seem to arrive too many guests at our parties* and the fully possible *There seem to be two policemen at the door*.

Chapter 7

1. Since these are structural relations, the terms *complement* and *specifier* have no special status, being simply the names of the structural relations: (i) a complement is the sister of the head, and (ii) a specifier is the sister of the syntactic object consisting of the head and its sister. Nonetheless, we will continue to use these traditional terms, as an expository convenience.

2. James Higginbotham, in the context of a Lexicon Seminar at MIT in 1997, developed an idea compatible with the view that the ending *-ed* in derived attributes like *saddled* corresponds to the head in a dyadic (b)-type projection; we take this *-ed* to belong to the category P.

3. The correlation does not extend to all subject-experiencer verbs; many verbs cannot appear in the *have*-construction, among them *fear, hate, like*. We maintain, however, that these have the same basic structure as that attributed here to *respect, love*, and *esteem*. It is perhaps interesting that some nouns that enter into the *have*-construction easily form adjectives with *-able*. And some nouns that do not enter into the *have*-construction also do not form adjectives with *-able*, for instance, **fearable, ?*hateable* (cf. *hateful*).

4. The structure depicted in (12) is problematic. Without some special provision, the label assigned to the upper maximal projection is ambiguous; that is to say, there is no way to determine which of P* and P is the head of the upper projection. We think, however, that the problem associated with this ambiguity is spurious and that (12) is well formed.

5. This argument depends, of course, on whether the stative variant of *respect the truth* can actually appear in the causative and in the *to*-infinitive construction of the type shown here. We assume that the complement in (13a), for example, is stative and that its telic interpretation is due to the construction; the truly active version, as in *Respect your parents*, means *Give your parents your respect*, not *Come to respect your parents*. In (13a), the meaning is that an event, or the like, made John come to respect the truth, not give the truth his respect.

6. We have not fully explored the possibility of a Case-theoretic explanation for (14) and the like. An explanation seeking to limit structural Case to just one internal argument, for example, would have to explain the range of constructions in which two VP-internal arguments are somehow licensed without resort to adpositions or other oblique case morphology (e.g., *I envy him his talent*). Such an explanation may well be possible, but we do not pursue it here.

7. This is not an autonomous principle, of course, but rather an integral part of the definition of these two relations, according to which a complement is the unique sister of a head and a specifier is the unique sister of the first projection (traditionally notated X') of the head. These notions may ultimately be shown to be wrong, linguistically fictitious, but they are fundamental to the proposals being entertained here.

8. Systems of the type represented by Hopi (Jeanne 1978), in which tense and aspect morphology selects the category P, as well as V, may or may not counter-

exemplify the principles of extended projection. This will depend on a variety of factors. In the related language O'odham, for example, the categories N and A take tense and aspect morphology, superficially, but it can be argued that these cases involve incorporation of bare nominal and adjectival stems into a morphophonologically suffixal copula -*k(a)* derived from the Uto-Aztecan verb **katï* 'sit, be'. It is this copula that takes tense and aspect morphology, not N and A directly. The case is not so simple for Hopi, inasmuch as, if this language has a copula, it is not overt and its detection will require more work. In general, however, the principles of extended projection are supported empirically to an extent that encourages us to assume that the Hopi system will eventually be shown to fall in with the general case.

9. There is an important property of the copula *be* that is not shared by the semantically more contentful verbs of (15). Even in its copular function, *be* behaves like an auxiliary in relation to inversion (I-to-C raising)—for example, *Is two and two four?*

Some of the verbs of (17) can passivize, of course, in a different use. And (17c,d) themselves are weakly possible, using *equal* and *comprise* in senses somewhat different from those attributed to them in the suggested copular use. The wellformedness of the passive verb form in *The collection is comprised of three books* is a different issue. In general, measure phrases of the type found in (15) sound rather bad as subjects of passives—for example, ??*Five dollars was earned by John*. This cannot account for (17), however, since in the corresponding *wh*-questions, the passive is possible with *earn*, as in *How much is earned by each worker?*, while with *cost*, for example, it remains ill formed, as in **How much is cost by that house?*

Chapter 8

1. The diagrams in (8) and (9) do not represent the structures assigned by Den Dikken, for whom members of the category we have labeled μ are modifiers adjoined to P. We treat them as heads taking π or P as their complements, since this, rather than adjunction, is the default analysis in our view.

2. But see Svenonius 1996 for discussion of a different view of this matter, to which we return later.

3. The item *free* is an l-selected "particle" here, not strictly speaking an adjective (despite its obvious relationship to the undisputed adjective *free*); hence **They set the tortoises freer (than ever before)*.

4. The precise nature of the enclisis of particles, if it is real, needs to be investigated. It is likely that it is a lexical matter; that is to say, the lexicon must be assumed to include complex verbal entries of the form *turn-out, end-up*. The enclisis cannot be so "tight" as to block verbal inflection, however—witness *turned-out, ended-up*. But lexical enclisis seems likely in view of (39b) and (40b).

5. These are Basilico's ideas in principle, but not in technical detail, given certain important structural differences assumed in his framework and ours.

References

Abney, Steven. 1987. The English NP in its sentential aspect. Doctoral dissertation, MIT.

Ackema, Peter, and Maaike Schoorlemmer. 1995. Middles and nonmovement. *Linguistic Inquiry* 26, 173–197.

Aissen, Judith. 1997. On the syntax of obviation. *Language* 73, 705–750.

Baker, Mark. 1988. *Incorporation: A theory of grammatical function changing.* Chicago: University of Chicago Press.

Baker, Mark. 1996. *The polysynthesis parameter.* New York: Oxford University Press.

Baker, Mark, and Ken Hale. 1990. Relativized Minimality and pronoun incorporation. *Linguistic Inquiry* 21, 289–298.

Basilico, David. 1998. Object position and predication forms. *Natural Language and Linguistic Theory* 16, 541–595.

Belletti, Adriana, and Luigi Rizzi. 1988. Psych-verbs and theta-theory. *Natural Language and Linguistic Theory* 6, 291–352.

Bittner, Maria. 1994. *Case, scope, and binding.* Dordrecht: Kluwer.

Bittner, Maria, and Ken Hale. 1996a. The structural determination of Case and agreement. *Linguistic Inquiry* 27, 1–68.

Bittner, Maria, and Ken Hale. 1996b. Ergativity: Toward a theory of a heterogeneous class. *Linguistic Inquiry* 27, 531–604.

Bok-Bennema, Reineke, and Anneke Groos. 1984. Ergativiteit. *GLOT* 7, 1–49.

Borer, Hagit. 1998. Deriving passive without theta grids. In Steven G. Lapointe, Diane K. Brentari, and Patrick M. Farrell, eds., *Morphology and its relation to phonology and syntax.* Stanford, Calif.: CSLI Publications.

Bowers, John. 1993. The syntax of predication. *Linguistic Inquiry* 24, 591–656.

Chomsky, Noam. 1972. Remarks on nominalization. In *Studies on semantics in generative grammar.* The Hague: Mouton.

Chomsky, Noam. 1981. *Lectures on government and binding.* Dordrecht: Foris.

Chomsky, Noam. 1982. *Some concepts and consequences of the theory of government and binding.* Cambridge, Mass.: MIT Press.

Chomsky, Noam. 1986. *Knowledge of language.* New York: Praeger.

Chomsky, Noam. 1991. Some notes on economy of derivation and representation. In Robert Freidin, ed., *Principles and parameters in comparative grammar,* 417–454. Cambridge, Mass.: MIT Press.

Chomsky, Noam. 1995. *The Minimalist Program.* Cambridge, Mass.: MIT Press.

Chomsky, Noam. 2000. Minimalist inquiries: The framework. In Roger Martin, David Michaels, and Juan Uriagereka, eds., *Step by step: Essays on minimalist syntax in honor of Howard Lasnik.* Cambridge, Mass.: MIT Press.

Clark, Eve, and Herbert Clark. 1979. When nouns surface as verbs. *Language* 55, 767–811.

CODIUL/UYUTMUBAL. 1998. Diccionario del Ulwa (Sumu Meridional). Ms., CIDCA (Managua) and MIT.

Condoravdi, Cleo. 1989. The middle voice: Where semantics and morphology meet. In Phil Branigan, Jill Gaulding, Miori Kubo, and Kumiko Murasugi, eds., *Student Conference in Linguistics 1989.* MIT Working Papers in Linguistics 11. Cambridge, Mass.: MIT, Department of Linguistics and Philosophy, MITWPL.

Craig, Colette, and Ken Hale. 1988. Relational preverbs in some languages of the Americas: Typological and historical perspectives. *Language* 64, 312–344.

Déchaine, Rose-Marie. 1996. Compositional morphology. Paper presented at the 7th International Morphology Meeting, University of Vienna.

Déchaine, Rose-Marie, Teun Hoekstra, and Johan Rooryck. 1995. Augmented and non-augmented *HAVE.* In L. Nash and G. Tsoulas, eds., *Langues et grammaire: Actes du Premier Colloque, Paris VIII, June 1994.* University of Paris VIII.

Dikken, Marcel den. 1995. *Particles: On the syntax of verb-particle, triadic, and causative constructions.* Oxford: Oxford University Press.

Dixon, R. M. W. 1972. *The Dyirbal language of North Queensland.* Cambridge: Cambridge University Press.

Dowty, David. 1979. Toward a semantic analysis of verb aspect and the English "imperfect progressive." *Linguistics and Philosophy* 1, 45–78. (Reprinted in Minoru Yasui, ed., *Kaigai eigogaku ronso* [English linguistics papers from abroad]. Tokyo: Eichosha.)

Fabb, Nigel. 1988. English affixation is constrained only by selectional restrictions. *Natural Language and Linguistic Theory* 6, 527–540.

Fagan, Sarah. 1988. The English middle. *Linguistic Inquiry* 19, 181–203.

Fagan, Sarah. 1992. *The syntax and semantics of middle constructions.* Cambridge: Cambridge University Press.

Friederici, A. D. 1982. Syntactic and semantic processes in aphasic deficits: The availability of prepositions. *Brain and Language* 15, 249–258.

Grimshaw, Jane. 1990. *Argument structure.* Cambridge, Mass.: MIT Press.

Grimshaw, Jane. 1991. Extended projection. Ms., Brandeis University.

Gruber, Jeffrey. 1965. Studies in lexical relations. Doctoral dissertation, MIT.

Hale, Ken. 1965. Some preliminary observations on Papago morphophonemics. *International Journal of American Linguistics* 31, 295–305.

Hale, Ken. 1972. A new perspective on American Indian linguistics. With appendix by Albert Alvarez. In A. Ortiz, ed., *New perspectives on the pueblos*. Albuquerque: University of New Mexico Press.

Hale, Ken. 1981. Preliminary remarks on the grammar of part-whole relations in Warlpiri. In James Hollyman and Andrew Pawley, eds., *Studies in Pacific languages and cultures in honor of Bruce Biggs*. Auckland: Linguistic Society of New Zealand.

Hale, Ken. 1986. Notes on world view and semantic categories: Some Warlpiri examples. In Pieter Muysken and Henk van Riemsdijk, eds., *Features and projections*. Dordrecht: Foris.

Hale, Ken. 1992. Subject obviation, switch reference, and control. In Richard K. Larson, Sabine Iatridou, Utpal Lahiri, and James Higginbotham, eds., *Control and grammar*. Dordrecht: Kluwer.

Hale, Ken. 1995. Universal Grammar and the necessity of linguistic diversity. Presidential address delivered at the annual meeting of the Linguistic Society of America, New Orleans.

Hale, Ken. 2000a. Remarks on the syntax of the Navajo verb. In Theodore Fernald and Ken Hale, eds., *Diné bizaad naalkaah: Navajo language investigations*. Working Papers on Endangered and Less Familiar Languages 3. Cambridge, Mass.: MIT, Department of Linguistics and Philosophy, MITWPL.

Hale, Ken. 2000b. A Uto-Aztecan (O'odham) reflection of a general limit on predicate argument structure. In Eugene H. Casad and Thomas L. Willet, eds., *Uto-Aztecan: Structural, temporal, and geographic perspectives. Papers in memory of Wick R. Miller by the friends of Uto-Aztecan*. Universidad de Sonora, División de Humanidades y Bellas Artes. Hermosillo, Sonora: Editorial Unison.

Hale, Ken. 2001. Navajo verb stem position and the bipartite structure of the Navajo conjunct sector. *Linguistic Inquiry* 32, 678–693.

Hale, Ken. In progress. Navajo verb structure and noun incorporation. Ms., MIT.

Hale, Ken, and LaVerne Masayesva Jeanne. 1999. Hopi *-na*. In Karlos Arregi, Benjamin Bruening, Cornelia Krause, and Vivian Lin, eds., *Papers on morphology and syntax: Cycle one*. MIT Working Papers in Linguistics 33. Cambridge, Mass.: MIT, Department of Linguistics and Philosophy, MITWPL.

Hale, Ken, and Samuel Jay Keyser. 1993. On argument structure and the lexical expression of syntactic relations. In Kenneth Hale and Samuel Jay Keyser, eds., *The view from Building 20: Essays in linguistics in honor of Sylvain Bromberger*. Cambridge, Mass.: MIT Press.

Hale, Ken, and Samuel Jay Keyser. 1997a. *Have:* Linguistic diversity in the expression of a simple relation. In Dick van der Meij, ed., *India and beyond: Aspects of literature, meaning, ritual, and thought. Essays in honor of Frits Staal.* Leiden: International Institute for Asian Studies, and London: Kegan Paul.

Hale, Ken, and Samuel Jay Keyser. 1997b. The limits of argument structure. In Amaya Mendikoetxea and Myriam Uribe-Etxebarria, eds., *Theoretical issues at the morphology-syntax interface.* Bilbao/Donostia-San Sebastian: Universidad del País Vasco/Diputación Foral de Gipuzkoa.

Hale, Ken, and Samuel Jay Keyser. 1997c. On the complex nature of simple predicators. In Alex Alsina, Joan Bresnan, and Peter Sells, eds., *Complex predicates.* CSLI Lecture Notes 64. Stanford, Calif.: CSLI Publications.

Hale, Ken, and Samuel Jay Keyser. 1998. The basic elements of argument structure. In Heidi Harley, ed., *Papers from the UPenn/MIT Roundtable on Argument Structure and Aspect.* MIT Working Papers in Linguistics 32. Cambridge, Mass.: MIT, Department of Linguistics and Philosophy, MITWPL.

Hale, Ken, and Samuel Jay Keyser. 1999. Bound features, Merge, and transitivity alternations. In Liina Pylkkänen, Angeliek van Hout, and Heidi Harley, eds., *Papers from the UPenn/MIT Roundtable on the Lexicon.* MIT Working Papers in Linguistics 35. Cambridge, Mass.: MIT, Department of Linguistics and Philosophy, MITWPL.

Hale, Ken, and Samuel Jay Keyser. 2000. Conflation. In Ana Bravo Martín, Carlos Luján Berenguel, and Isabel Pérez Jiménez, eds., *Cuadernos de lingüística VII 2000, Documentos de trabajo. Lingüística Teórica.* Madrid: Instituto Universitario Ortega y Gasset.

Hale, Ken, and Paul Platero. 1996. Navajo reflections of a general theory of lexical argument structure. In Eloise Jelinek, Sally Midgette, Keren Rice, and Leslie Saxon, eds., *Athabaskan language studies: Essays in honor of Robert W. Young.* Albuquerque: University of New Mexico Press.

Hale, Ken, and Danilo Salamanca. 2001. Theoretical and universal implications of certain verbal entries in dictionaries of the Misumalpan languages. In William Frawley, Kenneth Hill, and Pamela Munro, eds., *Making dictionaries: Preserving indigenous languages of the Americas.* Berkeley: University of California Press.

Halle, Morris, and Alec Marantz. 1993. Distributed Morphology and the pieces of inflection. In Kenneth Hale and Samuel Jay Keyser, eds., *The view from Building 20: Essays in linguistics in honor of Sylvain Bromberger.* Cambridge, Mass.: MIT Press.

Hardy, Frank. 1979. Navajo aspectual stem variation. Doctoral dissertation, University of New Mexico.

Harley, Heidi. 1995. Subjects, events and licensing. Doctoral dissertation, MIT.

Hill, Jane, and Ofelia Zepeda. 1992. Derived words in Tohono O'odham. *International Journal of American Linguistics* 58, 355–404.

Hoekstra, Teun. 1988. Small clause results. *Lingua* 74, 101–139.

Hoekstra, Teun. 1991. Small clauses everywhere. Ms., University of Leiden.

Hopi Dictionary Project (HDP). 1998. *Hopi Dictionary/Hopìikwa Lavàytutuveni.* Tucson: University of Arizona Press.

Hudson, Richard. 1992. So-called "double objects" and grammatical relations. *Language* 68, 251–276.

Jackendoff, Ray. 1983. *Semantics and cognition.* Cambridge, Mass.: MIT Press.

Jackendoff, Ray. 1990. *Syntactic structures.* Cambridge, Mass.: MIT Press.

Jeanne, LaVerne. 1975. Hopi causatives. Ms., MIT.

Jeanne, LaVerne Masayesva. 1978. Aspects of Hopi grammar. Doctoral dissertation, MIT.

Jeanne, LaVerne Masayesva, and Ken Hale. 2000. Transitivización en Hopi. In *Memorias del Quinto Encuentro Internacional de Lingüística en el Noroeste,* Tomo 1. Hermosillo: Universidad de Sonora.

Kaplan, David. 1992. *Language: Structure, processing, and disorders.* Cambridge, Mass.: MIT Press.

Kayne, Richard. 1984. *Connectedness and binary branching.* Dordrecht: Foris.

Kemmer, Suzanne. 1993. *The middle voice.* Amsterdam: John Benjamins.

Keyser, Samuel Jay. 1968. Review of "Adverbial Positions in English," by Sven Jacobson. *Language* 44, 357–374.

Keyser, Samuel Jay, and Thomas Roeper. 1984. On the middle and ergative constructions in English. *Linguistic Inquiry* 15, 381–416.

Keyser, Samuel Jay, and Thomas Roeper. 1992. Re: The abstract clitic hypothesis. *Linguistic Inquiry* 23, 89–125.

Koizumi, Masatoshi. 1994. Secondary predicates. *Journal of East Asian Linguistics* 3, 25–79.

Koopman, Hilda, and Dominique Sportiche. 1991. The position of subjects. *Lingua* 85, 211–259.

Larson, Richard. 1988. On the double object construction. *Linguistic Inquiry* 19, 335–391.

Levin, Beth. 1993. *English verb classes and alternations: A preliminary investigation.* Chicago: University of Chicago Press.

Levin, Beth, and Malka Rappaport Hovav. 1995. *Unaccusatives: At the syntax–lexical semantics interface.* Cambridge, Mass.: MIT Press.

Li, Yafei. 1990. X^0-binding and verb incorporation. *Linguistic Inquiry* 21, 399–426.

Marantz, Alec. 1995. "Cat" as a phrasal idiom: Consequences of late insertion in Distributed Morphology. Ms., MIT.

Marantz, Alec. 1997. No escape from syntax: Don't try morphological analysis in the privacy of your own lexicon. In Alexis Dimitriadis, Laura Siegel, Clarissa Surek-Clark, and Alexander Williams, eds., *Proceedings of the 21st Annual Penn Linguistics Colloquium.* University of Pennsylvania Working Papers in Linguistics 4.2. Philadelphia: University of Pennsylvania, Penn Linguistics Circle.

Mathiot, Madeleine. 1974. *A dictionary of Papago usage*. Language Science Monographs 8:1–2. Bloomington: Indiana University Publications.

Minkoff, Seth. 1994. How some so-called "thematic roles" that select animate arguments are generated, and how these roles inform control. Doctoral dissertation, MIT.

Mithun, Marianne. 1986. On the nature of noun incorporation. *Language* 62, 32–38.

Moro, Andrea. 1997. *The raising of predicates: Predicative noun phrases and the theory of clause structure*. Cambridge: Cambridge University Press.

Myers, Scott. 1984. Zero-derivation and inflection. In Margaret Speas and Richard Sproat, eds., *Papers from the January 1984 MIT Workshop in Morphology*. MIT Working Papers in Linguistics 7. Cambridge, Mass.: MIT, Department of Linguistics and Philosophy, MITWPL.

Oehrle, Richard. 1976. The grammatical status of the English dative alternation. Doctoral dissertation, MIT.

Pensalfini, Rob. 1997. Jingulu grammar, dictionary, and texts. Doctoral dissertation, MIT.

Perlmutter, David. 1978. Impersonal passives and the unaccusative hypothesis. In *Proceedings of the Fourth Annual Meeting of the Berkeley Linguistics Society*. Berkeley: University of California at Berkeley, Berkeley Linguistics Society.

Perlmutter, David, and Paul Postal. 1984. The 1-Advancement Exclusiveness Law. In David Perlmutter and Carol Rosen, eds., *Studies in Relational Grammar 2*. Chicago: University of Chicago Press.

Pesetsky, David. 1995. *Zero syntax: Experiencers and cascades*. Cambridge, Mass.: MIT Press.

Pustejovsky, James. 1995. *The generative lexicon*. Cambridge, Mass.: MIT Press.

Rapoport, Tova. 1997. The English middle and agentivity. Ms., Ben-Gurion University of the Negev.

Rice, Keren. 2000. *Morpheme order and semantic scope: Word formation in the Athabaskan verb*. Cambridge: Cambridge University Press.

Ritter, Elizabeth, and Sarah Rosen. 1991. Causative *HAVE*. In Tim Sherer, ed., *NELS 21*. Amherst: University of Massachusetts, GLSA.

Romero, Juan. 1995. Estructura argumental y sintagma flexión. Ms., Universidad Autónoma de Madrid.

Romero, Juan. 1997. Construcciones de doble objeto y gramática universal. Doctoral dissertation, Universidad Autónoma de Madrid.

Rothstein, Susan. 1983. The syntactic forms of predication. Doctoral dissertation, MIT.

Safir, Kenneth. 1982. Syntactic chains and the definiteness effect. Doctoral dissertation, MIT.

Saxton, Dean. 1982. Papago. In Ronald Langacker, ed., *Studies in Uto-Aztecan grammar*. Uto-Aztecan Grammatical Sketches 3. Arlington: University of Texas, Summer Institute of Linguistics.

Stanley, Richard. 1969. The phonology of the Navajo verb. Doctoral dissertation, MIT.

Svenonius, Peter. 1996. The verb-particle alternation in the Scandinavian languages. Ms., University of Tromsø.

Takano, Yuji. 1996. Object shift and scrambling. Ms., Keio University.

Talmy, Leonard. 1985. Lexicalization patterns. In Timothy Shopen, ed., *Language typology and syntactic description*. Cambridge: Cambridge University Press.

Tenny, Carol. 1987. Grammaticalizing aspect and affectedness. Doctoral dissertation, MIT.

Tenny, Carol. 1994. *Aspectual roles and the syntax-semantics interface*. Dordrecht: Kluwer.

Travis, Lisa. 1984. Parameters and effects of word order variation. Doctoral dissertation, MIT.

Tuttle, Siri G. 1996. Direct objects in Salcha Athabaskan. In Eloise Jelinek, Sally Midgette, Keren Rice, and Leslie Saxon, eds., *Athabaskan language studies: Essays in honor of Robert W. Young*. Albuquerque: University of New Mexico Press.

Wechsler, Stephen. 1995. *The semantic basis of argument structure*. Stanford, Calif.: CSLI Publications.

Williams, Edwin. 1980. Predication. *Linguistic Inquiry* 11, 203–238.

Young, Robert W., and William Morgan. 1980. *The Navajo language*. Albuquerque: University of New Mexico Press.

Young, Robert W., William Morgan, and Sally Midgette. 1992. *Analytical lexicon of Navajo*. Albuquerque: University of New Mexico Press.

Zepeda, Ofelia. 1983. *A Papago grammar*. Tucson: University of Arizona Press.

Index